Hartlepool
in the Great War

About the Author

Stephen is a retired police officer having served with Essex Police *as* a constable for thirty years between 1983 and 2013. He is married to Tanya and has two sons, Luke and Ross, and a daughter, Aimee. His sons served five tours of Afghanistan between 2008 and 2013 and both were injured. This led to the publication of his first book, *Two Sons in a Warzone – Afghanistan: The True Story of a Father's Conflict*, published in October 2010.

Both Stephen's grandfathers served in and survived the First World War, one with the Royal Irish Rifles, the other in the Mercantile Marine, whilst his father was a member of the Royal Army Ordnance Corps during the Second World War.

Stephen collaborated with Ken Porter on a book published in August 2012, *German PoW Camp 266 – Langdon Hills*. It spent six weeks as the number one best-selling book in Waterstones, Basildon in 2013. They have also collaborated on other books in this local history series.

Stephen has also co-written three crime thrillers, published between 2010 and 2012, which centre around a fictional detective named Terry Danvers.

Hartlepool in the Great War is one of numerous books which Stephen has written for Pen and Sword on aspects of the Great War, including several in the Towns and Cities of The Great War series which commemorate the sacrifices made by young men up and down the country. He has also written *Against All Odds: Walter Tull, the Black Lieutenant* about a professional football player, who became the first black officer to lead white soldiers into battle in the First World War.

Hartlepool
in the Great War

Stephen Wynn

Pen & Sword
MILITARY

First published in Great Britain in 2018 by
Pen & Sword MILITARY
An imprint of Pen & Sword Books Ltd
Yorkshire – Philadelphia

Copyright © Stephen Wynn, 2018
ISBN: 978 1 47382 860 5

A CIP catalogue record for this book is available from the British Library

Printed and bound in the UK by TJ International, Padstow, Cornwall, PL28 8RW

Pen & Sword Books Limited incorporates the imprints of Atlas, Archaeology,
Aviation, Discovery, Family History, Fiction, History, Maritime, Military, Military
Classics, Politics, Select, Transport, True Crime, Air World, Frontline Publishing, Leo
Cooper, Remember When, Seaforth Publishing, The Praetorian Press, Wharncliffe
Local History, Wharncliffe Transport, Wharncliffe True Crime and White Owl.

For a complete list of Pen & Sword titles please contact
PEN & SWORD BOOKS LIMITED
47 Church Street, Barnsley, South Yorkshire, S70 2AS, England
E-mail: enquiries@pen-and-sword.co.uk • Website: www.pen-and-sword.co.uk
Or
PEN AND SWORD BOOKS
1950 Lawrence Rd, Havertown, PA 19083, USA
E-mail: Uspen-and-sword@casematepublishers.com
Website: www.penandswordbooks.com

Contents

Chapter One   A Brief History of Hartlepool 1

Chapter Two   1914 – Starting Out 2

Chapter Three   1915 – Deepening Conflict 31

Chapter Four   1916 – The Realisation.. 50

Chapter Five   1917 – Seeing it Through 82

Chapter Six   1918 – The Final Push... 108

Chapter Seven   The Aftermath 123

Chapter Eight   Hartlepool War Memorial.. 129

Sources 183

Index 184

A Brief History of Hartlepool

Hartlepool has a long and interesting history which can be traced back some 1400 years to 640AD when the town had a monastery founded by the Irish Abbess Hieu which, unusually, was home to both monks and nuns. A village formed around the perimeter of the monastery, which was the beginning of what is today the town of Hartlepool.

St Hilda became the monastery's second Abbess in 649 before she moved on to the abbey in the neighbouring town of Whitby in about 658. After Hilda left nothing much else was heard of the town for centuries afterwards; it was as if it simply hadn't existed for about 500 years.

It was not until the year 1174 that the first mention of the town by its current name of Hartlepool, occurred. It was King John in the year 1200, who created the town of Hartlepool as a Royal Borough. It used to be a walled town and due to its geographical location played a prominent part in some of the troubled times across the centuries. Over the years its importance and its prosperity waned. It wasn't really until the development of the railway around 1830 as a viable proposition, for both travel and the delivery of goods, that the people of Hartlepool realized the full potential and worth of the locomotive. With this in mind a Bill was promoted in Parliament for the building of a dock and a railway line for Hartlepool. The Bill was successful and passed into law in 1832, and within just three years the dock was finished and open for business. The railway was established soon after and the town's prosperity soon began to grow; so flourishing was the trade, that a second dock was opened in 1840.

By 1845 business was booming and more and more people were moving into the town. A stretch of land that was a barren swamp, where only an old farm house stood, was developed to such an extent that an entire new town grew, known as West Hartlepool. In no time at all the new town had flourished and within two years it had a harbour, followed a short while later by a dock, both of which were linked by the railway to other nearby towns and cities.

Despite continued competition from its powerful and wealthy neighbours on the Tyne and the Humber, Hartlepool continued to prosper and by the outbreak of the First World War its docks were equipped with some of the most up-to-date equipment which allowed for the rapid loading and unloading of vessels. Added to this was the repairing and building of ships, industries which not only helped make the town even more affluent, but also provided more work opportunities for many of the townspeople.

CHAPTER TWO

1914 – Starting Out

The outbreak of war in 1914 wasn't really a shock to most people. It had been coming for a long time and it was more a case of when, rather than if, war broke out. But as with everything in life, when a situation becomes a reality, it is always a shock to a greater or lesser degree. From the start of the war on 4 August until 31 December 1914, British and Dominion forces lost more than 42,000 men who had been killed in the fighting. That equates to 8,400 men for each of the first five months of the war. These figures included men from Hartlepool.

The first major battle of 1914 and therefore of the First World War was the Battle of Mons. It took place on 23 August as the British attempted to hold back the rapidly advancing German Army at the Mons-Condé Canal. It was followed by a two-week retreat, which saw the British Expeditionary Force (BEF) pushed all the way back to the outskirts of Paris. The retreat was only halted by a counter-attack in unison with French forces in what became known as the Battle of the Marne.

There were other battles during the course of those first five months of the war, with the First Battle of Ypres being the major coming together of the two opposing sides. It took place between 19 October and 22 November, and saw British, French and Belgian forces pitting their strength against the might of the Germany army, across a front that stretched from Arras in France all the way up to the Belgian coastal town of Nieuport.

To show the size of the problem that Britain found herself up against at the beginning of the war, one only had to take a look at the strength of the opposing forces. Whilst Germany and France each had armies which numbered one million men, Britain had an army of only 80,000 men, which included a combination of volunteers and reservists.

If the reports in local newspapers were anything to go by, war was the last thing on the minds of most residents of Hartlepool. It was sport, or so it seemed. The day war broke out, there was a local tennis tournament going on, with competitions for both men and women. The Northern Cyclists group had an important meet, which involved competitors from both West Hartlepool and Hartlepool areas, and football was in the news as well.

With the outbreak of war, it was not surprising that a number of individuals who lived in Hartlepool and its surrounding areas, and who were of German descent, were rounded up and detained by the British military authorities in the interests of national security as well as for their own safety. They were held at the town's Stranton Ice Rink. One of those detained was the former German consul for the Hartlepool district; others, including local residents of many years standing, were also detained.

On Tuesday, 11 August 1914, with the war just a week old, Hartlepool recorded its first military-related death, when Captain James Arrowsmith of C Company, Northern Cyclist Corps, a Territorial unit, was killed in a traffic accident at the corner of Mainsforth Terrace and Surtees Street in West Hartlepool. Captain Arrowsmith was riding a motor bike when he was in collision with a motor trolley. One of the vehicle's wheels ran over his body. He was immediately conveyed to the Cameron Hospital by PC Hillier by ambulance, but was pronounced to be dead on arrival, from severe internal injuries. He also had fractures to both legs. He was buried at the Oxbridge Lane Cemetery at Stockton-on-Tees.

The first naval man from Hartlepool to be killed during the war was Able Seaman J/1782 James William Dale, part of the crew of the light cruiser HMS *Arethusa*. He was 23 years of age when he was killed in action on 28 August, during the Battle of Heligoland Bight, when the *Arethusa* came under attack by the German cruisers SMS *Frauenlob* and SMS *Stettin*. Both vessels caused serious damage to the *Arethusa*, to such an extent that she had to be towed back to Hartlepool. James Dale is buried at the Woodlands Cemetery in Gillingham, Kent.

On Sunday 30 August Mr Horsley of West Hartlepool, organized a fleet of some twenty automobiles, which had been lent by their patriotic owners, to travel to the outlying villages in the East Durham coalfield areas, collect young men, and deliver them to the recruiting offices in West Hartlepool to enlist. The town had done so well with its recruitment drive that Lord Kitchener had written to the mayor personally, to thank him.

Owing to the lack of facilities, recruits from some of the outlying districts were unable to get to Hartlepool, and accordingly Mr J.J. Prest, Chief Agent of the Horden Collieries, on Monday morning sent a telegram to the War Office:

> *Kitchener, War Office, London. Hundreds of young miners, physically fit and excellent recruits, unable to join your Army at Hartlepool or Sunderland, owing to inefficient arrangements of recruiting staff. – Prest, Castle Eden, Durham.*

By noon on Wednesday 2 September, the total number of recruits who had passed their Army medical at West Hartlepool was 2,200. Of these 400 had enlisted on the Tuesday. The time spent attending one of the recruitment offices to enlist in the Army could be a long and arduous process. To try and assist with the smooth running of the day, men were provided with meals paid for by private donations.

By noon on Saturday 5 September, the total number of recruits who had enrolled in the Army at Hartlepool stood at the staggering figure of 3,200. The previous day had seen a total of 270 men enlist in the town, and during the course of the Saturday afternoon and the following Monday, a similar number from surrounding districts were also expected. Throughout West Hartlepool it was hoped that a local corps could be formed, similar to what had been proposed at nearby Darlington and other surrounding towns. Councillor E.O. Bennet had communicated with the commanding officer of the Northern Division on the matter and was awaiting a reply.

With the war just over a month old, Sunday 6 September saw the sudden and tragic death, and in the strangest way, of Hartlepool's Member of Parliament, Sir Stephen Furness, whilst on a short holiday with his wife at a sea front hotel in Broadstairs, on the Isle of Thanet. They had a room with a sea view and were situated on the fifth floor. It would appear that at about one o'clock in the morning, Sir Stephen attempted to open the large bedroom window, as it was a warm and sticky evening, and in doing so, overbalanced and fell some 60 feet to the pavement below, breaking his back and dying almost immediately.

He had won the Hartlepool seat in the by-election of June 1910, for the Liberal Party, by a hair's breadth, with a margin of just 48 votes, polling 6,017 against the 5,969 of the Unionist Party's candidate, Mr W.G. Howard Gritten. The original General Election which had taken place in January 1910, and which had been voided as a result of an electoral petition, had been won by his uncle Sir Christopher Furness. Although by the time of his death he had been a Member of Parliament for four and a half years, according to Hansard records, he had not made one single speech on behalf of his constituents during that period.

When Sir Christopher died in 1912, Sir Stephen succeeded him as the chairman of the company Furness, Withey & Co, which included ship building, collieries and ironworks. He became a member of the West Hartlepool Town Council in 1897, the Durham County Council 1898, a Justice

Sir Stephen Wilson Furness

of the Peace, as well as a member of the Hartlepool Port and Harbour Committee. At 42 years of age, he was a comparatively young man and was married to Eleanor Forster, the daughter of Matthew Forster, of Adelaide in South Australia. They had three sons, Christopher, Stephen and Frank, and a daughter, Eleanor. The family lived at Tunstall Grange in West Hartlepool, along with Stephen's brother, Einar, both of whom were born in Sweden. Stephen was made a baronet on 18 June 1913.

Sir Stephen was buried just three days after his death at Cundall. Three memorial services were held simultaneously at the Burbank United Methodist Church, St Hilda's Church, both of which were in Hartlepool, and the other at Christ Church in West Hartlepool. There were many signs of mourning throughout the district. Flags were flying at half mast from all municipal buildings, as well as the Constitutional and Liberal Clubs and numerous different businesses. The civic service, held at Christ Church, was an impressive affair, attended by the mayor, members of the corporation and many other prominent citizens.

I found records of a Carl Einar Furness, evidently Sir Stephen's brother, who was conscripted at Newcastle on 2 June 1917 as Driver 240565 in the Royal Field Artillery, but the next day he was transferred to the Royal Garrison Artillery at Hartlepool, initially serving as a driver, before becoming a gunner. He was living in Gateshead at the time he was called up and was 30 years of age, single and a ship owner and managing director. He spent six days as a patient at the Western General Hospital in Manchester, between 29 June and 5 July 1918. The reasons for his admission was not legible on his Army Service Record. On 28 October 1918 he was discharged from the Army as no longer physically fit for wartime military service due to fracturing his skull.

After Sir Stephen's untimely death, he was replaced as the town's Liberal MP by Sir Walter Runciman, who at the time was also the President of the Northern Liberal Federation, after a meeting of Hartlepool's Liberal Six Hundred on Friday 18 September. In keeping with the agreement of all political parties during the First World War, the Hartlepool Unionists agreed to abide by its terms and not to contend any elections, meaning that Hartlepool would politically remain in the hands of the Liberal Party for the duration of the war.

On a personal level it must have been a difficult time for the Unionist candidate, Mr W.G. Howard Gritten, a London barrister, who had previously contested the Hartlepool parliamentary seat on three occasions, but who was unsuccessful each time. He finally had a realistic chance of winning the constituency, only to be thwarted by the wartime agreement between the leading political parties, not to contest by-elections, so as to keep political stability during wartime.

On Tuesday 15 September, a vessel belonging to Furness, Withy & Co, *The Clan Matheson*, which was first launched in 1906, was sunk by the

German cruiser, *Emden*, in the Bay of Bengal. The crew were transferred to the *Dovre*, and were then taken to Rangoon.

The first soldier who had connections with Hartlepool to be killed whilst fighting on foreign soil was John Robert Richardson, who was born in the town in 1887. As a young man he joined the army and initially became a gunner (57561) with the 144th Battery, stationed at Wellington Lines, Aldershot. He was promoted and eventually became a corporal (57561) with the 45th Battery, Royal Field Artillery, which was the unit he was serving with when he was killed in action on 4 October 1914. He is buried in the Bergen Communal Cemetery at Mons, in the Hainaut region of Belgium.

In the early weeks of the war the men of Hartlepool responded to the national call to enlist. The town's recruiting office in Tower Street was open for twelve hours a day from 9am to 9pm. It came under the charge of Captain Osler and his staff of fifteen men, who dealt with the extremely busy workload. The idea was to encourage as many men as possible to enlist, and by providing them with a twelve-hour time slot and sufficient staff to deal with them on their arrival at the recruiting office, it was felt that more and more would sign up. Here are the numbers of those men who enlisted at the Hartlepool recruiting office during the seven days between 19 and 23 August 1914.

Wednesday 19 August – 34 men enlisted
Thursday 20 August – 45 men enlisted
Friday 21 August – 54 men enlisted
Saturday 22 August – 39 men enlisted
Sunday 23 August – 19 men enlisted
Monday 24 August – 76 men enlisted
Tuesday 25 August – 57 men enlisted

Between Wednesday 12 August and Tuesday 25 August, Captain Osler and his trusty staff had registered a total of 324 recruits. Prior to these dates 116 local men had already enlisted, making a grand total of 440 men who had been recruited since the beginning of the war. On top of this a further 12 men who had wanted to enlist had been rejected as being medically unfit for military wartime service. Men were required for many different roles. Understandably, they were needed in their tens of thousands for all front-line infantry units. The Royal Engineers required sappers and pioneers, whilst the Royal Field Artillery needed both drivers and gunners. The military authorities quickly realized that despite the overflow of national pride, fervour and an innate desire of men wanting to do their duty, what they were really lacking was experience. As a carrot to try and rectify the problem, they offered men under 42 years of age, who had previously been in service with the colours, to rejoin at their former rank.

Mr Harry Picken of Milton Street, West Hartlepool wrote a letter home to his family. It was dated 28 October, and was about the Battle of Penang, which took place that same day, and was a naval action in the Strait of Malacca, that saw the German Cruiser SMS *Emden*, sink a Russian cruiser and a French destroyer, killing 135 Allied sailors, and wounding a further 157.

Mr Picken wrote:

> *We witnessed this morning the most terrible spectacle I ever saw or wish to see. Not two hundred yards from our stern the Emden was emptying her broadsides into a Russian warship at anchor.*
>
> *It was just before dawn. She had stolen up in the dark, dodged the scouts, and came into harbour, steaming once round the Russian, when she started. All the Russians were asleep, except the watch. They thought I suppose, that she was Japanese, as she rigged up a dummy funnel.*
>
> *After firing her broadsides she turned, and nearly hit our stern in doing so, and then, letting the Russian have her other broadside, blew up her magazine. There was a tremendous crash, and the Russian was no more. All this was within an eighth of a mile from us, and all over in thirteen minutes. If one shot had hit us it would have blown us up. Had the Russian moved we should have been damaged, all her shells going over our stern; so we all crowded forward.*

The letter then took some time describing the efforts that were made to rescue the survivors from the Russian cruiser, *Zhemchug*, before continuing:

> *It was an awful sight. A lot of them would never know, the first shot going in to her sleeping quarters. After she blew up, and the smoke cleared, it was awful to hear the cries of drowning men and the cheers of the Germans. It seems like a dream to think that at 5.30 am, 340 men were sleeping and at 5.45 am, half were gone, and most of the others injured.*
>
> *They have 160 in hospital, and 60 of them died today. I don't think a naval battle was ever fought at such close range, about 200 yards, since the days of Nelson. I am sure no one ever witnessed one so close without being engaged.*
>
> *All now left of the Russian is the top mast about 6 feet out of the water. All ships passing it today have lowered their flags as a mark of sympathy. There were three French torpedo boats in harbour at the time, but had no steam up. Had there been a general battle we should certainly have been blown up. The Emden can't have seen the Frenchmen, but he met one as he went out, and sunk her with four shots.*
>
> *The Emden met another ship in the open, and had an awful battle, but we can't get any news about it. They say there was no battle; but we know better, as we could both see and hear it. People ashore say the Emden torpedoed the Russian. He did nothing of the sort; he blew up their magazine.*

Mr Picken was an engineer on board the SS *Nyganistan*, at anchor in the same harbour where the battle took place, and it just goes to show that even though he was thousands of miles away from home, the worry and concern of his family would have still been paramount; such feelings were not exclusive to the battlefields of France and Belgium.

An interesting letter appeared in some of the northern newspapers on and around Thursday 3 December. It was based on a letter which Guardsman 5460 John Edward Hartland of the 1st Battalion, Scots Guards had written to his wife, Katherine, at their home, 27 Middlegate Street, Hartlepool. Before the war John had been a Police Constable in Hartlepool. He had been wounded in action whilst serving in France and had been sent home to be treated in England. At the time of writing his letter he was a patient at Leeds General Hospital:

> *They can talk about South Africa as much as they like. They did not know what fighting was there. A few with ribbons that went out to France can tell you that all the time the South African war was on, there wasn't one day's fighting to compare with one day out in France or Belgium. There have been more shells fired out here in one day than there were fired in twelve months in Africa. That just gives an idea of what it is like.*
>
> *I suppose you will have read the letter I sent to the Police office. There was one special incident I forgot to put in it. It happened whilst we were retiring from one position, and had to run for our lives, with the German Maxim gun only about 50 yards behind us, and the Germans coming in their thousands. On jumping out of the trench I ran about 50 yards and dropped on top of several more behind a hedge who had got there first. I had my bayonet fixed at the time, and on dropping on these others I caught my bayonet in some part of one of their coats and being in such a scramble I could not get it free.*
>
> *The same fellows were shouting 'mercy', so with not being able to get under cover I dropped my bayonet and rifle there and made another run for it. The Germans were firing their Maxim guns and rifles from about only 50 yards away. They had stopped in trenches which we had just left.*

His letter made for a truly enthralling read and vividly brought to life what he had experienced. My heart was racing as I dived in and out of the trenches with him as he made good his escape from the advancing swarm of German soldiers.

> *It happened when I got up to make another run for it, there was a bit of a dyke run up the side of the road only about a foot deep and not much more than a foot wide. After running a short distance, I threw myself headlong into this dyke, and lay there for a few minutes, not knowing what to do next.*

I intended escaping capture, or being hit if I could help it; so whilst lying down I undid my belt, and threw everything off, knowing quite well it was easy enough to get some more. You could always pick up dead men's equipment and rifle anywhere about there. After throwing them off, I crawled on my stomach for about 150 yards to a farmhouse which was on the other side of the road, so I had to get up and chance it again. Making a mad dash I managed it without being hit, although the firing was proceeding fast.

On reaching the house there happened to be more of our fellows there who also had made a run for it. Whilst there I saw across the field on our right, about 100 yards away, an officer of the Black Watch and nine men come from behind a hay stack and extend out from each other. They had just nicely extended out when every man dropped. There were five killed. Three of the others managed to crawl back, but the other man and the officer had to lie there. It was a queer thing the officer had only gone out the day before.

The next on the scene while I was standing there was one of the Black Watch coming round the corner of the house against which I was standing, dragging a box of ammunition. He came to me and asked me if I would give him a hand to carry it across a field to where his battalion were entrenched.

I said, 'Don't be foolish man. You had better wait until the firing ceases a bit.' I asked him if he had carried it himself. He said no. His chum who had been helping him had just dropped on the other side of the house. He was right, he had been shot down. Well, he begged me to help him across with it, so I got hold of one side and he the other, and we ran for all we were worth across the same field where the nine men had been knocked down. I was lucky again. I don't know how I escaped being hit. I seemed that I didn't seem to care much whether I was hit or not.

After landing at the trench, I managed to get a complete equipment with rifle and bayonet, which one of the Black Watch had done with. I then went to seek our companions. I found about half a dozen left of my company. One of our Sergeants was shot through both legs. I got hold of him and helped him across the field to the farm house, risking my life again. It was then beginning to get dark, and we all had to retire further back to keep up another position.

Sometime after having been discharged from hospital in Leeds, John Hartland eventually returned to France, but sadly his luck deserted him, and he was killed in action on 14 August 1916. He is buried at the Sucrerie Military Cemetery in Colincamps, in the Somme region of France.

The inquest took place on Monday 7 December of 17-year-old Douglas Jardine, a labourer of 40 Durham Street, Hartlepool. Evidence was presented to the court that the young man in question was employed on the north basin extension works at Hartlepool harbour. Early on the morning of Friday 4

Sucrerie Military Cemetery.

December, whilst returning to work after having just finished his break, he tripped over a piece of timber whilst stepping on to a temporary gangway, which crossed the entrance to the basin.

He fell to the bottom of the lock, a distance of some 40 feet, sustaining a fractured thigh and internal injuries. Although quickly conveyed to Hartlepool's General Hospital, he died later the same day.

Having heard all of the available evidence, the jury retired, and after only a few minutes consultation the foreman remarked that they could not come to a decision without first visiting the scene of the accident. The coroner acquiesced to their request and adjourned the inquest until later the same day.

The Bombing of Hartlepool

Along with the neighbouring towns of Scarborough and Whitby, Hartlepool experienced, at first hand, the destructive and devastating effects of war when it came under attack from three ships of the Imperial German Navy, the armoured cruiser, SMS *Blucher*, and the battlecruisers SMS *Seydlitz* and SMS *Moltke*, about 9am on Wednesday 16 December. By the time the attack was over, the German naval vessels had fired an estimated 1,150 artillery shells at the town, killing 9 soldiers and 86 civilians, with a further 438 who

Blake Street -Bomb damage.

had received injuries, 14 of whom were soldiers. Although Hartlepool wasn't exactly in ruins, a great deal of damage had been done to the town's buildings, at a cost of tens of thousands of pounds, including homes, churches, the steelworks, the railway station, the gasworks along with many of the local churches.

One of those who was killed during the attack on Whitby, was 30-year-old local Coastguard Boatman, FREDERICK RANDELL, a married man with four children. He died when he stepped out of his home, one of the cottages near to the coastguard signalling station, just as a shell exploded nearby, blowing his head off. His death was particularly poignant as he had been serving with the Royal Navy, when he had been awarded the Naval General Service Medal, and had been discharged so that he could return to his pre-war position with the Coastguard.

He was buried at the Larpool Cemetery in Whitby. By the time the Commonwealth War Graves Commission had begun collating its records in the early 1920s, Frederick's parents were living at 13 Clarence Place, Gosport, Hampshire, and his wife, Eliza Jane Rendell and their children, had also moved to Hampshire, living at 8 Clark's Buildings, Quay Street, in Fareham.

There were nine British soldiers killed on that fateful December day, six of whom were from the 18th Battalion (Durham Pals) Durham Light

Cliff Terrace after bombardment.

Infantry, which had only been formed in September 1914 by a committee, the chairman of which was the Earl of Durham. Once permission had been granted by the War Office to begin recruiting for the battalion, monies were quickly raised to equip the young men who had eagerly joined up. By the time of that initial committee meeting, which took place on 21 September 1914, Colonel Burdon reported that 570 men had already enlisted, and that the names of sixteen suitable 'gentlemen' had been obtained as prospective temporary officers.

The battalion's headquarters were the illustrious surroundings of Cocken Hall, which was Lord Durham's home. In what seemed like no time at all, an encampment for the men had been erected in the tranquil grounds, allowing them to undertake their military training, whilst at the same time providing them with suitable living accommodation.

Although not having completed their basic training, 500 of the battalion's men were sent to Hartlepool in November 1914 to help bolster the sea defences, because of the fear that Germany might imminently engage in naval raids along the North Sea coastline of Great Britain. Sadly, these fears would become a reality quicker than anybody could have possibly imagined.

The nine soldiers who were killed on that fateful day, were:

Private 18/295 THEOPHILUS JONES, of the 18th Battalion, Durham Light Infantry, had the unwanted claim to history of being the first British serviceman to be killed on British soil, as a result of enemy action during the

THIS TABLET MARKS THE PLACE
WHERE THE FIRST SHELL FROM THE
LEADING GERMAN BATTLE CRUISER
STRUCK AT 8·10 A.M. ON THE
16ᵀᴴ OF DECEMBER 1914
AND ALSO RECORDS THE PLACE WHERE
(DURING THE BOMBARDMENT)
THE FIRST SOLDIER WAS KILLED
ON BRITISH SOIL BY ENEMY ACTION
IN THE GREAT WAR 1914-1918

Memorial to Private Jones.

course of the First World War, when he was hit by a German shell at 8.10am on 16 December 1914.

He was 29 years of age and his parents lived at 44 Ashgrove Avenue, West Hartlepool. He was buried at Stranton Cemetery in Hartlepool. His brother, Alfred, who also served as a private (18/1419) with the 18th Battalion, Durham Light Infantry, also became one of the war's casualties, when he was killed in action during the Battle of Arras on 3 May 1917. He has no known grave and his name is commemorated on the Arras Memorial, in the Pas de Calais region of France.

Gunner 5693 WILLIAM STEPHEN HOUSTON, was 22 years of age and serving with the Durham Royal Garrison Artillery, which was part of the Heugh Battery at Hartlepool, when he was killed in action during the bombardment of the town by SMS *Seydlitz* and SMS *Moltke,* vessels of the German Imperial Navy. His parents, Adam and Sarah Houston, lived at 75 Union Road, Central Estate, Hartlepool, and he was buried at the town's West View Cemetery.

Acting Corporal 18/107 ALIX OLIFFEE LIDDELL, was 25 years of age and serving with the 18th Battalion (Durham Pals), Durham Light Infantry.

Private 18/398 LESLIE DOBSON TURNER was 24 years of age and prior to joining the 18th Battalion, had lived with his parents William and Mary Turner, at 'Dalmeny', 10 Rectory Drive, Gosforth, Newcastle-Upon-Tyne. He was buried at St Patrick churchyard at Winlaton, Durham.

Private 18/369 WALTER ROGERS was 25 years of age and a single man who also served with the 18th Battalion, Durham Light Infantry. He was a

Hartlepool West View Cemetery.

native of Bishop Auckland, where he was buried in the town's cemetery. His home was at South View, Bishop Auckland.

Private 18/328 THOMAS MINKS was 25 years of age. He was initially wounded, but died of his wounds the following day. He was buried at the St Patrick Churchyard and Hookergate Cemetery in Winlaton, Durham. Before the war Thomas had been an assistant schoolmaster and had lived with his mother, Elizabeth and his five brothers and sisters at Melbourne House, Rowlands Gill, County Durham. Another brother lived at Woking in Surrey. He had enlisted in Newcastle on 21 September 1914, with enthusiasm, pride and a desire to do his bit for his King and country sadly for him, less than three months later he was dead.

Thomas's younger brother, Robert Sydney Minks, who was only 18 years of age in 1918, also served his country during the the war, firstly with the Northumberland Fusiliers and during the latter stages, with the Royal Air Force.

In a booklet entitled *The German raid on the Hartlepools, December 16th 1914*, that was printed soon after the event by Sage, Bookseller and Stationer, of 6 Lynn Street, West Hartlepool, one of the soldiers who was killed on 16 December 1914, is recorded as being Lance Corporal Clark. The same man is recorded on the Commonwealth War Graves Commission website as being Private 18/707 C.S. Clarke. This is in fact CHARLES STEPHEN CLARKE, who enlisted at Hartlepool on 1 October 1914 when he was 25 years of age. His Army Service Record shows that when he enlisted he lived at 11 Collingwood Road, West Hartlepool, although by the time of his death he had moved across town and was living at 47 Sheffield Street, and his rank was that of acting lance corporal. He was buried at North Cemetery in Hartlepool. He was a married man having wed Elsie Ireland in West Hartlepool on 5 August 1911. They had a son, also Charles Stephen Clarke, who was born on Christmas Eve 1912.

Gunner 5428 ROBERT SPENCE was 22 years of age and serving with the Durham Royal Garrison Artillery. At the time of his death his home was at 19 Prissick Street, Hartlepool, but by the time that the Commonwealth War Graves Commission began amassing their records in the early 1920s, his parents, James and Amelia Spence, were living at 4 Alfred Street, Hartlepool. He is buried in the town's West View Cemetery.

Sapper 558 SAMUEL LITTLE was 20 years of age and was serving with the Durham Fortress Company of the Royal Engineers at the time of his death. Before he enlisted in the Army he lived with his parents, Walter and Susan Little, at 8 Clyde Street, Jarrow. He was the youngest of four children. Mary, who was the eldest, followed by his brothers James and John.

James, who was 25 years of age at the outbreak of the war, also enlisted in the Royal Engineers, on 21 September 1914 at Jarrow, when he became Sapper 53091 of the 18th Signal Company, the unit with which he went to France as part of the British Expeditionary Force on 24 July 1915. On 24 August 1915 he was admitted to the 55th Field Ambulance near Rouen for treatment to an abscess. Whilst still serving in France he was transferred to the Base Signal Depot on 3 May 1916, before moving on to the 12th Signal Company five days later. He remained on the Western Front for a further four months, during which time he was treated at No.9 Stationary hospital between 15 March and 3 April 1916, finally returning home on 15 September 1916. He was immediately admitted to Stoke-on-Trent War Hospital at Newcastle in Staffordshire, to be treated for an abdominal wound, where he remained until 25 September. From there he was transferred to the Red Cross Convalescent Hospital at Leek until 24 October. According to his Army Service Record, he was then sent to another hospital, the name of which was not legible, where he remained until 6 November 1916, when he returned to the Red Cross Hospital at Leek, before finally being released on 15 December 1916.

He was discharged from the Army on 26 October 1917 as no longer physically fit for wartime military service, having served for a total of 3

HMS *Doon.*

years and 36 days. His condition, it would appear, was connected to a bout of appendicitis he had suffered in December 1914 at Colchester, which had resulted in internal stomach problems, most likely a ventral hernia, which is a bulge in the wall of the abdominal muscles. It was deemed to be sufficiently serious and debilitating, that he was not required to present himself for re-examination of his condition a year later as per the guidance of the Military Service Act.

The first committee meeting of the 18th Battalion, after the German bombardment of Hartlepool, took place on Boxing Day and of course, most of the discussion centred around the attack and the confirmation that the battalion had lost six of its men. Five were killed outright and a sixth died later of his injuries. A further ten men were wounded, most of whom it was believed would eventually be fit enough to return to active duty.

Sadly, it does not appear that the names of the men who were either killed or injured in the attack had their names recorded in the minutes of the meeting, and neither does it appear that a minute's silence was called for in their memory, and for the sacrifice they made.

Nine sailors also lost their lives during the bombardment of the town.

Stoker 1st Class SS/109383 JAMES FRASER, Royal Navy, was 23 years of age and one of the crew of HMS *Doon,* a Hawthorn Leslie type River-class destroyer, when he was killed in action during the raid by the Imperial German Navy on Hartlepool. The *Doon,* under the command of Lieutenant Commander H. McLeod-Fraser, was damaged by German shell fire which

HMS *Patrol*.

resulted in one of her guns and her torpedo tubes been put out of action. Besides the three men who died, six others were wounded.

The next of kin for James Fraser was his brother George, who lived at 26 Victoria Road, North Berwick, Scotland. James's body was never recovered so he has no known grave. His name is commemorated on the Chatham Naval Memorial.

Able Seaman J/8662 ERNEST CHARLES CUMMINGS was just 20 years of age and one of the crew of HMS *Patrol*, a Pathfinder-class scout cruiser, when he was killed in action during the German bombardment of Hartlepool. As she made her way out of the harbour, the *Patrol* was spotted by the German cruiser *Blücher* and struck by two of her heavy shells, leaving Captain Bruce no option but to run his ship aground to save her from sinking. Four of her crew were killed whilst a further seven were injured.

Ernest Cummings was buried in the Holy Trinity Churchyard at Seaton Carew, one of only four men from the First World War laid to rest there.

Another crew member of HMS *Patrol*, killed on that fateful day, was Armourer CH/345449 GEORGE M. FLYNN, who served under the surname of Martin. He is buried at the Linthorpe Cemetery in Middlesbrough.

Leading Seaman 224557 RALPH WESTON HOOK was 28 years of age and also one of those killed whilst serving on HMS *Patrol*. He was a married man, his wife May Lavette Hook lived at 42 Godwin Road, Cliftonville, Margate. Like George Flynn, he was buried at the Linthorpe Cemetery in Middlesbrough.

Holy Trinity Churchyard. (Commonwealth War Graves Commission)

The fourth crew member of HMS *Patrol* to be killed during the German bombardment of Hartlepool, was Engine Room Artificer 1st Class P.J. SHERIDAN. He was buried at St Joseph's Roman Catholic Cemetery, in North Ormesby, Yorkshire.

Below is a list of the town's civilian population who also tragically lost their lives on that December day in 1914:

Allen, Annie (25) 14 Victoria Place, Hartlepool

Allen, Robert A. (18)

Ambrose, Robert L. (33) 65 Everard Street, Hartlepool

Arnold, Hannah (33)

Ashcroft, Edwin (29) 19 Penrith Street, Hartlepool

Ashquith, William (51)

Austrin, Beart Beaumont (32) 4 May Street, Hartlepool

Avery, William Gordon (49) 7 Victoria Place, Hartlepool

Backham, Cuthbert J. (42) Darlington Terrace, Hartlepool

Bell, Henry S. (11) 31 Belk Street, Hartlepool

Binns, Samuel (68) 21 Ramsey Street, Hartlepool

Brennan, Margaret

Brookbanks, Charles A. (35)

Bunter, James (32) 13 Commercial Street, Hartlepool

Capeling, Nicholas (25)

Caw, Dorothy (25)

Chappell, William (15) 18 Slake Terrace, Middleton

Churcher, William H. (26) 29 Clarendon Road, Hartlepool

Clark, John (54) 5 Kinburn Street, Hartlepool

Claude, Alfred C.B. 12 Gordon Street, Hartlepool

Cook, Harold (10) 40 Turnbull Street, Hartlepool

Cook, James (37) 28 Rokeby Street, Hartlepool

Cook, Robert W. (8) 40 Turnbull Street, Hartlepool

Cook, Thomas C. (14)

Cooper, Edward (14)

Corner, Bridget (37) 1 Dock Street, Hartlepool

Cornforth, Charles (63) 3 Lilly Street, Hartlepool

Cornforth, Polly (23) 3 Lilly Street, Hartlepool

Cornforth, Jane Ann (17) 2 Lilly Street, Hartlepool

Cox, John Garbutt (26) 2 Durham Street, Hartlepool

Crake, John William (15) 19 Woods Street, Hartlepool

Cressy, Albert E. (29) 48 Turnbull Street, Hartlepool

Dixon, George E. (14) 30 William Street, Hartlepool

Dixon, Margaret E. (8) 30 William Street, Hartlepool

Dixon, Albert (7) 30 William Street, Hartlepool

Dring, George (47) 30 Elliot Street, Hartlepool

Evans, John (32) 30 Charlotte Street, Hartlepool

Frankland, Catherine (4)

Gray, William (23)

Geipel, Ethel Mary (36) 17 Cliffe Terrace, Hartlepool
Hamilton, Jessie (21) 50 Malton Street, Hartlepool
Harper, Elizabeth A. (49) 4 Moor Terrace, Hartlepool
Harris, Etta (30) Ivy Lodge, South Crescent, Hartlepool
Harrimin, Mary A.
Healey, John (63) 18 Hart Street, Hartlepool
Henderson, Joseph (47)
Henighan, Margaret
Herbert, Selina (3) 5 William Street, Hartlepool
Heslop, Thomas (7)
Higham, Thomas (11)
Hodgson, John (62) 58 Stephenson Street, Hartlepool
Hodgson, Sarah
Hodgson, William (43)
Horsley, Hilda
Hudson, Charles W. (21) 43 Mary Street, Hartlepool
Hunter, Margaret
Hunter, Samuel (16)
Jackson, Edith
Jackson, Joseph (13)
Jefferey, Thomas (48) 10 Dock Street, Hartlepool
Jobling, Hannah (4)
Jobling, Sarah (6)
Kay, Annie M. (34) Rockside, Cliffe Terrace, Hartlepool
Kay, Florence J. (32) Rockside, Cliffe Terrace, Hartlepool
Lee, Clementina (25) 6 Victoria Place, Hartlepool
Leighton, James S. (56) 16 Clifton Street, Hartlepool
Lofthouse, Benjamin (7 months) 25 Belk Street, Hartlepool
Lynett, James (43)
Marshall, Catherine (87) 41 Mary Street, Hartlepool
Measor, Christopher (10) 11 Wells Yard, Hartlepool
McGuire, John (15)
Moon, Julia (64) 11 Dover Street, Hartlepool
Mossom, Thomas (54)
Necy, Eleanor (6 months)
Oliver, Joseph (45)
Owen, Mary E. (17)
Owen, Rose (43)
Pearl, William 5 Turnbull Street, Hartlepool

Pearl, Charles 2 Turnbull Street, Hartlepool
Pearson, James W. (25) SS *Phoebe*, Robin Hoods Bay
Phillips, Thomas (16)
Ramsay, Charles L.C. (37) 24 Osbourne Road, Hartlepool
Redshaw, Margaret A. (47) 50 Watson Street, Hartlepool
Reynold, Hannah
Sarginson, William (22)
Scarr, Thomasina (44)
Sharp, Margaret (18)
Simmons, Stanley (5)
Skelton, Matthew (54)
Sta, John (41)
Stewart, Stanley (6) 20 William Street, Hartlepool
Stoker, Jane (41)
Stringer, Ethel (12) 10 William Street, Hartlepool
Sullivan, Daniel (47) 3 Harrison Street, Hartlepool
Swales, Matthew (36)
Theaker, Richard (26) 63 Turnbull Street, Hartlepool
Unthank, Frank (14) 24 Woods Street, Hartlepool
Walker Albert (9) Turnbull Street, Hartlepool
Walker, Stanley (6) Turnbull Street, Hartlepool
Watson, Mary E. (40) 164 Hart Road, Hartlepool
Wainwright, Freda (19) 10 Henry Street, Hartlepool
Watt, Amy (22) 2 Marine Crescent, Hartlepool
Wheelwright, Barwick (15)
Whitecross, Peter (8) 34 William Street, Hartlepool
Whitecross, John M. (6) 34 William Street, Hartlepool
Wilkinson, Laura (13)
Williams, Ivy (31) 8 Beaconsfield Square, Hartlepool
Witty, Stanley W. (18)
Woods, Josiah (33) Harbour Terrace, Hartlepool
Woods, Martha Jane (6) Harbour Terrace, Hartlepool
Woods, Samuel N. (19) 18 Lumley Street, Hartlepool
Wright, William (41) 4 Crook Street, Hartlepool
Young, Bertie (13) 13 Princess Street, Middleton

My apologies if I have inadvertently missed anybody off the list. I have taken the original list that was issued and then added to it, mainly by looking through newspapers of the day to find the names of those who subsequently died as a result of their injuries.

Durham Royal Garrison Artillery.

Ethel Mary Geipel is included in the above list, although she was not killed on 16 December 1914. She was injured in the bombardment, but subsequently died of her wounds a month later on 15 January 1915 at Hartlepool General Hospital. She was a single woman, and in her will she left the sum of £418 1s 11d to her brother, Arthur Geipel. Ethel was the youngest of nine children, her mother, Margaret Geipel, gave birth to Ethel when she was 43 years of age. By the outbreak of the war Ethel's seven brothers were too old for war service, their ages ranging between 42 and 53.

The bombardment wasn't all one way, the battery situated at the Lighthouse managed to return fire with its one 6-inch gun, striking the *Blücher*, and killing nine of her crew, whilst the nearby Heugh Battery, consisting of two 6-inch naval guns, did her best to repel the attack. They were manned by 166 officers and men of the Durham Royal Garrison Artillery.

Even though the Hartlepool batteries were given warning of the likelihood of a German naval bombardment of their positions, the first they knew of it was at 0430 on the morning of the attack. Four hours later nine of them would be dead. Just over three hours later they were further informed that German vessels had been spotted off the North East coast close to their position, although remarkably this information had not been passed to Royal Navy vessels on patrol in the same area. The situation was compounded by the inclement weather conditions which prevailed at the time, making for poor visibility which only added to the already confused situation. The Royal

Navy had seven vessels stationed in Hartlepool Harbour. Four destroyers – HMS *Doon, Moy, Test,* and *Waveney,* along with two Scout Class cruisers, HMS *Patrol* and *Forward,* and the submarine HMS *C9.*

All four of the destroyers were on patrol at the time of the bombardment, whilst the others were still at their moorings in the harbour. HMS *Forward* was unable to start her engines as she had no steam in her boilers. HMS *C9* managed to get underway, sailing along on the surface, but as the German shells began raining down, she had to submerge, and by the time she broke the surface again, the enemy vessels had finished their bombardment and left. HMS *Patrol* barely made it out of the harbour before she was struck by two 8-inch shells fired from one of the three German attackers, leaving Captain Bruce with no other option but to run his ship aground to save her from sinking.

It was only when the shells from the guns of the German vessels started to land in the town that the batteries fully realized that they were under attack and returned fire. Sadly, the small calibre of the weapons at their disposal meant that even when the shells they fired hit their intended targets, most of them simply bounced off the heavily armoured sides of the German vessels. Fortunately for the people of Hartlepool, many of the German shells that landed in the town, failed to detonate, because they had been fired too close to their intended targets, resulting in a much flatter trajectory, which meant many of the shells skimmed across the ground rather than landing nose down.

The bombardment commenced at 0810 and ended forty-two minutes later at 0852. During the attack, the three German vessels fired an incredible 1,500 shells into the town, which is nearly 36 a minute, or roughly one every one and a half seconds. More than 300 hundred buildings were struck, including churches and residential properties.

The heroic defence of the town by the men at the Heugh and Lighthouse batteries, who between them managed to fire more than 120 rounds at the German attackers, was rewarded with two Military Medals and a Distinguished Conduct Medal.

The aftermath of the bombardment was interesting. It generated a negative public opinion of the Royal Navy for not being able to prevent the attack from taking place, whilst the British Government seized the opportunity to use the attack for propaganda purposes to increase the number of men enlisting in the armed forces. It was a strategy that certainly worked as far as the men of Hartlepool were concerned, with some 22,000 of them joining up in the weeks immediately following the bombardment of their town.

The inquest of those killed in the bombardment took place on Thursday, 17 December 1914, but because of the numbers of involved, two inquests were held, one at West Hartlepool and one at Hartlepool.

The Deputy Coroner was in charge of the inquests held at West Hartlepool. He made the observation that the German bombardment was an attack on England, by an enemy, the likes of which hadn't been witnessed for hundreds of years. Because of the uniqueness of the situation, he determined that there was no precedent that allowed him to provide any guidance to the jury, but at least they would have some idea of what the people of France and Belgium had experienced when they had been invaded by German forces. The previous day he had gone on a tour of the town to witness at first hand the damage which had been caused by the bombardment. Although he couldn't help but notice how calm and quiet it was as he walked about the town, he commented on how totally different it must have been during the attack.

The first person to give evidence at the West Hartlepool inquest, Mr William Ropner, told the jury that at 8.35 on Wednesday morning he was at home when the bombardment began, and he at once went down into his cellar to join his family. According to his watch it was 8.50 before it finally came to an end. When eventually he left the cellar and saw the damage caused to his home, he came across the lifeless body of his cook, Jane Stoker, who had been hit by a shell. Why she wasn't in the cellar with the Ropner family does not appear to have been explored.

Charles Leonard Clayton Ramsey was employed at a local factory. One of the shells struck the roof of the premises where he was working, so along with all of the other workers, believed to have been about forty in number, they made a dash for the door which led out into the rear yard, but because they could see and hear other shells landing, they went back inside the premises. Ramsey then made the decision to leave so as to return to his home nearby, and look after his wife and children, but sadly he was not seen alive again.

The father of a young woman named Dorothy Caw, who was 25 years of age, said that he, his wife and their daughter Dorothy were sitting down to breakfast in the kitchen of their home when a shell came through their ceiling, killing Dorothy instantly.

The daughter of Mrs Julia Moon told the inquest how she and her husband had gone to her mother's home in Dover Street to check on her wellbeing, only to discover that her home had been destroyed by one of the shells, and her mother was lying dead in a passageway at the rear of the property.

The husband of Mrs Rose Owen told the jury how he had found his wife's body, lying face down with her arms outstretched and a large hole in her body where a piece of shrapnel had passed through.

The aunt of two siblings by the name of Jobling stated that their father was a stoker in the Royal Navy. The children's grandfather also gave evidence to the inquest that when he heard the noise of the guns he went to his front door to see what the commotion was all about. It was mayhem, with people running about all over the place:

I never thought it was the Germans, I thought our ships were practising.
I turned into the house again and was just going to get a drop of tea when
all at once, smash went the corner of the house. It took me a few minutes
to recover. When I did so I went to the door and found three children
among a lot of bricks, two of them being my son's children. They had
been killed by a shell which struck my house.

The husband of Bridget Corner was a gunner in the Royal Field Artillery. His
wife was found dead face down on the pavement.

The father of Thomas Phillips explained how his son went out to look for
his mother, his brother and sister. When the father was making his way back
home from work, he discovered the body of his dead son, which had been
absolutely riddled with what he took to be pieces of shrapnel.

Margaret Hunter's son told the inquest how at the time of the
bombardment, his mother had been out collecting sea coal. When she did not
return as expected, he went out looking for her and found her body near to
the railway line.

Similar evidence was provided to the inquest from the relatives of other
victims of the bombardment. After hearing all of the accounts the jury decided
that under the cover of a dense fog ships from the Imperial German Navy
fired artillery shells into the town of Hartlepool, killing a number of unarmed
civilians, including the above-mentioned persons. In a gesture of kindness,

Father of these children was killed.

Hartlepool German Shells.

each member of the jury voluntarily forfeited their fees to the coroner, to be used for the most deserving family or person, who it was deemed was in most immediate need, as a result of the bombardment.

At Hartlepool, the coroner, Mr J.H. Bell, commented that the civilian victims of the catastrophe had taken no part whatsoever in war-like operations, yet they were still cut down in their prime whilst simply going about their day to day lives.

Mr Anderton, headmaster of the Henry Smith School, had the unenviable task of identifying the dead body of one of his young teachers, Etta Harris, aged 30, who had worked at the school for the previous eighteen months, teaching English and Latin. She was killed at her lodging house in South Crescent.

The body of 47-year-old George Dring, a married man of 30 Elliot Street, West Hartlepool, was identified by one of his sons, Johnson, who told the inquest that his father had been killed by a piece of shrapnel from one of the exploding German shells whilst he was working at the docks. He left a widow, Jane Dring, and their seven children.

Elizabeth Agnes Harper, aged 49, who lived at 4 Moor Terrace, Hartlepool, with her husband, George, and their four daughters, was injured when a shell struck their house and died later whilst having her wounds treated at the town's Cameron hospital.

Hartlepool German unexploded bombs.

Albert Edward Cressey, aged 29, lived at home with his younger sister, Edith, and his parents, Arthur and Sarah Cressey, at 30 Middleton Road, West Hartlepool. His occupation was that of a wire mattress maker at a local factory. It was Albert's mother, Sarah, who identified his body. She told the inquest that on that fateful December day, Albert did not return home for dinner as he usually did. Inquiries were made as to his whereabouts, and it was then that it was discovered that he had been killed by one of the German shells that had landed on his place of work.

Mary Elizabeth Watson, a 40-year-old woman, who lived at 164 Hart Road, Hartlepool, was seen by a local constable walking in the middle of the road when she was struck by a falling shell.

The jury heard the sad case of Charles Cornforth, who was 63 years of age, and his two daughters, Polly (23) and Jane (17). They were all having breakfast when one of the shells hit the back of their house in Lilley Street, demolishing the kitchen. Charles's wife, Elizabeth and their other children survived.

Their son, John Robert Cornforth, served in the Army during the First World War. He enlisted as a Private (463) in the 18th Battalion, Durham Light Infantry on 17 September 1914 at Hartlepool. He was promoted to the rank of corporal on 15 July 1916 and to that of Sergeant a month later on 28 August. He was eventually discharged from the Army on 3 June 1919, not on being demobilized, as one might think, but as a result of a gunshot wound to the face and other injuries which had left him classified as being 60 per cent disabled. He had served for four years and 260 days. During this time he had served as part of the Mediterranean Expeditionary Force in Egypt between 6 December 1915 and 4 March 1916. Rather than returning home to Britain, he and his comrades in the 18th Battalion were sent to France, where he remained until 21 September 1918. Whilst serving there he was wounded twice. The first time in 1916 saw him shot in the head, by what would appear to have been a glancing blow rather than a penetrating wound, not sufficiently bad enough to end his time as a soldier. He was wounded for a second time in 1918, when he received gunshot wounds to his face and one of his arms. He was awarded Silver War Badge No.279332 and certificate on 15 September 1919.

He had a daughter, Jessie Mary Cornforth, who was born on 30 October 1909, but according to his Army Service Record, his wife Hannah was already dead by the time he had enlisted. Having checked the Civil Registration Marriage Index, which covered the years 1837 – 1915, I found that John and Hannah were married in the period covered by October – December of 1909 which was also the period in which 23-year-old Hannah died and their daughter was born, which would strongly suggest that she either died in childbirth or very soon afterwards.

A lady who according to the local newspapers went by the name of Mary Watt, was identified by her father, who told the court that his daughter was in

Damage in York Road.

the process of getting dressed, when a shell landed on their home killing her. Amy Watt, aged 22, who lived at 2 Marine Crescent, Hartlepool, was also one of those killed during the bombardment.

An employee of the North-Eastern Railway Company, Richard Theaker was 23 years of age and worked as platelayer. At the time of the German bombardment, Richard was working on the railway in Hartlepool, when a shell landed near to where he was working, killing him outright. He lived at 63 Turnbull Street, Hartlepool.

The jury at the Hartlepool inquest determined that:

> *Between 8.15 and 8.55 am on December 16, under cover of a dense fog, an enemy ship fired shot and shell from Hartlepool Bay into the twin Boroughs, killing several unarmed civilians, including the above named.*

The reality of the situation was that Hartlepool was an obvious location for the Germans to target. At the time it had one of the busiest ports in the British Isles. The local engineering sites were key for the British war effort, as were the numerous factories which produced much needed munitions, but despite this, it was extremely poorly defended from attack from the sea.

In the aftermath of the bombardment four men were awarded medals of the gallantry and distinguished service which they displayed on the day of the German attack. These awards were not announced in the *London Gazette* until the evening of Friday, 7 April 1916, some sixteen months after the bombardment of Hartlepool had taken place.

Lieutenant Colonel Lancelot Robson, of the Durham Royal Garrison Artillery, Territorial Forces, was awarded the Distinguished Service Order.

Sergeant T. Douthwaite, also of the Durham Royal Garrison Artillery, Territorial Forces, attached to the 41st Siege Battery, Royal Garrison Artillery, was awarded the Distinguished Conduct Medal.

Sergeant F.W. Mallin, of the 16th Battalion, Welsh Regiment, formerly 47th Company Royal Garrison Artillery, was awarded the Military Medal.

Acting Bombardier J.J. Pope, No.4 Company, Durham Royal Garrison Artillery, Territorial Force, was also awarded the Military Medal.

On 6 January 1915 at the Houses of Parliament, Lord Kitchener, in his capacity as Secretary of State for War, paid tribute to the people of Hartlepool for what they had endured on 16 December 1914 during the German bombardment of their town:

> *On our coasts, on the morning of December 16, German battle-cruisers bombarded for half an hour, Hartlepool, Scarborough and Whitby. At Hartlepool a battery replied with some effect, though it was outclassed by the heavy guns of the cruisers. No military advantage was gained, or could possibly have been gained, by wanton attacks on undefended seaside resorts, which attacks had as their chief result fatal accidents to a certain number of civilians, among whom women and children figured pathetically. The people in three towns bore themselves in this trying experience with perfect courage and coolness, and not the least trace of panic could be observed.*

The first five months of the war up until the end of 1914 had already been a terrible time for the people of Hartlepool. At least thirty-nine of the town's young men who had enlisted in the Army or Navy and gone off to fight in the war, had already been killed. On top of this there was the bombardment of 16 December, which had a long term and lasting affect on the town as a whole, with a significant number of properties and premises damaged and soldiers, sailors and civilians killed or wounded.

One thing was certain, the war had not started well for the people of Hartlepool.

CHAPTER THREE

1915 – Deepening Conflict

On Monday, 4 January 1915, the following letter appeared in a northern newspaper. It was from Mr F.H.R. Alderson. In it he passed on some useful advice from the Duke of Northumberland as to what the residents of Hartlepool should do in the case of another naval bombardment by the German navy. Is it useful advice, somebody being wise after the event, with the benefit of hindsight, or somebody just being downright condescending?

To the Editor
Henry Smith School, Hartlepool.
Sir, I went through the recent bombardment of Hartlepool, and strongly advise all persons to read carefully and follow out the excellent advice given them by the Duke of Northumberland.

I decided some months ago, that in the case of bombardment the only safe thing to do was to go down into the cellar kitchens and turn off the gas, so that when on the 16th ult. after watching with my family for ten minutes what we thought were British cruisers, we suddenly got a shell through our terrace, just four doors from us, we at once disappeared to the basement, and although our drawing room on the 1st floor was shattered by a shell, and most of the windows in the house broken, we all, I am thankful to say, escaped without a scratch.

I have visited the wounded in both hospitals and in every case I find they had been hurt in the streets or else in an upper room. I have not found a case yet of anyone, even on the ground floor being injured, so I conclude it is safer to stay on the ground floor rather than run the risk of reaching a house with cellars.

So many people in the Hartlepools never seem to have thought out any plan in case of bombardment, that I hope all householders on the east coast will be told what to do, either by Special Constables or by letter, and especially warned not to run out into the streets and to remember that no bombardment is likely to last more than 45 minutes; I only expected ours to last 30 minutes but they risked another 15 minutes, and I understand if they had only stayed another 15 minutes, they would now be on the bottom of the North Sea.

Hartlepool Great War.

I am not absolutely clear how the person who penned this letter came to his last conclusion. Some of those who were killed in the street during the Hartlepool bombardment weren't there for fun or to get a close up view of the incoming German artillery shells, they were either trying to get to safety, having been in the streets on their way to or from work when the attack started, or they were on their way to check on the wellbeing of a friend or relative.

HMS *Char* was sunk in the early hours of Saturday 16 January. Eight of her seventeen-man crew were from Hartlepool. The tragedy occurred as she attempted to assist a Belgian steamer/vessel, the *Frivan*, which appeared to be in some distress. Whilst assessing the situation in rough seas and high waves, she was pushed against the bow of the *Frivan* and was holed below the waterline. Those who lost their lives were:

E. Booth (Fireman)
W. Booth (Artificer)
R. Fergus (Petty Officer)
M. Hastings (Able Seaman)
W. Hatch (Fireman)
J.E. Hunter (Fireman)
G. Nossiter (Artificer)
J.P. Whale (Lieutenant)

HMS *Char* began life as the tugboat *Stratton*, and was based at Hartlepool, but was requisitioned by the Admiralty during the early months of the war. Her original eight-man crew, all of whom hailed from Hartlepool, wanted to continue with her, so became part of the Mercantile Marine Reserve and worked alongside nine other men who were already serving in the Royal Navy.

Her new home became Ramsgate in Kent and her new role was to check all vessels that travelled through the English Channel, between the Kent coast and the Goodwin Sands, which is a sandbank measuring some 10 miles in length about 6 miles off the Kent coastline opposite the town of Deal. The Sands were an extremely dangerous natural hazard for all shipping, situated just below the surface of the water and ranging in depth between 26 feet and 49 feet which, depending on the tides and currents in the area, were liable to change at any moment in time.

Although the German bombardment had taken place some three months earlier, the effects of the attack were still being felt amongst the local community, not all of whom had managed to dispel it from their minds. On Saturday 6 February there was an example of just how far reaching that effect could be, as the tentacles of death claimed yet another victim. Lilly Elizabeth Moore, who lived in Durham Street, Hartlepool, committed suicide by hanging herself. She was a married woman and had for many years lived in Canada, before returning to live in England. Up until a few weeks before her death she had been living with her mother, before moving into Durham Street. According to the 1911 Census she had a daughter, Doris, born in 1910.

On the Saturday in question a neighbour of Mrs Moore heard her child crying and called through the partition to see what the matter was. The young child told the man that her mother had gone away and left her. The neighbour went to the front door, opened the letter box, looked through, and saw the child sitting at the bottom of the stairs in its night clothes. Unfortunately, the child was not tall enough to be able to open the front door, but the neighbour knew where Mrs Moore's brother lived and went for him. On his arrival he entered the property and sadly found his sister hanging on the inside of her bedroom door.

Since the German bombardment of the town, Mrs Moore had been depressed, with most of her conversations with her friends and neighbours being about the attack. At the inquest in Hartlepool on Monday 8 February, the jury found that she had committed suicide whilst suffering from insanity, brought on by the shock of the German bombardment – yet another victim of the war.

By the end of 1915 at least 115 members of His Majesty's Armed Forces, who had connections with the town of Hartlepool in one way or another, had either died of their wounds, illness, or had been killed in action, with many others who were wounded.

At least nine of these young men were 18 years of age with a further two of them being 17 years of age. As we shall see, some of these individuals might not have even been the age they were claiming to be. I have written about them in the order in which they were killed throughout the course of the year, which means their names and stories can be found at different points throughout this chapter. Remember, officially a British soldier had to be 19 years of age to serve overseas, but that did not stop an estimated 250,000 under age recruits from joining up during the course of the war.

William John Storr was the first of these youngsters who became a casualty of the war in 1915. He was a Driver (T2/10537) in the 7th Cavalry Field Ambulance, Royal Army Service Corps, when he died of pneumonia on 27 February 1915. He was 18 years of age, one of eight children and the eldest son, born to William and Sarah Storr of 12 Collingwood Road, West Hartlepool. Before enlisting in the Army, he was a draper's errand boy. He is buried at the Hazebrouck Communal Cemetery, in the Nord region of France.

Ashley Shute was 18 years of age and a private (1923) in the 13th (Kensington) Battalion, London Regiment, when he was killed in action on 10 March 1915, which was the first day of the Battle of Neuve Chapelle. He is buried at Neuve Chapelle Farm Cemetery, in the Pas de Calais region of France. The cemetery was begun by the 13th Battalion, London Regiment, during the battle. He lived with his parents, William and Isabella Shute, and three siblings at 30 Percy Street, West Harlepool, although the family later moved to 136 Colwyn Road, West Hartlepool.

Ashley's brother, George Ashley Shute, was two years his senior. On the British Army's Service Medal and Award Rolls for the period covering the First World War, I found a George Ashley Shute who was a private (27711) in the Machine Gun Corps. I have no way of knowing if this is the same person, but he survived the war, being discharged on 14 December 1918.

An unusual article appeared in the newspapers on Saturday 13 March, concerning George Edward Dixon, a private (128730) with the West Yorkshire Regiment, who sadly had three of his children, Margaret, Albert and George, killed in the German bombardment of Hartlepool on 16 December 1914. His two surviving children, Joseph and Thomas, were also injured, as was his wife Margaret, who had to have her left leg amputated as a result of the injuries she sustained in the attack. George and Margaret had already experienced the sadness and pain of losing a family member. Their youngest child, Robert, died when he was only a year old, in May 1911.

George had enlisted in the army on 5 September 1914 at West Hartlepool, and was discharged on compassionate grounds on 10 March 1915, after having served for 187 days. This came about because of the intervention of Hartlepool's wartime MP, Sir Walter Runciman, who made representations to the War Office, on George's behalf. Thankfully, common sense prevailed and

Christopher Street.

he was discharged so as to be able to return home and look after what was left of his family.

On Saturday 3 April the normality of life was alive and kicking as Hartlepool played football against North Shields in an away fixture, in the North Eastern League, with the home team club renowned for the notoriety of their sloping pitch. The Hartlepool team that day was as follows: Gill, Taylor, Graham, Jameison, Hibbert, Macdougall, Boyle, Young, Johnson, Stringnell, Mahon.

Even though it was spring time there was a strong wind blowing the length of the pitch which made a kick and run style of play totally ineffective for either side. It was Hartlepool who had the better of the early exchanges, but North Shields also had their moments. It was more akin to a game of table tennis, the ball changing ends with frightening regularity, with neither side really gaining the upper hand for more than a matter of minutes. Chance after chance went begging, either because of shots whizzing the wrong side of the goals, or the keepers pulling off last gasp saves, to keep their team in with a chance. By some kind of miracle, both teams somehow reached half time without a goal having been scored, but it wasn't for the want of trying.

The second half began with North Shields coming out on top in the early exchanges, much like Hartlepool had done in the first half. A free kick followed for North Shields awarded for a foul on Buchanan, who got up to take the kick himself. The ball fell at the feet of the apparently surprised Chambers who quickly fired in a shot on the Hartlepool goal, Gill fumbled the shot, leaving Kirton with the easiest of opportunities right in front of goal. He did not disappoint and dispatched the ball effortlessly into the back of the Hartlepool net. The visitors did not give up or throw in the towel, they continually pressed the North Shields goal, but to no avail. With no more goals from either side, the home team won the match with Kirton's earlier goal.

With the war into its second year, it was a great surprise that there were so many young, fit men available for there to be so many games taking place. Besides the North Eastern League, which North Shields and Hartlepool played in, there were the neighbouring leagues of the Northern Alliance, the Blyth and District League, and the Shields and District Junior Alliance League, to name but a few.

On Wednesday 28 April two cases under the Aliens Registration Order came before the West Hartlepool Bench. The first to be heard was that of Albert Thompson, a sailor who lived at 8 Windsor Street in the town. He was charged with having failed to report himself to the Registration Officer, which might seem slightly strange with a name such as his, but it got even stranger. The main witness against him was his sister-in-law, Mrs Charlotte Schroeder, with a very German-sounding name. She told the court that Thompson had lived in Hartlepool for about sixteen years but that he had been born in Germany. She further stated that he had been back from his last trip for about two weeks.

Local Police Sergeant Young, who was the Registration Officer for Hartlepool, attended Albert Thompson's home address the night before his appearance in court and informed him that he was in possession of information which suggested that he had been born in Germany. In reply to this, Thompson confirmed his name, stating that he was 33 years of age, that he had been born in Australia, and had lived in Hartlepool for the past 20 years. He had run away from home when he was a boy of 13 and although he did not possess a birth certificate he claimed that his parents had told him that he had been born in Sydney.

Sergeant Young suggested to him that his name wasn't in fact Thompson but Rodenburg and that he had been born in Hamburg, Germany. Thompson denied this and said that as he was from New South Wales in Australia, he did not need to register himself as an alien, because he wasn't one.

Mrs Schroeder gave further evidence to the court that the defendant could barely speak English when she first knew him; he spoke German instead.

Sergeant Young was able to help on this point and gave evidence that he had known the man for some time and that he had been working on a Furness liner and had eventually been discharged in London. From asking around over the years he had got to know that Albert's surname was Rodenburg.

Having listened to all the evidence, the members of the Bench found in favour of the prosecution, and imposed a £20 fine, or if unable to pay such an amount, three month's imprisonment with hard labour.

Cleveland Road.

The other case involved a man by the name of William Leopold Schroder, who was a shipyard labourer, of Mary Street, Hartlepool. He was charged with making a false statement to the Registration Officer, on 11 August 1914. Superintendent McDonald told the court that the defendant had registered himself with the local police station and had at the time claimed to have been born in Australia.

Sergeant Young confirmed he had visited Schroder at his home the night before the court case, and told him that he believed he had been born in Germany rather than Australia as he had previously claimed. Young then took Schroder to Hartlepool police station where he continued the interview, where he strangely claimed that although he did not know, or could not prove where he had been born, he knew that he was Australian. He had not known his father, but confirmed that his mother, Augusta Schroder, was a Prussian. He was unable to produce a birth certificate, but claimed that he had been brought up as a young boy in Australia, before moving to England 26 years previously. He had been married to his wife, an English woman for the past 16 years, and neither of them knew of anybody who was German.

The case was adjourned to allow the police to carry out further enquiries in relation to what Schroder had claimed.

In early May 1915 the crew of the West Hartlepool based Steam Ship *Mobile* were landed at Stornoway by the government patrol steamer *Pearl* from Grimsby. The *Mobile*, which was carrying Welsh coal out of Barry, was held up by the German submarine *U-30* about 40 miles west of Butt of Lewis. The U-boat's captain, Erich von Rosenberg-Grusczyski, gave the *Mobile's* crew only ten minutes to collect their belongings and abandon their ship. The twenty-three-man crew didn't need telling twice and took to the boats as quickly as they could.

The *Mobile*, which was owned by Furness, Withy & Co Ltd of West Hartlepool, was then torpedoed and sank.

After sailing for about nine hours the exhausted crew finally found land at Carloway on the Isle of Lewis, which is about 24 miles by land from Stornoway. Luckily for the crew of the *Mobile* they did not encounter any rough seas or inclement weather, and the winds were in their favour.

James William Bell was 17 years of age and a Private (3/10007) in the 1st Battalion, West Yorkshire Regiment (Prince of Wales's Own) when he was killed in action on 6 May 1915; he is buried in the Erquinghem-Lys Churchyard Extension, in the Nord region of France. He lived with his parents, George and Sarah Bell, at 165 Alma Street, West Hartlepool and his three younger siblings.

The death took place on Saturday 5 June, of Alice Kennedy who lived with her family at 65 High Street, Hartlepool. She was found by her husband, Robert, in the early hours of the morning. He had gone to bed at about 11.30pm and some time in the early hours of the morning, he heard his wife call out.

She was as he freely admitted, 'addicted to drink' or in today's parlance, an alcoholic. He got out of bed and went downstairs to see what all of the commotion was about and found her lying on her back with a bottle next to her. He gave her a drink of water with some salt, with the intention of it acting as an emetic, to make her sick. He then left the house and ran to fetch the doctor.

Doctor Robertson told the inquest that on returning to the house he attended Mrs Kennedy in the kitchen, but she was already dead. He found signs of what he believed to be belladonna poisoning on her body. This is also more popularly known as 'deadly nightshade'.

Mrs Kennedy, who with Robert, had five children, had been fretting for some time about the wellbeing of her elder son, John Robert Kennedy, who had only recently enlisted in the army. The jury returned a verdict that 'death was due to poisoning from belladonna, self administered, while under the influence of drink'.

A good example of everybody wanting to do their bit for the war effort came about at a meeting held at the Hartlepool Works on Tuesday 15 June. Mr Donald Barns Morison, the managing director of Messrs. Richardson, Westgarth & Co, an engineering company, and one of the largest builders of marine engines in the world, addressed his work force in what can only be described as a direct and forthright manner, as he become aware that some of his staff were not quite giving their all.

Dene Street.

He told the workers present that in their midst were a small minority of men who seemed totally devoid of a sense of responsibility, but rather than threaten them with being sacked, he decided to appeal to their sporting instincts, with the presentation of a silver cup on Peace Day, to the department with the best record for time keeping and general efficiency. He hoped that those to whom his comments were aimed at came on board, as from that night onwards, those who continued to be what he classed as slackers, would not be treated so leniently.

Despite the company's long history in the business of engine building, it was necessary to write to the Admiralty at the beginning of the war, outlining its services before it received any orders appertaining to naval vessels. Throughout the war years the company made engines for some 200 vessels, which were used by the Admiralty, the Mercantile Marine and the Ministry of Shipping. The Admiralty also requested that the company manufacture artillery shells for the war effort, which they did, opening a factory in nearby Middlesbrough, where they produced 4, 6 and 8-inch shells at the rate of 1,000 a week.

It was reported in the local press on Tuesday 22 June, that Thomas J.E. Stanley Robson from Hartlepool, had been killed in action whilst serving in Gallipoli. He was a sergeant in the Naval Division of the Royal Engineers. Before the war he had worked at the Middleton Shipyard in Hartlepool, before going on to manage the Taikoo Dry Dock in Hong Kong. He had also worked in a similar capacity in Brazil. He was a well-known sportsman having played fullback for the Hartlepool Rovers Rugby Football Club.

Six months after the bombardment of Hartlepool on 16 December 1914, there were still people dying as a direct result of the raid. On Saturday, 26 June 1915 Margaret Sharp, who was 18 years old, the daughter of a Royal Navy stoker, died from meningitis due to being struck on the head by shrapnel from one of the German artillery shells which landed on the town. An inquest into Margaret's death was held on Monday 28 June, the findings of which officially connected the cause of her death to the bombardment, making her its 121st victim.

The Coroner, Mr Bell, held an inquest at Hartlepool Hospital on Monday 5 July, into the circumstances of the death of John William Horsley, a gunner with the 1st (Durham) Royal Garrison Artillery, and stationed at the Heugh Battery in Hartlepool. He died on Sunday 4 July in Hartlepool.

Lieutenant George Horsley, who served with him in the same battery, had been shooting birds from the battery commander's post, with a small calibre rifle. Gunner Horsley picked up a bird that Lieutenant Horsley had previously shot in the Hartlepool Rovers football field. A short while later Lieutenant Horsley fired two shots at a sparrow which had suddenly appeared close to where he was; he wounded it with his first shot and then took aim again, looking down the length of the rifle, and fired to try and kill it outright. He hit the bird and saw it fall before he heard one of his men, Gunner Robinson shout out, 'You've hit him, sir.' He dropped the rifle before running down into the football field and saw Gunner Cooper and others lifting Gunner Horsley, who was wounded in the neck. He was quickly removed to the Hartlepool General Hospital where he was pronounced dead on arrival a short time later. Lieutenant Horsley told the inquest that he had not instructed Gunner Horsley to collect up the birds, it was something he had done of his own accord.

On being informed of the incident, Lieutenant Colonel Robson immediately made his way to the hospital. He later informed the civilian police of the incident and placed Lieutenant Horsley under open military arrest.

Lieutenant Robertson of the Royal Army Medical Corps, who was attached to the Heugh Battery, described the wound, which was in the neck, as one that a bullet might cause. Gunner Robinson who saw Lieutenant Horsley fire the fatal shot, and saw Gunner Horsley fall, also gave evidence at the inquest.

The jury returned a verdict of accidental death and expressed their sympathy to the relatives of the deceased, who had enlisted with his brothers George and Henry. There were three other brothers, Arthur, Thomas and Robert, and four sisters Mary, Charlotte, Jane and Hannah.

Although one of John's brothers was a George Horsley, there was no clarification in any of the newspapers which carried the article, to confirm whether Lieutenant George Horsley, was in fact his brother. If that was the case it added even deeper sadness to John's death, dying at the hands of his elder brother.

Lieutenant Colonel Robson, on behalf of the officers and men of the battery, offered his expression of deep regret at Gunner Horsley's tragic death who, he said, was a very promising young soldier.

John William Horsley was 21 years of age when he enlisted in the Army on 4 January 1915 at Hartlepool, when he became Gunner 5766 in the Durham Brigade, Royal Garrison Artillery. His Army Service Record records that he 'died of bullet wound accidentally received'.

A Court of Enquiry was held into the circumstances of John's death on 12 July 1915 at the Heugh Battery, by order of the commanding officer of the Durham Brigade, Royal Garrison Artillery, Lieutenant Colonel L. Robson. The purpose was to investigate the circumstances connected with John Horsley's death, 'who was accidentally killed' according to the front page of the enquiry document which had already been completed before the enquiry actually began. Having listened to all of the available evidence, the enquiry found the circumstances of Gunner John Horsley's death to be an accident.

John's brother, Henry Davis Horsley, served in the Royal Navy throughout the war. He had enlisted as a boy sailor in 1908 aged 13 and retired in 1955 when he was 60 years of age – a truly remarkable achievement. His parents,

John William and Hannah Horsley, lived at 18 Clayton Street, Hartlepool. John was buried at the West View Cemetery in his home town.

On Friday 9 July at West Hartlepool, His Honour Judge Bonsey heard an application from engine driver, John George Cooper, who worked for the North Eastern Railway Company, for compensation for injuries he received during the German naval bombardment. He was making the claim for compensation against his company. At first glance it appeared a strange claim to bring. How a man's civilian employer could be held in any way responsible for a naval artillery bombardment by a foreign enemy, in a time of war, was not at all clear. The reality was that no employer in the town or anywhere else in the country could have taken any kind of measures to protect their employees against a potential threat and danger that they could have never reasonably have expected to take place.

With the greatest of respect to Mr Cooper, and with no disrespect inferred or intended to his memory or that of the legal profession of the day, it is highly unlikely that this was a matter that had been self driven, it is more likely that this case, and other such compensation claims, were driven by solicitorial direction, to test the law in relation to such matters, which at the time, was an extremely grey area and uncharted waters for all concerned.

Mr Edmund Brown, who was acting on behalf of the National Union of Railwaymen, told the hearing that the whole point at issue was whether the injuries caused by an enemy's shell could be regarded in certain circumstances as arising out of, or in the course of, a man's employment. The case was not an unsavoury affair, as both sides simply wanted the principle discussed and decided upon.

On the morning of the German bombardment, John Cooper, who was coming to the end of his night shift, and was in his engine on the unusually named Slag Island, between the island and the sea, when a shell fell close to his engine, just after eight o'clock. A colleague of Mr Cooper's, a shunter, was killed, whilst the footman ran away.

Mr Cooper jumped off the foot plate of the engine and took shelter by the side of the trucks attached to the engine. He suddenly remembered that he had not opened the engine's injector, so he ran back to the engine and quickly remedied the situation. As he then ran to find somewhere he could take cover, he was struck by a piece of shrapnel from one of the artillery shells, sustaining a compound fraction of his left arm in the process. When he arrived at hospital so severe was the wound that fragments of the shrapnel had to be removed from his arm before it could be cleaned up. As a result of the injury Mr Cooper had not been able to work as an engine driver in the previous seven months, although he was willing and able to undertake light work.

Mr Meynell, acting on behalf of the North Eastern Railway Company, contended, without any personal malice, that by leaving his engine for his

Dene Street.

own personal safety, Mr Cooper had in fact abandoned his duty, and that he was, in relation to the German bombardment of the town, in the exact same position and at no greater or lesser risk than any other member of the public who found themselves embroiled in the events of that never to be forgotten day. Judgement was reserved.

The incoming German shells were indiscriminate in the death and destruction which they caused on 16 December 1914. Social class had no advantage in such an environment. For those who were killed or injured, it was sadly a case of being in the wrong place at the wrong time. Whether a person was at work, on their way to work or school or still at home in bed or having breakfast, each and everyone of them faced the same threat. It was simply a lottery of who lived and who died. These were not the laser-guided missiles available to today's combatant nations, they were very large artillery shells which were fired in the direction of Hartlepool, and where they landed was anybody's guess. It really was a case of fingers crossed and pray.

Another of the young men who were 18 years of age or younger, was James Lancelot Huntley, who lived at 17 Cromwell Street, Hartlepool, with his parents, William and Eleanor Huntley. He enlisted as a private (15482) in the 8ᵗʰ Battalion, King's Own Scottish Borderers, and subsequently died of his wounds on 3 August 1915. The Commonwealth War Graves website records that he was only 17 years old, but according to the Christening Index for England and Wales, he was possibly even younger, as he was actually born on 19 October 1898. If that information is correct, he could have only been 16 years of age at the time of his death, which would mean that, allowing for the period it would have taken him to complete his basic training after enlistment, he could have well have been just 15 years of age at that time.

The War Diaries entry for the 8ᵗʰ Battalion, King's Own Scottish Borderers for 26 July 1915 shows the following entry.

> *Private J. Golding, 'D' Company was accidentally shot in a dug-out in sector X.2 about 10 am, by No.15445 Pt. H Guest.*
> *No. 15482 J L Huntley gunshot wound in chest on 26ᵗʰ. A & B companies relieved by C & D companies in sector X.2.*

The remarkable thing about this entry is that Private Golding and Private Huntley are referred to by their names and initials, along with their service numbers. It is the first time I have ever read a War Diary of any battalion, where privates are referred to by name. They are referred to as just 'Other Ranks' and it is usually only officers who had their rank, initials and surnames mentioned in War Diaries.

It is now clear that Private Huntley spent nine days in hospital having his wounds treated before he sadly passed away. Private Huntley is buried at Le Tréport Military Cemetery, in the Seine-Maritime region of France.

Although James Huntley wasn't killed in action on 3 August 1915, I thought it would still have value to look at the War Diaries entry of that date for his battalion:

> *Marched from Allouagne to Mazingarbe, halting at Houchin for dinner and tea. Arrived Houchin 11.30 am. Weather unsettled, heavy showers, at intervals. Men were made comfortable in a large threshing shed with*

plenty of clean straw. Marched from Houchin at 9 pm. Headquarters attending Mazingarbe about 11.45 pm. Heavy marching through mud and rain. Interval of five minutes between companies. Billet very poor and left in a very dirty condition by the relieved corps (Territorial). Brigade in Divisional Reserve, 44th & 45th Brigades in firing and support trenches.

There was an interesting entry for 2 August 1915, but although it doesn't have anything to do with James Huntley, or anybody else from Hartlepool, it was about a Field General Court Martial of three soldiers and was well detailed. It is the first such entry I have seen included in a First World War regimental War Diary, and it provides the reader with a flavour of the circumstances and conditions that young soldiers suddenly found themselves in once they had been sent off to war. It quickly became very real indeed and not the fun-filled experience they maybe thought it was going to be.

The entry was timed at 10am:

Field General Court Martial assembled for trial of Private Guest, 'neglect to the prejudice of good order and military discipline'. Sergeant Pike 'drunkenness when warned for duty'. Corporal McKinnon, 'drunkenness on parade'. Private Guest sentenced to one year's imprisonment with hard labour and suspension of punishment applied for. Sergeant Pike and Corporal McKinnon, sentenced to be reduced to the ranks.

It is also clear that the reason behind why Private Guest faced a court martial was because of his accidental shooting of Private Golding.

Ralph William Twizell was 18 years of age and a private (10267) in C Company, 2nd Battalion, Durham Light Infantry when he died of his wounds on 8 August 1915. He is buried at the Lijssenthoek Military Cemetery, in the West Vlaanderen region of Belgium.

The 1911 Census shows Ralph Twizell as a 14-year-old errand boy who delivered confectionary. The family home was at 73 Cornwall Street, West Hartlepool, although by the end of the war, his parents, Ralph and Rasina, were living at 24 Fenny Street, Stockton-on-Tees. Ralph had a younger brother named Albert. There was an Albert Twizell who was a gunner (66064) and later a sergeant in the Royal Field Artillery, who first landed in France on 30 August 1915, three weeks after Ralph had been killed. As far as I know Albert survived the war.

James Alfred Parkinson was 18 years of age and a private (10982) in the 6th Battalion, Alexandra Princess of Wales's Own (Yorkshire) Regiment, when he was killed in action on 9 August 1915. He has no known grave, but his name is commemorated on the Helles Memorial in Turkey.

The entry in the War Diary of 9 August 1915, for the 6th Battalion, reads as follows.

04.00. Battalion moved back for Hill 10 to St Oyanise. 12.00. Orders received to go forward to Sulayish. Battalion came under heavy rifle fire. Captain Chapman wounded and 10 other casualties. We went up into firing trench.

James was one of those '10 other casualties'. Before the war he had lived at 108 Alma Street, West Hartlepool, with his parents, John and Lucy Parkinson, his five brothers, John, William, Edward, Lawrence and Arthur, and his sister, Mary, the youngest member of the family.

James's brothers, John Joseph Parkinson, William Charles Parkinson, Edward Parkinson and Lawrence Parkinson, all served during the war although they have been impossible to positively identify from the British Army's Medal Rolls Index. There was one man with the name John Joseph Parkinson who served as a private with the Royal West Kent Regiment, who was medically discharged from the Army on 27 September 1916. There was also one entry for a Lawrence Parkinson, who was a sapper with the Royal Engineers.

John Ellison Clarke was 18 years of age and a private (13810) in the 10th Battalion, Cameronians (Scottish Rifles) when he was killed in action on 25 September 1915 at the Battle of Loos. He had initially served as a private (14257) with the King's Own Scottish Borderers. He has no known grave, but his name is commemorated on the Loos Memorial, in the Pas de Calais region of France.

He lived with his parents, John, who was a stone mason, and Mary Clarke, and his five younger siblings, at 5 Jesmond Gardens, West Hartlepool. One of his brothers, William Gammon Clarke, served as a private (317542) in the Royal Tank Corps. Having enlisted at Sunderland two weeks past his eighteenth birthday on 15 July 1916, he wasn't called up for service until 19 September 1918. Thankfully for William, the war was over before he had even finished his basic training at the Tank Corps Depot at Wareham in Dorset. He was demobilized on 13 February 1919 at the North Rippon Camp in Yorkshire.

James Marshall Matterson was 18 years of age and a private (14120) in the 8th Battalion, King's Own Scottish Borderers, when he first arrived in France on 10 July 1915. He was killed in action two months later on 25 September 1915, although his initial classification was recorded as missing, presumed dead. He has no known grave, but like John Clarke, his name is commemorated on the Loos Memorial. Prior to the war he had lived with his parents and five siblings, at 46 Tweed Street, West Hartlepool, although the family later moved to 24 Water Street, West Hartlepool.

Frank Hannaford Hurworth was 18 years of age and a private (32098) in the 43rd Field Ambulance of the Royal Army Medical Corps, when he died of his wounds on 28 September 1915. He is buried at the Poperinghe New

Military Cemetery in the West-Vlaanderen region of Belgium. Frank was the youngest of six children born to John and Mary Hurworth, who lived at 13 Granville Avenue, West Hartlepool. His elder brother, Bertrand James Hurworth, also served during the war, initially as a gunner (625912) with the Honourable Artillery Company, and later at the same rank (282945) with the Royal Field Artillery. Before military service he had worked as a bank cashier. He married Ellen Shelley in August 1917 in Kilkenny, Ireland. He died on 14 February 1938, still living in the town at 52 Linden Grove, and was survived by his widow, Ellen.

Joseph Henry Johnson was 18 years of age and a private (13677) in the 15th Battalion, Durham Light Infantry, when he was killed in action on 1 October 1915. He is buried at the Abbeville Communal Cemetery, in the Somme region of France. This was also the place where the British Red Cross had its No.2, No.3 and No. 5 Stationary Hospitals.

On Saturday 20 November an incident took place in Hartlepool, which resulted in the tragic deaths of two young children. The inquests of both children took place the following Monday, chaired by the coroner, Mr J. Hyslop Bell.

One of the victims was only 3 years of age and the daughter of Edward Carrigan, a stoker in the Royal Navy, who lived at 8 Exeter Street, Hartlepool.

Carrigan's wife, Annie, told the inquest that at 4.30 on the previous Saturday afternoon she left the house to go and buy a loaf of bread at the corner shop, leaving her three young children in the house with the front door open. She had only walked a distance of about 50 yards, when she heard her eldest child, Henry, who was 5 years of age, call out that his sister, Eliza's pinafore was on fire. Annie Carrigan immediately ran back to the house as fast as her legs could carry her. As she got to the front door she saw Eliza standing in the hallway with her clothes on fire. She grabbed hold of the door mat and wrapped it around her and shouted for help.

Two neighbours of the Carrigans also gave evidence at the inquest. Mrs Isabella Burns and Mrs Dorothy Cooper told how they assisted Annie Carrigan in extinguishing the flames and then helped to dress Eliza's burns, with oil and liniment. They could see that there was a small fire going and that there was a safety guard around it for protection. Apparently Henry had been playing with some paper and had put it through the wire of the guard to light it. The result of him doing this was Eliza's clothes caught on fire although how that actually came about is unclear.

Dr A.C. Strain explained that Eliza was admitted to the Cameron Hospital at 5.45pm on Saturday, but sadly died due to a combination of the extent of her burns and shock, at 8.30pm.

A verdict of accidental death was returned by the jury with the somewhat surprising addition by today's standards, that the parents were exonerated of any blame in the death of Eliza. An extremely sad case, but today a mother leaving three young children in the home, with the front door open, which then resulted in the death of one of her children, possibly would not be treated in a similar manner. It is odd to think that within what could have been no more than a minute from when Annie Carrigan left her home, her son Henry, found some paper, stuck it through the wire of the fireguard, managed to get it alight, pulled it back through, setting alight the pinafore of his sister Eliza, then ran or walked out of the house to call his mother.

The second inquest was that of 4-year-old Mary Scattergood of 19 Garibaldi Street, West Hartlepool. Her father was Samuel Scattergood, a smith's fitter. On Thursday 11 November Mary was playing in her parent's bedroom, when she picked up a box of matches from the dressing table. She managed to light one of the matches which set fire to her hair, and resulted in a burn to her forehead, but which did not appear to be of a serious nature. Mary's parents cleaned the wound by applying some oil and a dressing to it.

Two days later Dr Biggart visited the Scattergood's home to check on Mary's burn, and noted that it was no bigger than the size of a florin, an equivalent size today would be that of a £2 coin. The wound appeared to have improved but subsequent to the doctor's visit, Mary appeared to be suffering from septic poisoning. From this, bronchial pneumonia set in which caused her death on 20 November.

BUSINESS PREMISES WRECKED BY 6" SHELL GROSVENOR ST. WEST HARTLEPOOL.

Grosvenor Street.

The jury returned a verdict of accidental death and Doctor Biggart commented that the mother had done all that she could for her child. By today's standards leaving a 4-year-old child in a room where a box of matches was so readily available, would not have been received in the same manner.

William Bradley was 18 years of age and a stoker (8433S) in the Royal Naval Reserve, serving on board HMS *Natal*, a Warrior-class armoured cruiser, when he was killed on 30 December 1915. The *Natal*, under the command of Captain Eric Black, was at anchor in the Cromarty Firth in Scotland, hosting a party for some of the wives and children of the ship's officers, along with a small group of nurses from HM Hospital Ship *Drina*, at anchor nearby. At just before 3.30pm there were a number of internal explosions towards the rear of the ship. Confusion reigned, with the initial belief being that the vessel had either struck a mine or been torpedoed by a German submarine. A subsequent investigation determined that the explosion was caused by the ship's own exploding ammunition, which was possibly down to a quantity of faulty cordite.

The ship capsized in under five minutes and a total of 421 crew, along with some of their wives, children and visiting nurses were killed. The remains of the wreck of the *Natal* have been designated as a protected place under the Protection of Military Remains Act 1986, as a war grave.

William Bradley's body was never recovered but his name is commemorated on the Chatham Naval Memorial. His parents, Joseph and Jane Bradley, lived at 15 Wood Street, West Hartlepool.

CHAPTER FOUR

1916 – The Realisation

This was the year that for many was the turning point of the war. It was to be a defining year to a great extent because of the carnage of the Battles of the Somme and Verdun and the call for peace that was proffered by Germany late in the year.

By then Germany's leaders realized that the war had gone on much longer than they had expected it to; they had lost a great many men, both dead and wounded; and the cost of continuing the war was having a devastating financial effect on their economy, with certain basic food items becoming harder to come by.

The Battle of Verdun began on 21 February 1916 and went on for 9 months, 3 weeks and 6 days, making it one of the longest in history. By the time it came to an end on 19 December 1916, Germany had suffered an estimated 340,000 casualties, 160,000 of whom had been killed. During the same period from 1 July the German Army was fighting the Battle of the Somme which endured for four and a half months, finally coming to an end on 18 November 1916. This cost them a further 450,000 casualties, numbers that when added to those at Verdun, were simply not sustainable for much longer.

The big issue for the German leadership – and possibly what forced their hand in trying to agree a negotiated peace settlement at that time – was the real threat of America entering the war on the side of the Allies. Germany knew that if that happened, all hope of defeating the Allies was gone.

David Lloyd George became the British Prime Minister on 6 December 1916, taking over from Herbert H. Asquith. But both men agreed that the only way to guarantee a prolonged and sustainable peace throughout Europe was to defeat Germany militarily, once and for all.

It was against this backdrop that Hartlepool's part in the war during the year 1916 had to be looked at. According to the Commonwealth War Graves Commission, British and Commonwealth forces lost a total of 237,456 men and women who were either killed or died of their wounds, illness or disease.

Of these, at least 266 had connections to Hartlepool, which was a massive loss for the town, with 157 of them dying during the Battle of the Somme.

On the first day of the battle, 1 July 1916, at least sixteen men from the town were killed, and of these twelve were serving with the Durham Light Infantry, three with the Yorkshire Regiment and one with the King's Own Yorkshire Light Infantry.

Durham Light Infantry

Private 18/1611 PERCY BORRETT was 19 years of age and serving with the 15th (Service) Battalion which had been formed in Newcastle in September 1914 and moved to Halton Park in Lancaster. From there they went in to billets at Maidenhead in December 1914, before moving back to Halton Park in April 1915 and finally on to Witley in July 1915. Their training completed, the men of the 15th Battalion arrived in France on 11 September 1915, landing at Boulogne.

Percy's body was never recovered and he has no known grave, but his name is commemorated on Thiepval Memorial on the Somme. His parents, Mr J.R. and Mrs F. Borrett, lived at Southolme, Seaton Carew, West Hartlepool.

Lance Sergeant 18/246 JOHN CARR was 23 years of age and served with the 18th (Service) Battalion Durham Light Infantry, who were also known as the Durham Pals. The battalion was formed at Cocken Hall in Durham on 10 September 1914, with John enlisting soon afterwards. He was present at the bombardment of Hartlepool on 16 December 1914. After having completed their training, John Carr and his colleagues sailed from Liverpool on 6 December 1915 and arrived in Port Said, Egypt on 21 December 1915. The following year they were deployed to France, arriving there on 11 March 1916. He has no known grave and his name is also commemorated on the Thiepval Memorial. According to the 1911 Census, John's actual name was Clarence John Carr and he lived at 8 Albert Street, West Hartlepool with his parents, Thomas and Mary Jane Carr, three brothers Chester, Edward and Victor and two sisters, Edith and Eva.

Sergeant 763 JOHN HERBERT FURLONG HALL was 29 years of age when he was killed in action. He also served with the 18th Battalion and was buried at the Serre Road No.1 Cemetery, in the Pas de Calais. His parents, Edward and Mary Ann Hall, lived at 11 Arch Street, Hartlepool.

Private 18/1489 HERBERT WARD NEEDHAM was, according to the Commonwealth War Graves Commission website, just 17 years of age, and too young to have even been in the Army, let alone serving and fighting in France, when he was killed in action on the first day of the Battle of the Somme. He was another who served in the 18th Battalion and who is buried at Serre Road No.1 Cemetery.

His initial training lasted for eleven months before he was sent out to France, arriving there on 6 April 1916. Three months later he was dead, killed in action on the first day of the Battle of the Somme. He had served for a total of 1 year and 60 days. Initially he must have been reported as missing in action and then his official status was changed to, missing presumed dead because his Army Service Record shows that his body wasn't buried until 2 April 1917.

Herbert's Army Service Record survived and the first thing that it tells us, is that when he enlisted on 3 May 1915, he told the recruiting officer that he was 19 years of age, even though the Select Births and Christenings for England, 1538 – 1975, shows him as having being born on 8 April 1899. This means that when he enlisted he was actually just a month past his sixteenth birthday. Before the war Herbert had lived with his parents, David and Mary Needham, his brother Albert Ward Needham and his sister, Bessie Needham, at Thistlington House, Park Road, West Hartlepool.

Private 18/814 HENRY NEWBY was 21 years of age and another who served with the 18th Battalion. He is also buried at the Serre Road No.1 Cemetery in France. Before the war he was an apprentice compositer living with his parents, John and Faith Newby, and his two younger sisters, Mable and Maud, at 17 Gloucester Street, West Hartlepool.

Corporal 18/832 JOHN JAMES ROBINSON was 22 years of age and another of those who served with the 18th Battalion. His body was never found and nor does he have a grave, but his name is one of the thousands etched into the marble columns of the Thiepval Memorial. It commemorates more than 72,000 men from South Africa and the United Kingdom who were killed in the Somme region before 20 March 1918 and who have no known grave. His parents, John and Hannah Jane Robinson, lived at 186 York Road, Hartlepool, where John senior was a Police Constable. They had two other sons, Gordon and Victor, and a daughter Phyllis.

Gordon enlisted during the war and became a Private (TR/5/96501) in the 85th Training Reserve Battalion, but he was discharged on 14 April 1918 at York, having served in the Army for a total of 222 days so that he could take up a temporary commission in the newly formed Royal Air Force, when he was 18 years of age. He had initially enlisted in the Army on 5 September 1917 at West Hartlepool.

Sergeant 18/833 ROBERT HENRY ROBSON was 25 years of age, and another of the men who served with the 18th Battalion in D Company. Before the war he was an apprentice engineer. It is perhaps surprising that he didn't consider joining the Royal Engineers, rather than the Durham Light Infantry, but maybe he found the Pals aspect of things more appealing.

He must have enlisted with John James Robinson, as they have consecutive service numbers. How surreal that they joined up together and then died on the same day. He actually enlisted on 21 September 1914 at West Hartlepool, and had previously served with the 5th Battalion, which was a volunteer unit, for four years. He was promoted to the rank of corporal on 10 October 1914 and to sergeant on 6 December 1915, the day he arrived in

Egypt as part of the Egyptian Expeditionary Force, where he remained until 4 March 1916, before being re-deployed to France.

Robert Henry Robson was buried at the Euston Road Cemetery, Colincamps, on the Somme. His father, also Robert Henry Robson, and his stepmother, Catherine Robson, lived at 51 Thornton Street, West Hartlepool. Robert's biological mother, Mary Ellen Robson, died in the early part of 1904 when she was only 35 years of age, and Robert senior married Catherine Stephens, who was thirteen years his junior in August 1905.

Lance Sergeant 18/844 HENRY ARTHUR SCOTT was a 31-ycar-old married man, who lived with his wife, Mabel at 18 Back Lumley Street, Hartlepool, although he was born in Bow in the East End of London in 1886. When he enlisted at West Hartlepool on 18 September 1914, he was 28 years of age, although he didn't commence his military training until 2 October 1914. Prior to the war he had been employed as a tailor working in a local business. He had previously served for two and a half years in H Company, 2nd Battalion, East Yorkshire Regiment. He was discharged at his own request.

Possibly because of his previous military service, he was promoted to the rank of lance corporal on 24 October 1914. He was further promoted to corporal on 4 March 1915, and then lance sergeant on 16 November 1915. He arrived in Egypt as part of the Egyptian Expeditionary Force on 22 December 1914, where he remained until 5 March 1916, when he left, not to return home to England for a well-deserved period or rest and recuperation, but to be re-deployed direct to France, arriving there six days later on 11 March.

He was another from Hartlepool who served in the 18th Battalion and who is buried at the Serre Road Cemetery. On 13 January 1917 Henry's widow, Mabel, was awarded a war widow's pension of 21s per week for her and their three young children, Olive, Elsie and Henry junior, the latter being born two months after his father had enlisted in the Army. The pension commenced on 21 January 1917.

Private 13702 JOHN R. SKINNER was a 32-year-old married man whose home was at 19 Sarah Street, West Hartlepool, where he lived with his wife Sarah. He was one of those who served in the regiment's 15th Battalion, first arriving in France on 11 September 1915. He is buried at the Norfolk Cemetery at Beécordel-Bécourt in the Somme region of France.

Lance Corporal 961 ROBERT TAYLERSON who served with D Company in the regiment's 18th Battalion, was 22 years of age, a single man who lived with his parents Thomas and Elizabeth Taylerson, of 23 Chester Road, West Hartlepool, along with his three brothers, John, William and Edmund, and four sisters, Elizabeth, Monica, Winifred and Hilda.

He enlisted on 26 October 1914 at West Hartlepool when he was 20 years of age. On 14 September 1915 he was charged with an offence under the heading of 'conduct to the prejudice of good order and military discipline'. He was found guilty and punished by being confined to barracks for two days, although his Army Service Record does not record what it was that he actually did to face such a charge. Whatever it was, it couldn't have been severe, as two months later he was promoted to the rank of lance corporal. This took place on 16 November 1915, although he wasn't paid any more money for this additional responsibility.

The British Army Medal Rolls Index Cards that cover the period of the First World War, show a John Taylerson who served as a gunner (337747) with the Durham Royal Garrison Artillery, enlisting on 10 August 1914 and who was discharged on 23 February 1919. It shows another who served with the Royal Garrison Artillery, one who served with the Royal Army Medical Corps, and a John E. Taylerson who served with the Durham Light Infantry. The chances are that one of these four men was Robert's brother, which one, I do not know. Robert is one of those buried at the Serre Road No.1 Cemetery.

Private 18/1882 ALBERT CLENNETT THORNTON was 24 years of age and served with the regiment's 18th Battalion. He was the son of William Henry and Mary Ann Thornton, of Sydney Lodge, Stockton Road, West Hartlepool. He was one of those who had previously served with the battalion in Egypt before arriving in France. He is buried at the Serre Road No.1 Cemetery.

Private 18/909 ROBERT WILSON was 26 years of age and served with the 18th Battalion. He has no known grave and is one of the more than 72,000 names that have been recorded on the Thiepval Memorial, who served with the forces of either the United Kingdom or South Africa, in the Somme region before March 1918, and who have no known grave. His mother, Lily, lived at Haswell House, West Hartlepool.

Yorkshire Regiment

Private 8476 JAMES WILLIAM BUTCHER was 25 years of age and a married man who served with the regiment's 7th Battalion. His death left a widow, Eliza Butcher, who lived at 1 Laurence Street, West Hartlepool. Like many of his colleagues he has no known grave, but his name is commemorated on the Thiepval Memorial.

Below are some extracts from the War Diaries of the 7th (Service) Battalion, Yorkshire Regiment, 50 Brigade, for 1 July 1916.

> *The attached Battalion Operational Order No. 53 gives the general and detailed orders for the offensive for which the Battalion assembled in the trenches opposite FRICOURT VILLAGE on the afternoon of 27 June 1916.*
>
> *The first zero hour was 7.30 am on July 1st when the troops on our left and right attacked, and the 2nd zero hour was at 2.30 pm when the Battalion assaulted. Owing to an unfortunate mistake on the part of the officer commanding 'A' Company, his company assaulted at 7.45 am. As soon as they began to climb over the parapet, terrific machine gun fire*

was opened by the enemy, and the company was almost at once wiped out. The survivors lay in crump holes some 25 yards in front of our wire until after dark. As soon as it was discovered that 'A' Company had assaulted by itself, 'D' Company, the reserve company, was brought up into the assembly trench, to take 'A' Company's place.

At 2 pm on 1/7/16 our artillery began the half hour preliminary bombardment of FRICOURT VILLAGE. This bombardment was feeble and did little damage to the enemy as the Battalion soon learnt to its cost. At 2.30 pm the Battalion assaulted and was met by a murderous machine gun and rifle fire. Officers and men were literally mown down and were finally brought to a standstill about half way across to the enemy's trenches.

13 officers and over 300 men became casualties in about three minutes. The survivors lay in crump holes until dark with a few exceptions who managed to crawl back. Many magnificent deeds of courage were performed especially in bringing wounded and in carrying messages under fire.

The Battalion withdrew after dark on 1/7/16 and marched home 5 miles behind the lines......

What an extremely powerful account of one of the worst days in British military history. The entry would have been made by an officer, so to hear him lay the blame for 13 officers and 300 men becoming casualties, at the feet of a fellow officer, is as incredible as it is refreshing. It shows that regardless of how good the preparations and planning of an operation were, in the heat of battle, mistakes can be made and things can go drastically wrong with devastating consequences, as was the case here for the men of the 7th Battalion, Yorkshire Regiment. I found the sentence about the 13 officers and 300 men who became casualties, in the space of just 3 minutes, particularly moving and sad. So many young men, wiped out in the blink of an eyelid, many of whom didn't even make it out of the trenches.

The Commonwealth War Graves Commission records that 221 officers and men of the Yorkshire Regiment died on 1 July 1916, this number included three officers from the 7th Battalion, one of whom was 25-year-old Second Lieutenant Lionel Adolf David David, who was an officer with A Company. He is buried at the Dantzig Alley British Cemetery in Mametz. Is this the same officer referred to in the 7th Battalion's War Diaries for 1 July 1916, as the person who made the 'unfortunate mistake'?

Private 14170 MATTHEW GARDNER was 28 years of age and a married man, who before the war had lived at 8 Briar Street, West Hartlepool, with his wife Annie. He served with the Yorkshire Regiment's 10th Battalion, has no known grave and his name is commemorated on the Thiepval Memorial.

Sergeant 21484 ROBERT HENRY WHITE, 21 years of age and serving with A Company of the 7th Battalion, sadly was one of those who was wiped out as soon as he attempted to leave the trenches to commence the attack. He is buried at the nearby Fricourt British Cemetery. His parents, Henry and Mary White, lived at 173 Burbank Street, West Hartlepool, along with their other children, Hilda and James. According to the 1911 Census, the family, excluding Robert, were living at 78 Derwent Street, West Hartlepool.

King's Own Yorkshire Light Infantry

Private 12112 ARTHUR EDWARD WILLIAMS was 22 years of age, born in Clerkenwell, London. He was a single man, who served with the 9th Battalion. Before the war he lived with his mother, Harriet, known as Hettie, Banks, his stepfather Percival Thomas Banks, his half-sisters, Ethel and Ivy Banks, and his half-brothers, Albert and John. The 1911 Census shows them as living at 73 Edinburgh Street, Goole, in Yorkshire.

His father having died when he was very young, his mother remarried when Arthur was about 3 years old on 14 March 1897, at St Mark's Parish Church in Clerkenwell. At the time, Hettie was living at 24 Rosoman Street in the town, whilst Percival was living in the same street but at number 43. When they married his occupation was shown as being a publican, but by the time of the 1911 Census, he was shown as working as an insurance agent.

The Commonwealth War Graves Commission records, collated in the early 1920s, shows Arthur's mother using the name of Hettie Williams and living at Westholme, 4 Cleveland Road, West Hartlepool. This is somewhat strange as Percival didn't die until December 1937 at the age of 63. Either the Commonwealth War Graves Commission has its facts wrong, or Hettie and Percival were divorced sometime in the early 1920s.

Another interesting fact is that Percival enlisted on 21 November 1915 at West Hartlepool, a month before his forty-first birthday. Initially he was allocated to the 22nd Battalion, Durham Light Infantry as Private 3/12660. At the time the family's address was shown as being 9 Osbourne Road, West Hartlepool. He was promoted to the rank of corporal on 24 November 1915, to that of lance sergeant on 23 December 1915, and to acting sergeant on 8 June 1916 and thirteen days later he was posted to the 16th Battalion, Durham Light Infantry. On 1 September 1916, he was transferred to the 1st Battalion, Training Reserve, where he remained as acting sergeant. His service number changed to 184973, but he did not stay in one place for long. The transfers came thick and fast:

23 November 1916 – Durham Light Infantry, Depot; 5 April 1917 – 1st Battalion, Training Reserve; 29 April 1917 – 354th Home Service Labour Company; 1 May 1917 – 21st Infantry Works Company; 13 June 1917 – 353rd Home Service Works Company; 9 February 1918 – Posted to the Labour Corps.

Whilst still serving with the Labour Corps he was discharged from the Army as no longer physically fit for wartime military service, having served for a total of two years and 112 days. All his service had been on the home front. Percival had also previously served in the Royal Navy for one month between 22 July and 26 August 1890, as a steward on HMS *Galatea*, a 2nd Class Armoured Cruiser.

Having looked at how the people of Hartlepool were affected by the First World War during the year of 1916, on a more global scale, I thought it would only be right to look at the same but from a local perspective, because despite the war and everything that came with it, day to day life, or what passed for it, carried on as best it could. The next part of this chapter will focus on Hartlepool on the home front throughout 1916.

On Thursday, 13 January 1916 a steamer moored at Victoria Dock in Hartlepool, capsized, killing a father and son, 39-year-old John Robert Chapple and William Chapple. The pair, who lived at 24 Commercial Street, Middleton, were engaged in mooring the vessel, when the hawser that attached the boat to the quay, suddenly became taut and capsized the boat. Sadly, both men were drowned.

What made this even more tragic was that the Chapple family had already lost one of their sons to the war; not on the Western Front, Gallipoli or at sea, but in the bombardment of the town by the German navy on 16 December 1914. There is some confusion surrounding this, as the newspaper article reporting this incident clearly states that 'John Chapple and his son, William', were the victims. It then makes reference to a 'member of the same family' being killed in the bombardment, but he is also shown as being William.

The Chapple family had seven children, two of whom had died before the time of the 1911 Census. William, we know, died along with his father John, on 13 January 1916. Son, John Chapple, aged 12 years in 1911, died in 1972, at 73 years of age. Miriam Chapple, who was only 9 in 1911, was still alive in 1926, as that is the year when she was married. Charles Chapple, who was only 7 years old in 1911, died in 1965 at the age of 61. Thomas Chapple, who was 6 years old in 1911, was 74 years of age when he died in 1980.

Even allowing for the possibility that John and Ellen had more children after 1911, they wouldn't have named one of them William, as they already had a child with that name. I can only assume that the newspaper has made a mistake.

Late on the evening of Saturday 29 January a mysterious fire broke out at the buildings of Messrs. W. Gray and Co, shipbuilders, at the Old Shipyard in West Hartlepool. So fierce were the flames that the premises were totally demolished. The fire had been discovered around ten o'clock in the evening, but within a couple of hours, all that was left of the building were the outside walls.

Moored next to the riverside building was one of the ships that had been built by Messrs. W. Gray & Co, the steel screw steamer *Andree*, a cargo vessel, which for some time was in danger of being set on fire, but eventually members of her crew were located and she was moved out of harm's way before any damage was caused. The *Andree* was a new vessel, having been launched three weeks earlier on 6 January.

It was down to the joint efforts of the West Hartlepool Corporation and the North Eastern Railway Company fire brigades, in preventing the flames from spreading to nearby buildings. But it really was a team effort as assistance was also provided by soldiers, policemen and members of the general public. The cause of the fire was unknown – although the premises did hold a quantity of oils and inflammable materials – and the cost of the damage ran into the thousands of pounds. The fire was so intense that the flames and glow were seen from miles away, which attracted unwelcome spectators to the area.

The steamer *Andree* survived the fire and went on to have a long and illustrious career, which saw her have five different owners and two other names, the *Pensicely* in 1923, and the *Granicos* in 1938. Her time came to an end during the Second World War when she was sunk by the Italian submarine *Guiseppe Finzi*, when en route to Loch Ewe in the north-west Highlands of Scotland.

Tuesday 1 February saw the sinking of the steamer *Franz Ficher* that had left Hartlepool harbour earlier the previous afternoon, heading south. The circumstances of the sinking were unusual, as the vessel in question hadn't hit a mine, been struck by a torpedo, or attacked by a German naval vessel. The attack had come in the form of a Zeppelin dropping a bomb on to the unsuspecting ship. Ironically, the vessel they bombed was in fact a captured enemy ship which was being used as a coastal collier.

According to one of the crew, a noise was heard coming from the skies above them, and moments later the Zeppelin appeared. No warning was given nor was the opportunity to evacuate provided. A bomb was dropped which struck them amidships and within two minutes they had sunk. Out of a crew of sixteen, there were only three survivors, the chief engineer, the steward and Able Seaman Charles Hillier who wrote:

> There was no time to take to the boats, and all were dragged beneath the waves on coming to the surface. I caught hold of a life-belt, and a little while later, after swimming about, I came across the other two survivors, who also had life-belts.
>
> Cries of other men were heard, but we could do nothing to help them and the shouts gradually died away. We were in a state of collapse when a Belgian steamer came to our aid and lowered a boat which picked us up. We were later transferred to another vessel and taken to London.

The *Franz Ficher*, which was actually called the *Frank Fisher* by the British, was at anchor at the time it was attacked. Those of the crew who were killed are as follows:

Able Seaman HENRY PATTERSON, of the Mercantile Marine, was 42 years of age and his death left behind a widow, Elizabeth Patterson, who lived at 42 Westmorland Street, Hartlepool. His body was not recovered, but his name is commemorated on the Tower Hill Memorial, in the City of London.

Second Engineer HENRY ALEXANDER POWELL was also a member of the Mercantile Marine, and was 36 years old at the time of his death. He was a married man, whose wife Celia Annie Powell, was living at 148 Harrow Road, Paddington, London, in the years immediately after the end of the war. His name is also included amongst the lists of the brave sailors who are commemorated on the Tower Hill Memorial.

A Fireman in the Mercantile Marine, WILLIAM PRIOR was 40 years of age, a married man from South Shields, who is also remembered on the Tower Hill Memorial.

Donkeyman EMMANUELE VIDOLICH was 42 years of age and a married man from Malta. His home with wife Maria was at 27 Sda, Dietro la Chiesa, Casal Zabbar, Malta. A donkeyman is not as you might at first glance think, somebody walking up and down a beach with a herd of donkeys trying to persuade reluctant holiday makers to pay to ride one of his loveable beasts. The term refers to a naval rating who worked in the engine room and who attended to the Donkey boiler. It was a role which required experience, and who had the title, tended to be older men. Emmanuele's name is also commemorated on the Tower Hill Memorial.

ABRAHAM NOBLE was a Mess Room Steward on the *Franz Fischer*, and at 59 years of age was the joint oldest of the ship's crew. His name is commemorated on the Tower Hill Memorial.

Able Seaman ALBERT HILLIER was another of the multi-national make up of the ship's crew, hailing from Newfoundland.

Master JOHN L. DAVIES, at 59 years of age, the man in charge of the *Franz Fischer*, was the crew's other old man, a Welshman who lived with his wife Letitia at 1 Rhyddings Park Road, in Swansea. As with the rest of the crew who perished, his body was never recovered, and his name is commemorated on the Tower Hill Memorial, in the City of London.

Second Mate WILLIAM INKSTER, who at 56 years of age, was one of the crew's older members, was a married man who lived with his wife Louisa, at 45 Agnes Street, in South Shields, although by birth he was Scottish, born in Shetland, an archipelago, which lies north east of Scotland.

Fireman DAVID BEVAN JENKINS aged 27 was a single man, and another of the crew who was from Wales. His mother, Margaret Jenkins, was living in Fishguard by the end of the war.

Fireman JOHN KYRIAKOS was 21 years of age and from Cyprus.

Lamps CHRISTOPHER CHARLES LENNARD was 54 years of age and a married man, who lived with his wife at 121 Arcadia Street, Poplar, London. He was a Londoner by birth, born at Woolwich, just south of the River Thames.

Able Seaman ALFRED WILLIAM CHARLTON was aged 28 and the husband of Mary Charlton. They lived at 3 Albany Street, West Hartlepool.

Mate GEORGE SKIMIN was 48 years of age. His home with his wife Jane was at 48 Holborn Avenue, Bangor, County Down. His name is also commemorated on the Tower Hill Memorial.

What follows is, I believe, an interesting story, particularly when compared with today's standards and the official outcomes imposed in relation to youth crime. On Friday 11 February brothers, John and Barney Crosby, hawkers, of no fixed abode, found themselves appearing before the Hartlepool Bench, charged under the Larceny Act, which is today referred to as theft.

The boys' crime was the theft of 4 feet of canvas. They went into the Co-operative Society's store in North Gate Street, Hartlepool, and purchased 8 yards of canvas, for which they paid 16 shillings. Later the same day one of the brothers returned to the shop claiming that the measurement of the canvas was wrong and that they wanted their money back, which was duly agreed, upon the return of the roll of canvas. Luckily for the boys, the shop assistant did not bother to check the length of the returned canvas straight away, and they walked out of the shop with 16 shillings and four yards of canvas. The discrepancy wasn't noticed until sometime later and, when it was, the Police were informed and the boys were found and arrested.

When they appeared in court both boys pleaded guilty to the charge against them and were each sentenced to 14 days imprisonment. This appears extremely harsh by today's standards, when considering that such an offence would just about warrant some kind of Police caution, no more than a proverbial smack on the wrist.

When at court the boys were each charged with a further two offences of obtaining property under false pretenses. One charge was of obtaining 24s 6d from Lilian Stonehouse, who lived at Durham Street, and the other victim was Mary Goodwin, of Charles Street who was duped out of 24 shillings, both in similar circumstances to that experienced by the Co-operative Society.

The Coroner, Mr J. Hyslop Bell, held an inquest at West Hartlepool on Monday 14 February into the death of Frederick Dayi, a 21-year-old seaman from the Belgian Congo.

Charles Alfred Anderson, gave evidence to the inquest that he had known the deceased for some time. They were friends and when ashore, Frederick would frequently stay at his lodging house, at 24 George Street, which was formerly known as the Crown and Sceptre Inn. The deceased was part of the crew of the SS *White Swan* which was a Newcastle-based ship, that sailed regularly between Hartlepool and London.

Anderson had last seen Dayi on the morning of Friday 11 February, when Dayi told him that he would be sleeping on board the *White Swan* that evening, but at 11.30pm he was woken by him banging on the front door of his property, wanting somewhere to sleep for the night as he had arrived late back from Sunderland, and it was then too late to go back on board his ship, which was not due to sail until Saturday evening. Anderson agreed to Dayi's request, and gave him a lighted candle to take up to his room, but specifically asked him not to light the gas. Dayi informed Anderson that he would like to sleep until dinner time the next day as he was very tired, potentially a period of more than eighteen hours.

The next morning, despite Dayi's protestations as to wishing to sleep so later, Anderson went to wake him, but there was no reply when he knocked on the bedroom door, and it was bolted from the inside. Anderson at once broke the door down, and on entering the room was almost overcome by the powerful smell of gas. He rushed to the window and pulled it open to allow the gas to escape. Dayi was laying on the bed face up and his body was cold to the touch and the gas tap was in the on position, which was allowing it to escape into the room.

Doctor Morgan had been called for, and besides confirming Dayi's death, he told the inquest that he had no doubt that the deceased had passed away as a result of gas poisoning. The jury having made their decision, returned a verdict of death due to gas poisoning, but added that there was insufficient evidence to determine whether this was the result of an accident or a willful act.

On the evening of Thursday 24 February a meeting of the Volunteer Training Corps took place in Hartlepool, to present awards to members of the local corps. Seventeen men were awarded badges for marksmanship and a further nine were presented with awards for being first class shots.

The evening was presided over by Sub-Commandant J.N. Reed (West Hartlepool), whilst the awards were presented by Alderman T.W. Watson, the Mayor of Hartlepool, who was a big supporter of his local corps. With the threat of a German invasion still a real possibility in many people's minds, the Volunteer Training Corps were seen mainly in a positive light, especially in coastal communities.

The Mayor made comment that in his opinion disciplined, well trained bodies of men, regardless of their age, who had the right equipment, could provide a formidable and efficient defensive corps capable of defending their communities against a potential enemy invasion.

A further presentation was forthcoming to celebrate the occasion of the wedding of Sergeant Burnett, who had voluntarily rendered invaluable assistance as an Army instructor to the Hartlepool section of the Volunteer

MILITARY SERVICE ACT, 1916

Every man to whom the Act applies will on Thursday, March 2nd, be deemed to have enlisted for the period of the War unless he is exempted or exempt.

Any man who has adequate grounds for applying to a Local Tribunal for a

CERTIFICATE OF EXEMPTION UNDER THIS ACT

Must do so BEFORE

THURSDAY, MARCH 2

Why wait for the Act to apply to you?

Come now and join of your own free will.

You can at once put your claim for exemption from being called up before a Local Tribunal if you wish.

ATTEST NOW

Military Services Act Poster.

Training Corps. He was unable to accept the gift in person, a china dinner and tea service, as he was serving in France at the time, but it was gratefully accepted on his behalf by Sergeant Major Wilson.

Wednesday 8 March saw possibly the first meeting of the Hartlepool Tribunal after the introduction of the government's Military Service Act 1916, introduced by the Prime Minister, Herbert H. Asquith. It came into being on 3 March 1916. Prior to this there had been no legal requirement for men to join the Army, instead the government had relied on a man's personal choice as to whether or not he should enlist. The reason why the Act had been brought in was because so many men were being wounded and killed in the war, more were needed to replace them. Because sufficient numbers were not enlisting voluntarily, the government had been left with no option if they wanted to sustain their efforts on a war footing, but to make it a legal requirement for young men to enlist in the Army once they had reached a certain age.

The new Act meant that men between the ages of 18 and 41 were liable to be called up for military service in the Army, with a few exceptions. These included men from Empire nations who were resident in the United Kingdom purely for the purpose of their education, or some other special purpose; men already serving in His Majesty's Armed Forces; men who had previously served in His Majesty's Armed Forces, who had been medically discharged or on completion of their service; men who either held a certificate of exemption, or who had offered themselves for enlistment since 4 August 1914 and been rejected. Married men were exempt from having to enlist, as were those who were widowed with dependent children, already serving in the Royal Navy, or an ordained minister of any religious denomination. The last category included in this exemption were those men who were working in what had been officially designated as a reserved occupation.

Despite the implementation of this Act, an addendum, or second Act, was brought in as from May 1916, because even more men were needed to fight the war, so from May 1916, married men could now be called up. The Act was further extended in 1918, when the ceiling on age was extended to include men up to and including the age of 51.

Men, or their employers on their behalf, could object to an individual being called up. Any such appeal had to be heard by what was called a local Military Service Tribunal, which could, in certain circumstances, grant exemptions for a man to have to undergo military training. The grounds for claiming an exemption from military service were, if it was expedient in the national interests for a man to be engaged in other work, or, if he was in education or training for any other work that he should continue; if serious hardship would ensue owing to his exceptional financial or business obligations or domestic position; in ill health or infirmity, or on the grounds of conscientious objection to the undertaking of combatant service.

On War Service Badge – 1914.

A government department could also issue certificates of exemption to individual men, or bodies of men in their employ, where it was deemed more convenient to do this rather than for them to be obtained by individual application before a local tribunal. An appeal, if applied for, could be temporary, permanent, or conditional in its implementation. If the initial appeal was refused, there was the right to appeal this decision to a County Appeal Tribunal. Not many of the records of these tribunals have survived, as after the war the government of the day determined that they should be destroyed, with no particular reason given as to why this needed to be done.

On 19 February, the Army Council of the United Kingdom issued instruction 386, stating that official War Service badges that had been issued to those men who were employed by the War Office, the Admiralty or the Ministry of Works, before 1 March 1916, would count as being a certificate of exemption from the requirement to undertake military training.

The Military Service Tribunal in Hartlepool would have consisted of between five and twenty-five members who were appointed locally, and usually included such individuals as the town's mayor and a military representative.

They had to hear appeals by 134 voluntarily attested men. These included forty-four applications by employers who made claims on the grounds of the indispensability of their employees. Of these thirty-one were granted with thirteen being refused. There were twenty-nine individual claims approved on either business or financial grounds, with a further two being refused. A total of thirty-six appeals were made in relation to domestic circumstances, thirty of which were granted, five refused with the other case being withdrawn. Approval was given in fourteen cases on the grounds that those individuals were employed in certified occupations, whilst nine other cases were adjourned so that further evidence could be provided by the individuals in question, in support of the appeals.

The case of Mr S.G. Clark, the town's deputy librarian, which had previously been heard by the Hartlepool Tribunal and determined to be worthy of only a temporary exemption, had been sent forward to the Central Appeals Tribunal, as Mr Clark had appealed the decision of the local tribunal. It hadn't, however, done him any good, as the Central Appeals Tribunal had confirmed the original decision.

The inquest resumed in West Hartlepool on Thursday 20 April concerning the death of Edward Wallace Stidder, the three-week-old son of a music hall comedian and his actress wife, at their home in Westbourne Road, on Tuesday 18 April.

Dr Pearson who carried out the post mortem examination of the child's body, told the inquest that the youngster was very emaciated. The skin was blue in colour and the lips were cracked and dried. It was the doctor's opinion that the child had been unable to assimilate its food, as it had gastro-inflammation of the stomach and the intestines, and died from starvation and inanition, or exhaustion from a lack of nourishment. Sadly, it would appear that the child had been born with a congenital weakness, which meant there were no juices in the stomach, which meant that no matter how much food was eaten, it could not be digested.

The coroner in his summoning up said that there would have been no inquest in this case if there had not been a refusal on the part of the registrar to accept a certain statement that had been sent to him. The reason for that refusal was, said the coroner, 'one which they could not criticize, much less find fault with because the Registrar was obeying a distinct injunction placed upon him by the Registrar-General'.

The issue in question was the validity of the death certificate that had been issued, which was signed by 'R Turner, MD, Chicago. Dr Turner, of 15 Hope Street, West Hartlepool, was called by the coroner, Mr J. Hyslop Bell, and asked if he was a medical man. He informed the coroner that he was in fact a doctor, and produced a licence to practise as such, but one that was issued by the State of Michigan in America.

The coroner informed Dr Turner that he could not deal with him without his having a legal certificate of medical skill in this country. Dr Turner advised the coroner that he had been practising as a doctor for eighteen years, and that there had never been an issue in relation to any previous death certificates which he had issued in the area.

The coroner replied, 'You are not on the list of foreign doctors who are recognized in this country.'

Mr Bertrand James Hurworth, the registrar for the West Hartlepool sub-district, told the inquest that the child's father produced to him a paper reading, 'I hereby certify that I attended Edward W. Stidder, aged 21 days, that I saw him on the 18th inst., and that he died on April 18th at 3.30 pm, and that to the best of my knowledge the cause of death was inanition.' This was then signed and dated by Dr Turner.

It is only fair to point out that in part Dr Turner's diagnosis concurred with that which was produced by Dr Pearson, who carried out the subsequent post mortem examination on the child, which gave credence to his claim of being a qualified doctor, even if he wasn't cleared to practise in England. It was more of an administrative matter surrounding the validity of the death certificate and Dr Turner's right to be practising as a doctor in England.

One witness had provided a statement that the child's mother had made up her mind from when the child was born, that owing to her stage commitments, she would not give the child its natural food, fearing that this might result in the child suffering unnecessarily. Another witness, the health visitor, gave evidence to the inquest that she was more than happy with the food that was being provided for the infant.

The jury returned a verdict that the child had died as the result of inherited inflammation of the stomach and bowels. Addressing the father, the coroner said, 'Whatever happens, we have great sympathy with you. You have behaved like a good fellow.'

The best possible match in the 1911 Census is that the child's parents were Frederick Vincent and Gertrude Stidder, who are recorded as being Music Hall Artists, living at 41 Devonshire Road, Holloway, North London. There was a Rifleman (8/45124) Frederick Vincent Stidder, who served with the Royal Irish Rifles during the war, between 10 December 1915 and 24 May 1918, before being discharged as no longer physically fit for wartime military service. Even though his was an extremely unusual name, I do not see that this as being one and the same person because of the dates he served with the Royal Irish Rifles.

In the years after the war Frederick must have fallen on hard times as on 10 September 1927 at the age of 41, he was admitted to the St Pancras Workhouse. Oddly enough, his wife Gertrude was still alive at the time of his admission to the workhouse and was living at 24 Liverpool Road, West London. He died in Romford four years later aged 46, and Gertrude died just three years after him.

An article appeared in the *Middlesbrough Daily Gazette* dated Thursday 27 April, concerning the death of a well known local resident, 63-year-old Mr William Scott, of 87 Clifton Avenue, West Hartlepool. He was running to catch a tram in nearby Grange Road, when he had a seizure and died a few minutes later. At the time of his death he was the Secretary of the Hartlepool Gas and Water Company.

Mr Scott was a native of Peebles in Scotland where he spent his younger years. He went on to become a teacher, working in educational establishments in both Edinburgh and Newcastle, but in 1873 he decided on a change of career and began working for the Hartlepool Gas and Water Company in 1873, going on to take up the position of secretary in 1900, taking over from a Mr Trewitt. He was also a director of the Hartlepool Permanent Building Society; a position he had held for some years. He was a religious man, a staunch Presbyterian and a prominent member of the Park Road Church, and for many years he was the chairman of the board of managers, a position he held up until about a year before his death, which he gave up due to failing health.

He was said to be a true gent with a kind, retiring disposition who was well liked and highly respected by all who knew him. He left a widow, Elizabeth, three sons, William, Ronald, and James, as well as three daughters, Jane, Margaret and Jessie. One of his sons was serving in the Royal Navy and another with the Army, the latter of which had been wounded whilst serving at Gallipoli, and was at the time of his father's death, recovering in hospital at Manchester.

It was good to see that despite the war, there was still time for men to take part in sporting pastimes when the opportunity arose. Saturday 29 April was one such occasion. Except for charity matches which the Football Association and the Northern Union supported and had sanctioned, the football season came to an end that day.

A Rugby Union match had been arranged at West Hartlepool and saw Mr R.F. Oakes take a strong North of England military team to play the Tees and Hartlepool Garrison. Included in the North of England team were several leading Northern Union players who would certainly give their side an advantage.

The man in charge of the Hartlepool team was none other than the Rector of Hartlepool, the Reverend Bertram Jones. He had also managed to put together a strong team to represent the Garrison, for a match that had raised a lot of local interest, as did the recent game that took place between the North of England and a strong Anzacs side in Leeds, which raised a substantial amount of money for local charities.

On the afternoon of Tuesday 30 May a ceremony took place at the VAD Hospital in Perth, Scotland, when Colonel Mackintosh, the Commanding Officer of the No.1 Highland District, presented Sergeant F.W. Mallins of the East Lancashire Regiment with the Military Medal for his efforts during the bombardment of Hartlepool on 16 December 1914. Sergeant Mallins had enlisted in the Army in 1902, so was a very experienced soldier by the start of the First World War. Before joining the military, he had served as a police constable in his home town of Cardiff.

The presentation ceremony of the medal took place in the hospital's day room and was attended by a number of wounded and sick soldiers, who were patients there, along with members of staff.

Colonel Mackintosh told those who were present that the General Officer Commanding-in-Chief for Scotland had delegated him to present the medal to Sergeant Mallins, not for fighting on the Western Front in France, but as part of a gun battery stationed at Hartlepool when the town was on the receiving end of a German naval bombardment, on 16 December 1914. But that didn't mean the medal had any less worth, far from it. His actions that day were brought to the attention of his commanding officers, who having heard what he had done, decided to recommend him for the award.

After pinning the medal on the sergeant's tunic, Colonel Mackintosh congratulated him and expressed the hope that he would survive the war and be able to hand the medal on to his children in future years. Hearty cheers were raised in Sergeant Mallin's honour and thereafter, all of those present, patients and staff alike, enjoyed an afternoon tea.

An inquest took place on Friday 26 May at West Hartlepool, into the death of local man, Mr Hugh Rae, who had been shot dead. He was found dead on the floor of his office along with a 17-year-old former employee, who was found bleeding from a head wound.

The young lady in question, Norah Hopkins, told the inquest that she had worked for Mr Rae as a clerk, and that on Thursday 25 May between 12pm and 1pm, she was in an adjoining office to where the tragedy took place. The two offices were only separated by a small sliding window, and on hearing a shot and groans coming from Mr Rae's office, where he and a lady by the name of Miss Young were working, she tried to get into the office but couldn't open the door. Instead she opened the dividing window and saw Mr Rae lying by the foot of the door, which was why she had been unable to open it. She then noticed Miss Young leaning up against a table and bleeding from the head.

Norah Hopkins then climbed through the open window and asked Miss Young if she could do anything to help her. Miss Young nodded towards Mr Rae and although Norah couldn't be certain, she thought she heard her say 'him'. Norah took one look at Mr Rae and could tell that he was dead. She then set about helping Miss Young as best she could, who by now had started complaining of pain from the wound to the side of her head.

Norah also said that there were miniature rifles kept in the office, the type used by members of the Voluntary Training Corps. Miss Young, who like Norah Hopkins, had previously worked for Mr Rae, was only back for a three-week period. Mr Rae did not appear to want her to leave, but to carry on working for him after the end of the three weeks, but because of a new job she had acquired in London, this would not be possible for her to do. As for him, he was not sure as to how he was going to cope once Miss Young had left his employment.

He then picked up one of the rifles, aimed it at her and opened fire, catching her on the side of the head. He then called out, 'My God, I will do it also', and he then shot himself.

Police Inspector Hunter of Hartlepool Police gave evidence to the inquest that he saw Miss Young in hospital on the afternoon of the incident. She told him that she had been in Mr Rae's employment for 16 months and that on the day in question she was in the office with him. Out of the blue and without any prior indication of what he was about to say, he suddenly told her that he was going to shoot himself. She told him not to be so silly, he simply turned round, pointed a rifle at her and pulled the trigger; the bullet struck her on the forehead. She immediately heard the sound of another shot having been fired and heard Mr Rae fall to the floor, although she dared not look round.

It transpired that Mr Rae had been worried about the state of his business as well as having to go through an operation for appendicitis. He had told Miss Young the previously day that he intended shooting himself, whether she believed that he would carry it out, is not known.

The jury determined that Mr Rae took his own life by shooting himself while he was in a depressed state of mind.

On Friday 2 June Mr John William Carter, 64 years of age, a herbalist, was charged at West Hartlepool with having supplied a noxious mixture to procure a woman to have an abortion.

Mr W.J. Waugh, King's Council, was representing Mr Carter, and Mr Higson Simpson, the Town Clerk, was prosecuting the case.

Mary Griffiths, the wife of a dock labourer from Hartlepool, gave evidence that on 14 March, she had visited Mr Carter's shop, which was located in Scarborough Street, and asked him to make her up a 'bottle' as she thought she was pregnant. He duly obliged, telling her that she had eight days to get another bottle if she needed it. The cost of the item was 2s 6d, which Mrs Griffiths took away and passed on to a Miss Cook.

Mr Waugh, acting on behalf of Mr Carter, enquired of Mrs Griffiths, who Miss Cook was. 'She is a great worker in the town,' she replied.

Mr Waugh asked Mrs Griffiths if she had intended to use the 'medicine', provided by Mr Carter, to induce a miscarriage for herself or anybody else. She replied that she hadn't.

Mrs Griffiths admitted that what she had told Mr Carter was a lie, and a story that she had made up, as all Miss Cook had asked of her was to obtain a 'bottle' from Mr Carter. She had also been to see similar individuals in the town to obtain similar 'bottles'.

Mary Ann Robson, the wife of an outdoor porter, provided evidence that she had also visited Mr Carter's, on 22 March and asked for a 'bottle' for a married friend. She was charged 2s 10d by Mr Carter, and claimed he told her that if it did not put her friend right, she should come and see him again and he would give her a stronger bottle. This was also handed over to Miss Cook.

The mysterious Miss Cook was Agnes Ellen Cook. She also gave evidence that she had received the bottles from Mrs Griffiths and Mrs Robson, and handed them over to a Dr Cargin, who was the town's Medical Officer for Health, who in turn had forwarded them to the public analyst, to establish the contents of each of the bottles. Joseph Stock, the analyst in question, said that the main ingredient of each bottle was Aloes, and that the contents of the bottles contained 17.74 grains of Aloes per fluid ounce. When given in proper medical doses, it was between two to five grains, and the effect could not be described generally as being harmful, but if taken in sufficient quantities could cause an abortion in a pregnant woman.

Dr A.S. Biggart stated that Aloes in the proportion mentioned by Joseph Stock would be a noxious amount to a pregnant woman, and likely to cause an abortion.

Mr Waugh then asked Dr Biggart if he had ever heard of a woman suffering an abortion as a result of talking a dose of Aloes. When Dr Biggart replied that he couldn't say for definite, Mr Waugh jumped on his response by declaring, 'That is, your answer is no.'

In his summing up to the bench, Mr Waugh suggested that the prosecution had not made out a strong enough case which could possibly justify his client being sent for trial. He added it was extraordinary that it had taken the prosecution more than two months, after the bottle had been supplied, to bring the matter before the bench. Lastly, he questioned how the evidence of Mrs Griffiths could be relied upon after she had admitted in court to uttering deliberate falsehoods to his client in an attempt at incriminating him, thus making her an unreliable witness.

In essence, Mr Carter provided bottles to two women, one of whom claimed to be pregnant. When analysed the two bottles were found to contain high doses of Aloes, which was and is used for numerous pharmaceutical reasons, one being as a purgative. If taken in high enough doses by pregnant women, Aloes can bring about an abortion. This was the evidence presented by the prosecution against Mr Carter, which is quite damming. Having heard and considered the evidence provided by each of the witnesses, the bench determined that there was insufficient evidence to put Mr Carter on trial, and therefore dismissed the case.

Based on the fact that I served for thirty years as a police officer, I find that an absolutely incredible decision, one which appears to have been made for no other reason than Mrs Griffiths admitted having lied to Mr Carter as to her reasons for needing one of his 'bottles'.

Some eighteen months after the bombardment of Hartlepool on 16 December 1914, another victim was claimed. The inquest, chaired by the deputy coroner, Mr George Newby JP, took place on Wednesday, 21 June after the death of 48-year-old Mr Thomas Jeffrey of 10 Dock Street, Hartlepool, on Monday 19 June.

The first person to give evidence was Mr Samuel Oliver of Albany Street. He told the inquest that on the day of the bombardment, he, Mr Jeffrey, and others were going through Irving's harbour shipyard, looking for a safe place to take cover, when a shell passed over him, struck the railways ahead, and exploded, killing a man and a woman. Mr Jeffrey who was immediately in front of Mr Oliver, was struck by a fragment of shrapnel from the exploding shell, the force of which blew him some 45 feet away.

Mr Oliver was also caught in the blast, his wounds causing him to be laid up in bed for some three and a half months. As for Mr Jeffrey, his wounds were attended to at the scene before he was taken to the Cameron Hospital.

Dr Gibb, who had been looking after Mr Jeffrey's welfare since 6 May 1915, told the inquest that the deceased's wound was the result of a piece of shrapnel passing through his pelvis from the buttock to his groin. By November 1915, the wound was fully healed and, although this had left Mr Jeffrey with a limp, he was gradually getting stronger. On Saturday 17 June 1916, Dr Gibb was called to see Mr Jeffrey at his home, where it was discovered that he was suffering with a hemorrhage of the stomach. He died two days later due to a syncope caused by the hemorrhage. The medical description of syncope is a brief loss of consciousness associated with transient cerebral anemia, as in a heart block, or sudden lowering of blood pressure.

Dr Gibb confirmed that the injuries Mr Jeffrey sustained in the bombardment of Hartlepool on 16 December 1914, played a very large part in his subsequent death.

Friday 30 June saw the Annual General Meeting of the Hartlepool United Football and Athletic Club Co. Ltd, which took place at the Commercial Hotel in Hartlepool.

Councillor W.J. Coates, who chaired the meeting, said he thought that results showed that the club's decision not to have a football team whilst the war was still going ahead, was the right one, although they would still be continuing their membership of both the North-Eastern League and the Football Association.

As much as everyone concerned with the club greatly loved their football, they decided that they did not want to continue playing and risk being seen as a club that tried to prevent local young men from joining the colours. The military had taken over the field on which they usually played their games, for which they paid handsomely. There was also the added bonus that, with the Army encamped on the premises, the chances of a break in at the clubhouse were unlikely.

Mr Coates reminded those present at the meeting about the sad loss, whilst serving his country on active service, of Jack Gatenby, an individual who was well respected and much loved by all of his fellow players. The Commonwealth War Graves Commission records four men with the surname of Gatenby and the initial 'J'. Of these only one had been killed by the time this meeting had taken place. He was shown as John Gatenby, who was 25 years of age and a Rifleman (R/5531) in the 12th Battalion, King's Royal Rifle Corps, who died of his wounds on 18 October 1915. He is buried at the Merville Communal Cemetery in the Nord region of France. People with the Christian name John, are often also known by the name 'Jack', John Fitzgerald 'Jack' Kennedy for one.

At the end of the war his parents, John and Penelope Gatenby, were living at 80 Studley Road, West Hartlepool, although at the time of the 1911 Census the family home was at 1 Lydenham Road, West Hartlepool.

The chairman also said that he would like to thank Mr T.P. Robertson for the work he had done for the club over the years, and that it was sad that he had decided to quit his role, but in Mr George Morris they had found a more than suitable replacement.

It had come to the attention of the chairman that some townsfolk were saying that the war would be over by Christmas and then they could all get back to playing football again, but he was not so sanguine about it.

The annual meeting of the Hartlepool's Volunteer Training Corps took place on the evening of Wednesday 26 July. It was chaired by Mr J.H. Smith. The honorary secretary, Mr S. Strover, reported that the membership of the West Hartlepool Company stood at 344, and of the Hartlepool platoon, at sixty. The exact number of men posted to platoons at West Hartlepool, was 188, whilst the number of men in the Hartlepool section who had received uniforms was thirty-seven, making the overall strength 225, a figure which also included officers.

It was proposed at the meeting that the Hartlepool Companies should be attached to No.2 Sunderland Battalion of the county regiment, so that an effective coastal defence could be in place. Other duties would include both carrying out patrols and acting as guards at specific required locations.

The meeting was informed that the Hartlepool Company would be allocated two company commanders as well as platoon commanders, whilst Mr S. Strover was appointed as a senior company commander and Mr J.N. Reid, as a junior company commander.

The Honorary Treasurer, Councillor A. Casper, informed the meeting that financially they were in a sound position, with a balance of £230 18s 7d in their funds.

Friday 28 July saw two Hartlepool men lose their appeal against a previous decision made by the Southampton Munitions Tribunal refusing to grant them certificates to leave their employment with Messrs. J.S. White and Co., of Southampton, and return to Hartlepool to work. Mr E. Timlin and Mr C. Gardner were skilled munitions workers who had left Hartlepool after the German naval bombardment of the town on 16 December 1914 and obtained work in Southampton.

Mr Justice Atkin listened to counsel acting for the two men. It was put to the court that they had found work slack in their home town of Hartlepool after the bombardment, so they went to Southampton where they found work which provided them with good wages. They continued to work there for some fifteen months, but found it more and more difficult to be living and working in one place, whilst their wives and children were living in Hartlepool. They had heard that work was now more plentiful back home in Hartlepool and had asked for certificates so that they might be allowed to return there, which would also allow them to be re-united with their families. Their request fell on death ears, as the tribunal at Southampton decided that the work they were doing in the town was of such importance that they should remain there, and so refused their application for certificates which would have allowed them to return to Hartlepool.

Mr Justice Atkin dismissed their appeal, saying that the case was a hopeless one, for it was obvious that the original tribunal in Southampton had determined the case correctly, and that the two men would have to remain working for their current employer.

During the course of the war Hartlepool came under attack by German Zeppelins on three separate occasions, the first of these attacks took place on Tuesday 8 August, but thankfully it was nowhere near as devastating as the German naval bombardment of the town on 16 December 1914.

Even though it was a cloudy night, the sound of the airship's engines could be clearly heard on the ground some distance away and it was also visible to the naked eye. Only two bombs were dropped during the raid, both of which landed in a field at Longhill, causing minor damage to a few of the nearby surrounding houses. There did not appear to be any intended target, and there was nothing of any military significance in the area. It could have been a case that the Zeppelin was just about to begin its journey home and simply wanted to lighten its load which would then allow them to fly at a greater height, which in turn would afford them greater protection from any British aircraft who were determined to shoot her down.

In the early days of August 1916 a Hartlepool man was recovering in hospital at Birkenhead from wounds he had received whilst fighting in France. Lance Corporal T. Thompson, who was serving with the Northumberland Fusiliers, wrote a letter to Hartlepool Councillor J.T. Graham, JP, telling him about his ordeal. He wrote:

> *I was in the scrapping eleven days before I got the knock. Mr Vivian Horsley, also from Hartlepool, was my platoon officer, and even when I got hit he looked after me until the stretcher bearers carried me away. He is a trump, I'll tell you, and there was not a chap in the platoon who would not do anything for him.*

On the night of July 13th, when they were making a terrific counter attack against our newly won position, Mr Horsley was a treat. He was along the line from one place to another with, 'All right boys,' and as cool as a cucumber. When we had driven them back, and were all cleaning our rifles ready for the next move you should have heard the chaps praising him. Now and then when they said something about Mr Horsley I'd chime in with 'Well, what do you think, he comes from Hartlepool.'

We had our Captain wounded that night, and later the second in command was hit, and I am pleased to say Mr Horsley is at present in command of my company. I had a notification from him which ran on to state that the officers, NCOs and men of the company congratulated me on my good fortune of having been granted the military medal.

The message gave me more pleasure than the news of the award, because it showed me I had the good opinion of all my comrades. I knew I had been recommended for my bombing on July 3rd.

It would appear that both men survived the war. Mr Vivian Horsley, who in 1916 was 25 years of age, had been a bank clerk before the war in Whitley Bay, and was the younger child of Matthew and Ann Horsley of 2 Albion Terrace, Hartlepool. Their elder son John, also served during the war, as a private (40879) with the Canadian Army, with whom he enlisted on 10 June 1915 as part of the Canadian Expeditionary Force, when he was 20 years of age. John, who was a labourer, must have left for Canada sometime after the 1911 Census was completed, as he was certainly in the UK at that time. He survived the war.

On 24 August 1916, a group of soldiers had a bathing parade when one of them, Private William Millward, serving with the 3rd Battalion, North Staffordshire Regiment, from Burslem, got into difficulties in the sea. Recognising his dilemma, two of those swimming with him, Sergeant Frederick Shakespeare and Private William E. Dring, from Spalding in Lincolnshire, swam with him, heading back to the safety of the shore. As they approached a small boat, Private Dring let go of his grip on Private Millward, to try and climb aboard it, but almost immediately disappeared under the water. Despite the confusion, Sergeant Shakespeare kept hold of Millward and continued with him towards the shore, until the latter indicated that he felt better and should be able to now swim unaided. No sooner had Sergeant Shakespeare let go of him, than Millward, in what would appear to have been a bit of a blind panic, tried to take hold of the sergeant, but only managed to grab hold of his swimming costume, which he pulled down to his ankles. Sergeant Shakespeare, whilst trying to re-adjust his costume, momentarily lost sight of Millward, before looking up to see him being carried away by strong currents; before he could get to him, Millward disappeared below the waves.

Mr A. Winterbottom, the Chief Constable of Hartlepool, made the Carnegie Hero Trust Fund aware of the facts of the incident, which resulted in the fund's trustee's entering the names of Private Dring and Sergeant Shakespeare on to their roll of heroes. The parents of Private Dring were presented with a certificate, framed in oak, to commemorate their son's heroic deed on that day, whilst Sergeant Shakespeare was granted an honorary certificate along with the sum of £10, which was invested in Exchequer Bonds on his behalf. Both presentations were made by the mayoress, with Sergeant Shakespeare making a gracious speech in response.

What made Private 24083 William Dring's death even more poignant was his age; he was only 17. His body was recovered and he is buried at Spalding Cemetery.

Private 20586 William Millward served with the 3rd Battalion, North Staffordshire Regiment. His body was never recovered and his name is commemorated on the Hollybrook Memorial at Southampton.

Tuesday 5 September saw a meeting take place of the West Hartlepool Town Council. One of the matters which required some urgent and detailed discussion, was that of a resolution which had been submitted by other councils urging that all enemy aliens should be interned. The submission was seeking support from towns across the country to adopt their resolution. This caused more consternation than could have been believed possible. Members urged that the matter should be dealt with at once, but the mayor, Alderman Charles Macfarlane, ruled that in keeping with their own rules and regulations, such motions required the agreed period of notice before they could form part of a particular meeting's agenda.

Councillor Fryer protested this decision, saying that in dealing with an unscrupulous enemy, the council should not trouble themselves with standing orders, as these were not conventional times. The discussion continued with some heated debate as passions began to rise on the topic, with it becoming clear that not everybody was in agreement on the issue of internment, many being against it. Despite the lively debate, the mayor's ruling on the matter prevailed.

Other matters discussed included war bonuses for corporation workmen, which it was agreed would be an increase of one shilling per week, which made a total bonus of four shillings. A Local Government Board circular on the topic of post war public works was presented for discussion. The mayor reminded the meeting that before the war there had been talk within the group about a new road, north of the town, via Easington, and he believed that the government would advance sufficient amounts of money to pay for such schemes. The mayor urged the members that this should be the scheme which they should submit on behalf of West Hartlepool Town Council. The town clerk said he would communicate with neighbouring authorities to gauge their potential interest in the matter.

The following evening, Wednesday 6 September, saw the monthly meeting of the Hartlepool Town Council, which was chaired by the mayor, Alderman T.W. Watson. The first item for discussion was the closure of the local Labour Exchange. A letter had been received by the town clerk which had originated from the Board of Trade, stating that the question of re-opening the exchange would need to be reconsidered if there was a big increase in the workload of the Board of Trade at the end of the war.

The Town Council's Sanitary Committee reported that a letter had been received by the County Council on the subject of overcrowding in industrial districts, and the building of accommodation for workmen under the Housing of the Working Classes Act. The Town Council were already ahead of the game and had previously submitted such an idea to the Local Government Board for a loan, so that they could commence the intended work.

Those present at the meeting were informed of the death of Hartlepool Borough Police Constable John Edward Hartland, and Mr J. Brown, one of the corporation's workmen. Both had been killed in action. The council decided that the allowance provided by the corporation to the men's immediate family should be continued until the situation regarding the men's army pensions was ascertained.

Private (5460) JOHN EDWARD HARTLAND was serving with the 2nd Battalion, Scots Guards, when he was killed on 14 August 1916. He is buried at the Sucrerie Military Cemetery at Colincamps, in the Somme region of France. John Hartland was 29 years of age and a married man who lived at 27 Middlegate Street, Hartlepool, with his wife, Kathleen, their son Francis, and John's younger brother Joseph.

The British Army's Medal Rolls Index Cards shows that John first arrived in France on 13 August 1914. This indicates that at the outbreak of the war he was in the Army Reserve and recalled to the colours, therefore was one of the first to be sent out to France as part of the British Expeditionary Force. His individual card shows he was killed on 14 August 1914, rather than 1916, which is a mistake.

John's younger brother Joseph had enlisted in the Army on 9 August 1911 at Dudley in Worcestershire, when he was nearly 18 years of age, becoming a private (8728) in the 2nd Battalion of the Worcestershire Regiment, and immediately placed on the Army Reserve. He initially underwent five months' training, between 9 August 1911 and 8 January 1912. He remained on the Army Reserve for the next two years, carrying out four weeks training annually at summer camp. In 1914 he began his summer camp training on 13 July which finished a week early due to the outbreak of the war. Suddenly, it was all for real, there was to be no more playing at it. On 5 August 1914 he was mobilized and posted to the 2nd Battalion, Worcestershire Regiment.

Joseph's Army Service Record records some remarkable information about him, and highlights just how fortunate a young man he was, considering that he served in France from 24 November 1914 to 25 February 1917.

On 30 March 1915 he was tried by a Field General Court Martial, which was one of only two types of courts martial that had the authority to issue the death penalty as its ultimate sanction. His Army Service Record included the following text:

> In custody awaiting trial. Tried by Field Court Martial and sentenced to 2 years' imprisonment with hard labour for, when a soldier acting as a sentinel on active service, sleeping on his post.

The following entry has then been added and dated 4 April 1915.

> Sentence commuted to 3 months Field Punishment No.1 by General Sir Douglas Haig Commander 1st Army 12 April 1915.

Having committed an offence that could have seen him placed in front of a firing squad, you would think that a lesson had been learnt, and to put his breach of military discipline into perspective, here are a few relevant facts.

Between 1 September and 31 October 1915, whilst serving in Gallipoli fifty-two British servicemen were sentenced to death as a result of being placed before a court martial. Of these, forty-one of them were for being asleep whilst on sentry duty. Fortunately, every one of those men had their sentence commuted to lesser and non-lethal punishments.

Throughout the war a total of 3,362 British servicemen who faced court martial were sentenced to death. Of these 449 were for the offence of falling asleep at their post, the second most common breach of army discipline. Of these only two individuals were actually executed.

On 21 October 1915 Joseph was listed as 'Suffering from Gas poisoning' on the War Office Casualty list.

There is another entry for Joseph Hartland dated 9 February 1916, which says:

> In custody awaiting trial by Field General Court Martial for when on active service, leaving his post without orders from his superior officer. Found guilty, sentenced to one year's imprisonment with hard labour. Sentence confirmed by Brigadier General A W Baine.

On 28 March 1916 Joseph had his sentence suspended under the Suspension of Sentence Act 1915, as authorized by the General Officer Commanding I Corps. Once again he was extremely fortunate, and was dealt with relatively lightly in the circumstances, especially considering this was his second serious breach of military law in just under a year.

Less than four months later he was in trouble again, this time he was arrested on 10 July 1916, in custody awaiting trial. On 27 July he was tried by a Field General Court Martial, this time for whilst on active service, absenting himself without leave and drunkenness. He was found guilty of both charges and sentenced to two years' imprisonment with hard labour, with the sentence once again confirmed by the Brigadier General.

As was the case with his two previous convictions, his sentence was commuted, this time after having served just two weeks in detention he was released from prison on 11 August 1916. It was replaced with three months' Field Punishment No.1. This was where a convicted man was placed in fetters and handcuffs, or similar restraints and attached to a fixed object, such as a fence post or a large gun wheel, for up to two hours a day. During the First World War, this type of punishment was issued on just over 60,000 occasions.

There then follows an entry on his Army Service Record, which is obviously an error, as it shows that he died of wounds received in action as part of the British Expeditionary Force, on 8 November 1916. This is possibly connected to the fact that he was wounded in action on 2 November 1916 when he received a gun shot wound to his left leg. He had also received wounds to his wrist and left elbow on 24 August 1916, one would imagine these were only of a minor nature as he had already returned to full duty before the November of that year, although not for long, as on Christmas Eve 1916 he was 'dangerously ill' in No.34 Casualty Clearing Station suffering from double pneumonia. On 27 February 1917 he was sent back to England on the Hospital Ship *St David* and remained in hospital until 18 March.

Between 1 February 1918 and his discharge from the Army on 2 May 1919, he was transferred on six occasions. Firstly, he was posted to the 2nd/5th Battalion, Essex Regiment. On 11 June 1918, he was transferred again, but the writing on his Army Service Record was illegible. On 21 June 1918 he was on the move again, this time to the 3rd Battalion, Durham Light Infantry. He was with them for less than a month when he was transferred to the 18th Battalion, Scottish Rifles on 12 July 1918, becoming Private 55674. He was with them for only two weeks when he was transferred again. This time on 26 July 1918, he became a member of the 16th Battalion, Argyll & Sutherland Highlanders and on 31 October 1918 to the 16th Battalion of the same regiment. On 2 December 1918, with the Armistice now in place he was transferred to the 378th PoW Company, Labour Corps, becoming Private 443910 in the process, and on 2 March 1919, he found himself in the 376th PoW Company, Labour Corps, with which he was serving at the time of his discharge from the Army on 27 May 1919.

He had a well documented and chequered time in the Army, which was duly noted, with his Army Service Record on his discharge being marked up with 'Character Bad', which was possibly why he had to forfeit 3 years and 42 days of the 7 years 292 days he had actually served, in relation to his Army Pension.

On Monday, 9 October 1916 Mrs Jessie Robson appeared before the West Hartlepool Bench on a charge of assisting an army deserter to conceal himself.

Police Sergeant Smith told the court that about 7.30am on the morning of Saturday 30 September, he attended at 7 Moseley Street in the town, where

Robson had a room. He introduced himself and explained that he had been informed that she was hiding a deserter in her room. She told Sergeant Smith that she was alone and had no idea what he was talking about, but when he entered the room he found a man dressing himself. He quickly discovered that this was the man he was looking for, Mr Frank Spence, who admitted that he had been at the address for two nights.

Mrs Robson told the court that she was not aware that Spence was a deserter, and that she was a married woman, whose husband was a sailor in the Royal Navy. The bench did not believe her story and fined her £5 or one month's imprisonment.

News of lost Hartlepool sailors having been found alive and well, was reported in local newspapers on Thursday 12 October. The report was in relation to the crew of the Steam Trawler *Loch Ryan*, owned by J.T. Graham & Sons of Hartlepool, which had left the town's harbour on 21 September and had not been heard of since. In the circumstances it was feared that the ship had struck a mine or been torpedoed by a German submarine, and all of her crew had been lost.

She was finally discovered on 29 September, anchored off the Terschelling Coast, which is a municipality and an island situated in Northern Holland, and is part of what is known as the West Frisian Islands. The ship's name was not displayed, only that of the serial number, HL7, which correlated with that of the *Loch Ryan*.

Her crew were standing on the rear deck of the vessel as prisoners under guard by a naval officer and two sailors from the German submarine *U-64*. Remarkably the Dutch authorities did not appear to know of the presence of either vessel inside their territorial waters, and by the time Dutch naval vessels had responded, the *Loch Ryan* and the *U-64* had left their waters.

The British trawler was taken back to Germany as a prize and used as an auxiliary vessel by the Imperial German Navy, whilst her crew were taken to Berlin and paraded through the streets, finally being interned as PoWs at Durman in Germany, where they remained until the end of the war.

The ship's skipper was Richard Henry Whittleton, and whilst still under German control, it struck a mine and sank on 21 February 1917. Richard survived the war before dying in 1923, at the comparatively young age of 43.

A newspaper article dated Saturday 21 October reported the suicide of Private John Robinson, which took place at 10 Warden Street, Hartlepool, the previous day. Two police officers attended the address to arrest the man, due to him being absent without leave from his regiment. It would appear that once he realized that he was about to be apprehended, he shot himself in the head with a revolver.

Possibly because he had committed suicide, his details do not appear to have been included on the Commonwealth War Graves Commission records.

A meeting was held on Thursday 1 November at the Miners' Institute in Wingate, to discuss the formation of a local company of men in connection with the 2nd Durham County Volunteer Regiment. There was a fine turn out of interested local men, all of whom were keen to find out what was on offer with the Volunteers. Mr C.H. Leeds presided over the meeting.

On Thursday 9 November, Alderman T.W. Watson, was elected as Mayor of Hartlepool for the fourth successive year. Such occurrences were quite commonplace throughout the First World War, up and down the country. It was deemed that political stability within communities was a much better option that continuous political in-fighting, which would not have helped the war effort. The country needed to be a united force rather than a divided mess, and most towns throughout the country managed to achieve this.

As protocol dictated in such matters, the mayor gave an acceptance speech and response to having been elected. In reviewing the previous year's work and achievements, he commented on the strong financial position that the borough found itself in, which included having reduced the council's overall debt by £39,272. Despite the uncertainty of the war, Hartlepool had more than one building project in the offing, as well as much of the old housing stock needing to be demolished. This cost a great deal of money, some of which had been raised in the form of loans which ultimately needed repaying.

Although the town's overall trade had been very good, it didn't take a genius to work out that the one industry that would face hardship throughout the war, would be that of fishing. The mayor was more than confident that once peace finally returned, the fishing industry would once again thrive and continue to go from strength to strength.

Those present at the meeting were reminded about the deed of heroism carried out by two British soldiers, one of whom unfortunately died as a result of his efforts to rescue one of his comrades.

Monday 27 November saw the second German Zeppelin raid on Hartlepool, and this was a much more involved incident than the first one. The Zeppelin, the *L34*, was first caught in the glare of searchlights over Elwick, whose anti-aircraft guns then opened fire on the German invader. Whether as a direct response to the anti-aircraft fire, or because they wanted to jettison their bombs in case they were hit, is not clear, but either way, the *L34* Zeppelin jettisoned thirteen of its bombs, in and around Elwick, all of which thankfully for those on the ground, landed in fields, with the only casualties being two cows injured by one of the exploding shells.

As it tried to make good its escape, *L34* headed across Hartlepool en route to the North Sea and home. Having been caught by the glare of the searchlights, it was now in trouble, like a wounded animal that was cornered and knew that its chances of escape and ultimate survival were diminishing by the minute. Its route took it over Hartley Street and Lowthian Road, its crew throwing their bombs over board as quickly as they could, not aiming at anything in particular, just wanting to jettison its payload, so that it could rise to a height where the British aircraft wouldn't be able to follow, whilst reducing the chances of being blown out of the skies by lucky bullets striking its munitions.

It is estimated that the *L34* managed to drop at least a further twenty-five bombs before making its way out to sea, killing at least two individuals and injuring some thirty-four others in the process.

The man who was credited with finally bringing down the *L34* was Second Lieutenant Ian Vernon Pyott, of the Royal Flying Corps, whilst flying a BE2c aircraft (2738) out of Seaton Carew aerodrome, which was where C Flight of 36 Squadron were based. He attacked the Zeppelin at nearly 10,000 feet, and after he had finished emptying his ammunition into the body of the airship, the hydrogen ignited, causing a fire to break out, and it crashed into the sea just past the old lighthouse. Second Lieutenant Pyott was awarded the Distinguished Service Order for his efforts that evening. He survived the war and returned to his native South Africa.

The bodies of two of the airship's crew were washed up on the shore at Seaton Carew some time later, and although unidentifiable, due to the amount of time they had been in the water, they were buried with full military honours at Holy Trinity Church, Seaton Carew, on 11 January 1917.

Thursday 30 November saw the unveiling of two more war shrines in West Hartlepool. One was in Hill Street, where sixty-three men from sixty-seven houses had enlisted, and Portland Street, where twenty-eight men had enlisted from twenty-five houses. Two men from each of the streets had already lost their lives in the fighting. Both of the unveiling ceremonies were performed by Lieutenant Colonel W. Thomlinson JP, who at each location was presented with a memento to mark the occasion. In Hill Street, the residents had clubbed together and bought him a silver-mounted walking stick, whilst in Portland Street, they presented him with a fountain pen.

The services at both locations were marked with both reverence and dignity, which was to be expected and conducted by W.J. Knowlden MA, the Vicar at St Aidan's Church. Large crowds of local residents turned out in both streets to mark the occasion. Each of the shrines had the names of all of the men from the street who had enlisted. They were accompanied by the picture of a crucifixion, which stood for prayer and patriotism. The first shrine, which had only been set up the previous week, in Florence Street, was unveiled by the mayoress of West Hartlepool.

Monday 11 December saw the Deputy Coroner, Mr C. Newby, hold an inquest in connection to the death of 59-year-old shipyard labourer, John George Hunman of 8 George Street, Hartlepool.

Mr Hunman, who had worked at the town's Marine Engine Works for more than 30 years, fell into the hold of a ship where he was carrying out repairs. The accident had happened at about 6.30 in the morning of Friday 8 December. Dr Gibb who attended Mr Hunman in the ship's hold, informed the inquest that he had sustained a ruptured right lung, along with other internal injuries, and that sadly, he died in hospital a few hours after having been admitted.

George Crowther, a colleague, who had been working with Mr Hunman at the time of the accident, gave evidence that the deceased had tripped over a prop, fell and hit a beam on the third deck on his way down, before landing in the bottom of the ship, which was very dark.

George Crowther was 46 years of age and a married man who lived at 70 Frederick Street, Hartlepool, with his wife Martha, four sons and two daughters. The eldest son also had the name George Crowther, who at the time of the 1911 Census was 16 years of age. He would certainly have been old enough to have served during the First World War, but the British Army Medal Rolls Index Cards for the First World War have at least fifty-eight men with that name.

At the West Hartlepool Court on Friday 22 December, a Swedish man by the name of Victor Gummersol, faced five very serious charges – drunkenness, three counts of assault, and one of being ashore without a permit. Gommersol was initially arrested in Church Street for drunkenness and almost immediately became violent towards Police Constable Page, who was the arresting officer. During the ensuing struggle Page was kicked in the chest and hand by Gommersol, who also assaulted Richard Johnson, a taxi driver, and Martin Philbin, a tramways Inspector, who came to the police officer's assistance. Between them, the three men managed to carry the screaming and kicking Gommersol, to Hartlepool police station.

Once placed in a cell it was established that Gommersol was a Swedish sailor who had come ashore without the necessary permit. Having heard all the evidence, the bench found Gommersol guilty of all five charges against him. He was fined a total of £6 14s 6d. This included being fined £3 for not having the required permit to come ashore from his ship, 12s for being drunk, 20 shillings for the assault of PC Page, and 10s for each of the other two assaults. There was also an interpreter's fee of 2s 6d that he had to pay.

As 1916 came to an end, the initial enthusiasm of going off to war and giving the Germans a bloody nose, with it all over by Christmas, had long since dissipated. A reality had taken over, coupled with a steely determination. The cost to date in financial and human terms, with hundreds of thousands dead and wounded, was too high to now quit and hand a victory to Germany. The hope was that 1917 would prove to be a much better year. What people wanted most of all, was for the war and the senseless killing and suffering to stop.

CHAPTER FIVE

1917 – Seeing it Through

The fourth year of the war and the death and destruction that came with it, had arrived, with still no end in sight. By the end of the year more men from Hartlepool, or with direct connections to the town, had either been killed, or died of their wounds or disease, as a direct result of the war. At least 329 families from across the district had seen mothers lose sons, wives become widows, children fatherless and friends and other family members lose someone they loved dearly.

These figures, from the Commonwealth War Graves Commission website, provide a measured perspective of month on month losses for the district of Hartlepool. Here we look at some of those men who paid the ultimate price, the young and old alike.

January saw the death of eight Hartlepool men. From the first month of the year is JOSEPH PEAT, aged 22, a sergeant (34544) in the 115th Heavy Battery, Royal Garrison Artillery, who died of his wounds on 7 January 1917. He was also a holder of the Military Medal. He is buried in the Guards Cemetery, Lesboeufs, in the Somme region of France.

His mother, Mary Jane Peat, lived at 19 Uppingham Street, West Hartlepool. This was the home of her daughter Margaret and son-in-law, George Henry Marshall, and their son, also George Marshall. Mary had one of her sons, also a George, living with her as well.

In February twenty-one men with Hartlepool connections died. WILLIAM GAMBLE, who was born in West Hartlepool, was 17 years of age when he was killed on 23 February 1917. He was a wireless operator in the Mercantile Marine and was one of the crew of SS *Grenadier* at the time of his death. William has no known grave, but his name is commemorated on the Tower Hill Memorial, in the City of London, immediately opposite the Tower of London.

The *Grenadier* was a British merchant vessel and on 23 February 1917, she was 6 miles to the east of the Shipwash Light Vessel, in the North Sea off Harwich on the Essex coast. It is unclear as to whether she was struck

SS "Grenadier"   torpedoed & sunk   23 February 1917

SS Grenadier.

by a torpedo fired from a German submarine, or struck a mine; either way, there was no warning and she quickly sank with the loss of eight of her crew, including William Gamble. Although most of the crew were from the North-East, William was the only one from West Hartlepool.

Before the war William had lived with his parents, Robert and Elizabeth Gamble, along with his brothers and sisters, at 3 Walton's Buildings, Ushaw Moor, County Durham.

March saw the death of fifteen men from the Hartlepool area. One of these was WILLIAM HARDY, a driver (461011) with the 2nd Field Company, Royal Engineers, who was only 17 years old when he died on 16 March 1917. He is buried in Hartlepool's West View Cemetery. His parents, Horace and Louisa Hardy, lived at 190 Hart Road, Hartlepool. He also had two brothers, Angus, who was the eldest of the three, and Eric, who was the youngest.

William's brother Angus, aged 22, was a sergeant (756095) in the 251st Brigade, Royal Field Artillery who had been Mentioned in Despatches. He was discharged from the Army on 16 March 1919, died on 6 June 1919 and was buried at the West View Cemetery in Hartlepool.

The month of April saw fifty-one local men die. This was by far the worst month of the year for fatalities, as far as the town of Hartlepool was concerned. FRANK JONES, was only 15 years of age, a mere boy, an ordinary seaman in the Mercantile Marine, and a crew member of the SS *Sowwell,* when he died on 19 April 1917.

The *Sowwell,* a cargo steamer, was built by W. Gray & Co Ltd of West Hartlepool and had been launched in 1900 as the *Kenley,* but in 1913 she

Kapitanleutnant von Arnauld de la Perière.

was sold to Roth Brothers (Atlantic Traders Ltd, in London, and renamed. On 19 April 1917, she was on her way from Sagunto in Spain, to Glasgow, carrying a cargo of iron ore, when she was sunk by a torpedo fired by the German submarine, *U-35*, which was under the command of Lothar von Arnauld de la Perière, 170 miles west of Gibraltar.

The ship went down almost immediately, and her entire crew of twenty-one, including ordinary seaman Frank Jones, were lost. Another member of the crew, 17-year-old, ERNEST MORELAND HARRISON, who was an assistant steward, was also a native of West Hartlepool, having been born at Seaton Snook, although his parents, Thomas and Jane Ann Harrison, lived at 51 Hind Street, Stockton-on-Tees.

The bodies of neither Frank Jones or Ernest Harrison were recovered, but their names are commemorated on the Tower Hill Memorial.

His parents, Frederick and Louisa Jones, lived at 3 Whittle's Yard, Garbut Street, Middlesbrough, and Frank was a native of Hartlepool, having been born there in 1902.

In May 1917 twenty-seven men with links to Hartlepool were either killed or died of their wounds or disease. One of these was DAVID SMITH, an 18-year-old gunner (863) with the 44th Battalion, Y3A Medium Trench Mortar Battery, of the Australian Field Artillery, who was killed in action on 21 May 1917.

The 1901 Census shows David living at 46 York Road, West Hartlepool, with his mother Maria, three brothers, John, George and Leonard, along with his two sisters, Marion and Dora. Five members of the family, Maria, Leonard, Marion, Dora and David had emigrated to Australia in 1904, arriving at Freemantle on 19 June 1904, after having left from Liverpool on the SS *Runic*, some six weeks earlier, hence why David Smith had enlisted in the Australian Army. He became a private (863) in the 57th Depot Unit, Australian Imperial Force, enlisting at Perth, Western Australia on 27 March 1916, when he was 18 years old. His occupation at the time was that of assistant farmer, and the family's home was at 79 Stuart Street, Maylands, Western Australia.

After having completed three months of basic training, he boarded His Majesty's Australian Transport ship, *Suevic*, and headed for England, leaving with his colleagues on 6 June 1916 from Freemantle and arriving in Plymouth on 21 July 1916. He remained in England, undertaking further training until 22 November 1916, when he left for France.

On 3 March 1917, David went before the commanding officer, 3rd Divisional Artillery Company, in relation to a breach of military discipline, in that his conduct was to the prejudice of good order and military discipline. He was found guilty and sentenced to 28 days Field Punishment No.2, the maximum length of time a commanding officer could award. It consisted of the convicted man being placed in fetters and handcuffs, but he was not attached to a fixed object, which allowed him to move about with his unit. As punishments went, it wasn't too traumatic an experience, although added to this was an element of hard labour and a loss of pay. Only a matter of days after having returned to his unit, he was killed in action on 21 May 1917. He is buried in the Strand Military Cemetery, Ploegsteert Wood, near Messines, in the Hainault region of Belgium.

By the end of the war, his mother, Maria, who by now had remarried and had the surname Elliot, was living at 21 Tate Street, West Leederville, Western Australia. She advised the Base Records Office in Melbourne of the change of her address on 12 January 1920.

She also wrote a rather interesting letter to the same records office, in connection with his grave, dated 30 January 1920.

> *The pamphlet describing the work of the Imperial War Graves Commission, was not enclosed as stated. Will you kindly send me one? Also, my son-in-law made and erected a nice wooden cross over my boy's grave at Ploegsteert Wood. I would like to know what will be done with it when the headstones are erected?*

A reply arrived two months later in a typed letter dated 31 March 1920. The response was somewhat guarded in its tone:

> *Dear Madam,*
>
> *Your letter of 30th January has now been referred to this office, and doubtless you have in the meantime received the booklet referred to (The Graves of the Fallen).*
>
> *With reference to the temporary cross erected over the grave of your son, the late No.863 Gunner D. Smith, Y3A Medium Trench Mortar Battery. If you desire that same be forwarded to you, kindly inform this office and your request will be passed to the officer in charge, Australian Grave Services, London, for compliance if possible. At the same time, it is pointed out that owing to the climatic conditions, in many cases it is not practicable to forward these crosses.*
>
> *Yours faithfully*
> *Major*
> *Officer in Charge, Base Records.*

The matter was clarified four months later by the same office in a letter dated 29 July 1920.

> Dear Madam,
>   With reference to my communication of 31st March, and your letter of 18th July, relative to the return of the temporary cross erected over the grave of your son, the late No.863 Gunner D Smith, Y3A Medium Trench Mortar Battery, I have to state that the work of completing the erection of the permanent headstones will necessarily occupy a number of years, by which time the temporary memorials will in almost every case, have so far fallen in to disrepair as to render it almost a matter of impossibility to arrange for their return to Australia. Moreover, the transport difficulties in the way of giving effect to the scheme are so formidable that it has been found impracticable to comply with requests of this kind, and the authorities have therefore reluctantly decided to abandon the proposal.

In June, there were thirty-four men with Hartlepool connections who died and in July, thirty-six men. One of them was 18-year-old, EDWARD MORRIGAN, who was a Stoker (S/6641) in the Royal Naval Reserve, serving on board HMS *Vanguard*, a Dreadnought class battleship, when it was sunk as the result of an internal explosion whilst at anchor in Scapa Flow in the Orkneys, at just before midnight on Monday 9 July.

Out of a crew of 845 there were initially three survivors but one, Lieutenant Commander Albert Duke, died soon afterwards. The two survivors were Stoker 1st Class K.3300 Frederick William Cox, and Private CH/17710 John Williams. Twenty-two bodies were recovered, all of whom were buried at the Royal Naval Cemetery at Lyness, a village community on the island of Hoy. A sad irony of the disaster was that earlier in the day of the explosion, the crew had been practising the routine of abandoning ship.

The *Vanguard* had been launched in 1909, and her main claim to fame had been to take part in the Battle of Jutland as one of the vessels of the Royal Navy's Grand Fleet. The rest of her wartime service was spent mainly on routine patrols and training exercises in the turbulent waters of the North Sea.

As would be expected in such circumstances, a Board of Inquiry was held into the disaster with numerous theories being suggested as to the reason for the explosions, most of which were supposition and could not be proved either way. What could be proved was that initially there had been a small explosion which gave off a white glare, followed by two much bigger explosions. The official findings of the Board of Enquiry were that a fire started in one of the ship's magazines, causing a spontaneous ignition of cordite, which spread to another magazine, which then exploded.

In 2002, the wreck of the *Vanguard* was designated as a controlled site and comes under the Protection of Military Remains Act 1986. It can only be dived upon with permission of the Ministry of Defence.

HMS Vanguard.

August saw the deaths of thirty-four men with Hartlepool connections. Two of these were 17-year-old ROBERT CORBETT and 57-year-old SAMUEL McCREEDY.

Robert was an apprentice in the Mercantile Marine and at the time of his death on 26 August 1917, he was part of the crew of the SS *Marmion*, which was built at West Hartlepool and launched in 1912. On 26 August the SS *Marmion* was en route from New York to Bordeaux in France, with a crew of seventeen, when she was attacked and sunk by the German submarine *U-93*. Robert's body was never recovered, but his name is commemorated on the Tower Hill Memorial in the City of London. There was also a HMS *Marmion* which was sunk in October 1917.

Robert was one of five children born to Robert and Mary Corbett, but their only son. Together they lived at 10 Wesley Street, West Hartlepool, with Robert's father earning a living as a plasterer. The 1911 Census shows Robert as having been only 9 years of age, which if correct, would mean that he was only 15 years old at the time of his death and not 17 as some records show.

Samuel McCreedy was 57 years of age, and a private (84683) in the 2nd (Garrison) Battalion, The King's (Liverpool Regiment), when he died of malaria and pneumonia on 13 August 1917, at the 62nd General Hospital, Salonika. He is buried in the Salonika (Lembet Road) Military Cemetery which was the main base of the British Salonika Force. During the course of the war it became a very large medical centre for the treatment of wounded British and Allied soldiers, being home to both general and stationary hospitals.

He was a married man who lived at 73 Sarah Street, West Hartlepool, with his wife Mary and their son, Robert. By the end of the First World War, Mary and Robert had moved to 18 Portland Street, which was also in West Hartlepool.

In September there were twenty-one men from Hartlepool who died as a result of the First World War. GEORGE PARKER had enlisted in the Royal Navy on 7 September 1915, just two months before his sixteenth birthday, as a Boy 2nd Class. When he died two years later on 15 September 1917, he was still only 18 years old and a Signal Boy (J/44234), part of the crew of HMS *Clio*, a Cadmus-class sloop.

His Navy Service Record shows that he died on board HMS *Clio* at 0620 hours as a result of an 'accidental gunshot wound'. A subsequent court of enquiry into his death, determined that he died as the result of a self-inflicted gunshot wound fired from a revolver. There was no comment as to whether it was believed the shooting was intentional or accidental, although it does appear that his burial at sea, which was carried out just three hours after his death, was somewhat premature, as at that stage, assuming there were no witnesses of course, the full circumstances of his death could not have been ascertained. He was committed to the deep at 0920 hours the same day, at Latitude 13' 18" north and 42' 52" east. His name is commemorated on the Chatham Naval Memorial.

According to the Commonwealth War Graves Commission, his parents, J.W. and Maggie Parker, lived at 20 Albert Street, Hartlepool. On the 1911 Census I found a John William and a Maggie Parker, who lived at 19 Graham Street, Hartlepool. Ten years earlier the family home had been at 7 Warren Street, Hartlepool. One of their children was a son with the initial 'G' who was 11 years of age. If these are the same people, they had four other sons, John William Parker junior, Albert Parker, Fred Parker and Anthony Parker, as well as a daughter, and youngest of the family, Margaret.

October saw the number of local war-related deaths more than double from what it had been in September, with the loss of forty-three men from Hartlepool.

Because of the difference in their ages – Carl Christian Christensen was 60 and Albert Hanson only 16 – I thought that it might be interesting to take a closer look at both of them.

CARL CHRISTIAN CHRISTENSEN, was a 1st Engineer in the Mercantile Marine, serving on board the SS *Manchuria* when he died on 17 October 1917 with his wife Alvilda. Both of them were born in Denmark. The 1901 Census shows him as being a married man living at 14 Alderson Street, West Hartlepool, with his wife. They are shown as having four daughters, Lily (15), Jenny (13), Marguerethe (9) and Marjorie (4).

On the 1911 Census he is part of the crew of the SS *Butland*, where he was the chief engineer. The census also shows Alvilda living at 13 Wansbeck

Gardens in West Hartlepool, with their daughter, Marguerethe, who was 19, whilst four of their other children were recorded as having died.

ALBERT HANSON was a mess room steward on board the *Manchuria* when she was sunk on 17 October. Like all his colleagues, he didn't stand a chance as no warning was given by the German submarine. They were not given the opportunity to 'take to the boats', or to be taken prisoner. Their fate was, in effect, determined as soon as the *Manchuria* was spotted by the *U-53*.

Albert Hanson lived at home with his parents, John and Mary Hanson, his three brothers and a sister, in Greatham Street, West Hartlepool. The elder brother by four years, Herman Stanley Hanson, also served during the First World War. He was a Private in the Machine Gun Corps, having enlisted at West Hartlepool on 29 November 1915, just after his nineteenth birthday. On 30 November 1915, he was initially allocated to the 21st Battalion, Durham Light Infantry, (Local Reserve Battalion), and then on 1 September 1916 he was transferred to the Training Reserve Battalion, before finally ending up as a Private (81212) in the 19th Battalion, Machine Gun Corps, on 28 November 1916. He was finally demobilized on 9 March 1919, when he was transferred to the Army Reserve.

During his military service he had just one disciplinary matter against his name. On 14 August 1918, in what appears to have been a training exercise, rather than in real time, he removed his respirator mask on two occasions before the all clear was given by the officer in command. He was found guilty and punished by having fourteen days pay deducted.

Carl and Albert were on board the British registered steamship *Manchuria* that was en route from La Goulette in Tunisia, to her home port of West Hartlepool, with a much-needed cargo of iron ore, when she was attacked and sunk by German submarine *U-53*, some 60 miles north-west of Ushant. Twenty-five of the ship's crew were lost, including Carl and Alber; eleven of them were from the Hartlepool area.

The other Hartlepool men were:

Sailor JOSEPH SHEPHERD ANDREWS, aged 42 years and a married man, who lived with his wife Elizabeth and their two sons at 10 Dock Street, West Hartlepool. Elizabeth had given birth to two other children, who had both died prior to the 1911 Census, when they were living at Back Bridge Street, Hartlepool.

Fireman and Trimmer WILLIAM BELL, aged 27, was a single man who lived with his widowed mother, Mary, at 35 Durham Street, Hartlepool.

Fireman and Trimmer JOHN GARLAND, aged 33, was a married man who lived with his wife, Florence at 2 West Street, West Hartlepool.

Boatswain and Lamps WILLIAM LIDDLE, aged 43, was a single man who was born in West Hartlepool.

Fireman and Trimmer TOM PRINCE MACK, aged 29, was a single man, whose mother Mary, lived at 27 Dene Street, West Hartlepool.

SS *Dunrobin.*

Able Seaman CHARLES OSBERT MORDAUNT, aged 35, lived at 37 Robinson Street, West Hartlepool, with his wife, Elizabeth.

Sailor and Carpenter DANIEL NICHOL, aged 37, and his wife Annie lived at 3 King Street, Hartlepool.

Second Engineer ARTHUR ERNEST RUMSEY, aged 39, lived with his wife Sarah at 1 Crimdon Street, West Hartlepool.

Second Engineer WILLIAM STODDART, aged 29, lived with his wife Lily at 43 Colenso Street, West Hartlepool.

In November, nineteen men from Hartlepool died or were killed as a result of the war. JOHN GEORGE PERKINS, who was only 16 years of age, was one of them. He was a mess room steward in the Mercantile Marine, and a member of the crew of SS *Dunrobin*, when he died on 24 November 1917.

The SS *Dunrobin*, an armed British merchant cargo ship, was en route from Almeria to Newcastle with a somewhat mixed cargo of iron ore and grapes. As she approached the area of the Lizard in Cornwall, she was struck by a torpedo fired by the German submarine, *U-53* and sunk. No warning of the attack was given, and no opportunity to abandon their ship was forthcoming. As a result, thirty-one members of the crew of the *Dunrobin*, were killed and their bodies never recovered.

John was the only member of the crew who was from the Hartlepool area. He was the son of Joseph and Susannah Perkins, who by the end of the war were living at 16 Gordon Street, West Hartlepool. At the time of the 1911

Census, the family, which also included a younger brother, James William Parker, were living at 47 Flaxton Street, West Hartlepool.

John's name is commemorated on the Tower Hill Memorial in the City of London.

December saw the same number of local casualties as November, with nineteen Hartlepool men either having died or killed. JOHN THOMAS GRANGER was one of those killed. He was 61 years of age and a First Engineer in the Mercantile Marine, serving on board the SS *Mabel Baird* at the time of his death on 22 December 1917, when it was sunk by a torpedo some 4 miles off the Lizard on the Cornish coast. It was fired by the German submarine *U-57* at just before 7am, the vessel being under the command of Otto Steinbrinck. As was becoming the norm in these attacks, no warning was given and five members of the *Mabel Baird's* crew, including John Thomas Granger, were killed.

John was born and bred in West Hartlepool, having lived in the town all his life. He was a married man who lived with his wife Margaret, and their four children, John, Albert, Ethel and Jane, at 53 Granville Avenue, West Hartlepool. Although both John and Albert were old enough to have served during the First World War, I could find no definitive record to prove that they did. There had been a fifth child who had died some years earlier.

Of the four other crew members who were killed, WILLIAM WALKER COWARD, who was the ship's second engineer, was also from Hartlepool. He lived with his wife, Pauline Charlotte Ann Coward, at 18 Arch Street, Hartlepool, although at the time of the 1911 Census, William and Pauline were living with his parents at 5 Dock Street, Hartlepool, with their one-year-old son.

For every man that was killed in the war there was, on average, at least one other person who was wounded, some of these with life changing injuries.

There were approximately 1,150,000 Silver War Badges issued to British, Empire and South African soldiers who had been honourably discharged from the armed services due to wounds, sickness, or illness; in fact all of those who were no longer physically fit for wartime military service. The reason for the issue of these badges was a simple one. It stopped men who had served and fought for their country, but

Silver War Badge.

who through no fault of their own, were no longer capable of doing so, from being thought of as cowards. The wearing of the badge let other people know that although their outward appearance might not suggest that they had an obvious disability, they had already done their bit for King and country.

By way of comparison here are some of the more day-to-day routine matters that affected Hartlepool and its residents, who were carrying on as routinely as possibly in the circumstances.

An article appeared in the *Newcastle Journal* of Tuesday, 9 January 1917. It was about some of the men who had been Mentioned in Despatches by Sir Douglas Haig for their 'distinguished and gallant service and devotion to duty'. One of these men was from Hartlepool, IVAR THOREN, a Sergeant (624A) in the Australian Pioneers with which he had served since December 1914, seeing action with them in Gallipoli, Egypt and in France, where he died of his wounds on 31 July 1916.

Before the war he had lived in Hartlepool with his parents, Captain and Mrs Thoren at 38 Milton Road, and had worked as a clerk for Otto Trenchmann Limited. Although there is no mention of him in the 1911 Census, he is mentioned in the previous one when he was a 16-year-old pupil at the North Eastern County School for boys.

Mrs Thoren had received a letter from a comrade of her son, telling her how he had died:

> *A call was made for dispatch riders, who were detailed off by your son. He said to me, 'Well, I won't ask a man to do what I won't do myself.' I told him to wait a while, but he went ...Either he must have lost his way or got knocked in to a shell hole, but at daybreak he was quite close. His gas helmet was off, and the doctor pronounced him gassed, although he was still living. The next day we had the sad news that he had passed away. He died nobly, and his section would do anything for him. His Colonel also placed great confidence in him.*

He was buried in the Albert Communal Cemetery Extension, in the Somme region of France.

On Monday, 19 February Mrs Annie Collins of Brook Street, West Hartlepool, was charged at the town's court with neglecting her step-children. It was a particularly interesting case as it was not straightforward. She had been left a widow with two children to look after on the death of her husband and had subsequently re-married. Her new husband, who was a widower with four children of his own, had been called up for military service with the Army.

In early January, Inspector Leaver of the National Society for the Prevention of Cruelty to Children visited the Collins's home. There he found Frederick Collins who was 8 years of age and Mary, who was 5. The little girl was sitting by the fire looking very ill and emaciated and according to Mrs Collins, also had abcesses. Sadly, Mary had subsequently died and Dr

English, who had carried out a post mortem examination on her body, told the court that in his professional opinion her death had come about as a result of pneumonia, following inanition, which could have been caused by want of food or debilitating disease.

Several neighbours of the Collinses gave evidence that the children were often seen walking the streets looking for scraps of food that they could pick up, and that the defendant was often seen in a drunken state.

Annie Collins was in receipt of 29 shillings per week separation allowance whilst her husband was serving in the Army, as well as receiving financial compensation in relation to the death of her first husband. Having heard and considered all the evidence, the Bench found Annie Collins guilty as charged and sentenced her to six month's imprisonment with hard labour.

The article did not mention what happened to Annie's two children or her three remaining step-children whilst she was in prison or what happened to them afterwards.

Sunday 11 March 1917, saw the tragic deaths at their home, 22 Town Wall, Hartlepool, of two young sisters, Muriel Oliver, aged 3, and Sarah Jane Oliver who was only 2. The children had been put to bed at 7pm on Saturday evening. The following morning at 7.20am Muriel was found to be dead, and just twenty minutes later Mary Jane, who had awoken, had started to fit and convulse and died soon afterwards.

The children's mother, Mrs Mary Ann Oliver, who was a widow, had six children, the eldest of whom was 17, and the youngest having been Mary Jane.

An inquest into the children's deaths took place at Hartlepool's Town Hall, chaired by Mr George Newby JP. The jury heard that Mrs Oliver earned just over 19 shillings a week as a munitions worker. She managed to bring in a further 2 shillings each week by letting one of her bedrooms and received a further 13 shillings from her eldest son, who worked. From this she had to pay out 4 shillings and 6 pence a week in rent, and 2 shillings 6 pence per week to one of her neighbours, to look after her younger children when she was at work.

Mrs Oliver explained her routine of preparing the children's food for the following day, making sure that there was always sufficient food in the house. She explained that each of the children had sufficient clothing to wear and that she purchased new items for them as and when she could afford to. Despite her protestations on this point, witnesses came forward to state that the previous week, three of the children had been seen out in the street wearing neither stockings or shoes.

Inspector Carr from the National Society for the Prevention of Cruelty to Children, gave evidence that when he visited the Olivers' home on the evening of Friday 9 March, the house was fairly clean, though sparsely furnished. The two younger children, Muriel and Mary Jane, looked particularly ill, and Mrs Oliver commented that Mary Jane had never seemed to thrive like other children did. On seeing the condition of the two children, Inspector Carr advised her to call for a doctor to come out. He added that the best he knew, Mrs Oliver was both hard working and of sober mind and body.

It had been noted that Muriel had a burn mark on her right buttock, but this was not the first time she had sustained such an injury. Over a period of time she had acquired several other burn marks whilst her mother had been out at work, but they had not been regarded as being of a serious nature. Like her sister Muriel, Mary Jane was a rather delicate child from a medical perspective.

Dr Jubb, who was the Medical Officer of Health for Hartlepool gave evidence that when Inspector Carr had visited the Oliver's home, four of the family's children were insufficiently dressed as well as being dirty and apparently suffering from neglect.

Dr de Jong, who carried out the post mortems on both of the young girls stated that he attributed Muriel's death to blood poisoning as a result of the burns she had incurred, whilst in a weak and emaciated state. The cause of death in relation to Mary Jane, was a result of convulsions, following rickets, which had been caused by improper feeding.

The jury found that the causes of death of both girls were as per the findings of Dr de Jong, and added that no blame should be attached to Mrs Oliver.

These last two examples, which were a combination of sadness and family tragedy, highlighted how difficult everyday life could be for the civilian population, and how the harbinger of death did not hunt its prey exclusively on the battlefields of France, Belgium and further afield. It showed just how appalling the conditions were in which a lot of people lived, and how susceptible to illness and disease children were. Add to this the large number of families who were struggling to make ends meet, due in most cases to no fault of their own, and it was a horrifying picture. The number of widowed mothers, victims of the war, who were spread out amidst the communities they lived in grew by the day. A married soldier, sailor or airman who became a casualty of war, made his wife a widow and left his children to grow up fatherless. The longer the war continued, the more these figures and statistics rose.

On Friday 16 March an article appeared in a local daily newspaper about a meeting of the Hartlepool Board of Guardians and the different topics that were discussed.

The Workhouse and Finance Committee reported that they had discussed at their previous meeting the subject of the workhouse's dietary needs and the possibility of reducing individual food intake for the duration of the war. The outcome of those discussions had been the decision to make reductions, over a two-week experimental period, to individual food portions, by limiting the weekly flour intake to 3lb per head, with any necessary additions being made up by use of relevant substitutes, as were included in the list provided under the Local Government Board Order. In relation to meat and sugar intake per inmate, these had already been reduced on a weekly basis to below the suggested amount which had been set by the Food Controller's scales.

The food reductions also affected those who worked at the workhouse as well as those who were its inmates. The war had caused food shortages to become so severe, they had resulted in inmates of the Hartlepool Workhouse, having to endure food rationing.

Other topics which were discussed at the meeting included the Board of Guardians allowing officers of Hartlepool's Workhouse Union to enrol under the National Service Scheme.

The town clerk of West Hartlepool submitted a report which suggested that the Local Government Board had authorized the preparation of the town planning scheme with the exception of certain pieces of land, such as that which fell within the curtilage of the workhouse. Those who were interested could inspect the plan at the town's Municipal Building. Alderman Brown suggested that all members of the board should make the effort to inspect the plan as it would no doubt be discussed over time at future meetings.

Members were informed that an allowance of £13 per year had been agreed for payment to the family of a Sergeant Foster and his family. Prior to enlisting in the Army the man had been in the employment of the Hartlepool Union which had taken it upon themselves to provide relevant support to the family of one of their own, who had gone off to serve his country. This was dependent on him continuing in his rank of sergeant and there was no subsequent increase in the rate of his military pay and allowances.

The edition of the *Police Gazette* dated Tuesday 3 April 1917 included a list of men who under the Military Service Act 1916 were classified as being absentees from the army; most had been placed in this category because when their call up papers had been sent to them in the post, they had either ignored them and not surrendered themselves for the beginning of their military training, they genuinely had not received their papers, or had moved and not informed the authorities of their new address.

The list of those men recorded as being classified as absentees from the Hartlepool district, was as follows:

Henry Dobson (24) was a joiner whose last known address was Eastbourne Terrace, West Hartlepool.

George Duncan (38) was a labourer whose last known address was 24 Durham Street, West Hartlepool.

Frederick Edward (36) was a foreman whose last known address was 66 Frederick Street, Hartlepool.

Robert Ellesmore (31) was a salvage breaker whose last known address was 47 Brook Street, West Hartlepool.

George W. Elver (39) was a fried fish deliverer whose last known address was 46 Colwyn Road, West Hartlepool.

Thomas Fallow (39) was a general labourer whose last known address was 16 Marmion Road, West Hartlepool.

George W. Foster (35) was a market trader whose last known address was 29 Silver Street, Hartlepool.

William Gilliar (38) was a serving member of the Royal Navy whose last known address was 36 High Street, Hartlepool.

Harold Goulding (32) was a shunter whose last know address was 3 Hurworth Street, Hartlepool.

The authorities were certainly trying everything within their power to ensure that they had as many men as possible to carry on fighting the war. This was simply the most direct way of embarrassing men who, for what ever reason, had not answered the call to arms when they had been asked to by the authorities. It was believed that because it was such a sensitive issue, friends, relatives, or other members of the community would give these people up if they knew where they were living.

Monday 9 April saw two rather interesting football matches take place at the Victoria Ground, West Hartlepool, in front of an estimated crowd of some 5,000 excited and expectant spectators. A hard-fought match between a team made up of male munition workers and a local military eleven, surprisingly resulted in a goalless draw, despite the best efforts of all concerned. The other match was between female munition workers, with one team being from the Expanded Metal Company, who beat their female counterparts, from the Central Marine Company, by a score of one goal to nil. An enjoyable afternoon's entertainment was had by both the players and those who came to watch.

It was good to see that despite the war, and the extreme demands and pressure which this placed on all concerned, the effort to organize some leisure time for those workers whose daily efforts were high on the list of those doing their bit for the war effort on the home front, was commendable.

On Friday 13 April a meeting, organized by the local Advisory Board, took place in West Hartlepool, for trade union representatives. It was addressed by Mr Lynden Macasey, the Director of Shipyard Labour at the Admiralty, and covered the topic of the Admiralty's Shipyard Labour Scheme, as well as the better use of existing labour in all its different forms. This included the interchangeability of work, the question of demarcation, the better use of mechanical tools and appliances, the introduction of a system of payment by results, and the transfer of workmen to other required work.

It must have been a difficult speech for some of these staunch union men to have to listen to, as in essence his talk was about getting more from less, better productivity by increasing the skill set of individuals so that they could cover different roles. With so many men being called up for military service, manpower was at a premium, so getting the best out of those who were still available was imperative. The real problem that needed addressing was the old and entrenched habits, where the working man was concerned, which were hard to change. Some of those present would have viewed what was being said with deep suspicion, whilst for others it would have simply gone against their basic core principles to accept what was being suggested.

It was not all one sided, with some of those present prepared to allow common sense to win the day, rather than stick to their inflexible and somewhat outdated principles, some were more than sympathetic to what was being proposed, appreciating how the war had changed matters. Many had brothers, uncles, fathers, nephews and sons who were serving in the forces, so they would have wanted to make sure that their relatives had all of the correct equipment and manpower, as and when they needed it. The shipyard workers of Hartlepool were proud and patriotic men, it was a record that they were rightly proud of and one which they badly wanted to maintain.

A meeting took place on Tuesday 1 May which included the Port and Harbour Commissioners, discussing an alternative system to that of row boats at Hartlepool Ferry. Competing ideas were explained by the town's engineer. One of these related to purchasing a series of motor boats at an estimated start-up cost of £5,000 for the boats, with a further annual outlay of £2,000 in maintenance costs. The main objection to this proposal was the short distance these boats would have to travel, 200 feet at most, which meant that before the engines were fully warmed up, the ferry would have already left.

Other options which had also been considered were a swing bridge or transporter bridge, but these would have cost too much. Equally opposed was the idea of a travelling tramway which would be activated by underwater chains. The main objection to this idea was that the chains could too easily become caught up in a ship's anchor, the outcome of which didn't bear thinking about.

The idea which received most support was that of a subway, the crown of which would have to be at least 30 feet below the surface of the water, so that the port would not be handicapped for future development. There was however a major problem with this idea, and that was the cost. The commissioners could not afford to carry out the project on their own, and without the financial support of other interested parties, it was going to be difficult to raise sufficient funds to get the project off the ground. After the matter had been fully discussed by the committee, no decision was made and it was left in abeyance to be considered at a future meeting.

In May an extremely strange matter found itself being heard before the West Hartlepool County Court, His Honour Judge Bonsey presiding. The date of the hearing was Friday 11 May and involved a Robert Scougal and a case of compensation. He had originally been employed by Messrs Gray & Co, ship builders from Hartlepool, and whilst working for them he met with an accident for which the firm paid compensation. After recovering from his injuries he returned to working for the company for a short period of time, before allegedly being dismissed. A compensation agreement between Mr Scougal and the company was settled upon and he received 11 shillings and 2 pence per week. After this was put in place, Scougal found further employment working for Messrs Cameron & Co, Brewers, where he met with another accident and once again received compensation.

The issue of the case was whether the compensation Scougal had received from Messrs Cameron should be deducted from, or taken into account, the compensation payable by Messrs Gray & Co., who were the appellants in the case. They were understandably asking the question as to why they should be paying compensation to a man who had left their employ because of an injury which prevented him from being able to carry on working for them, yet was then able to acquire another job elsewhere that was just as physically demanding.

Judge Bonsey cited stated cases to show that a man could in fact receive compensation from two different employers in respect of two different and separate injuries. Commenting on the written agreement made between Scougal and Messrs Gray & Co, he stated that the true meaning of that agreement did not indicate that he, Scougal, was not entitled to receive more than £1 per week. Accordingly Judge Bonsey found in favour of Scougal, adding that it would still be open for Messrs Gray & Co to bring evidence before the court to prove that since the agreement to pay 11s 2d per week to Scougal, the man's incapacity resulting from the injury had diminished.

It was an interesting point to note that a man injured whilst undertaking work of a civilian nature, is paid out in financial compensation almost immediately by the firm he was working for at the time of the accident, whilst a wounded soldier, or the family of one who had been killed in action or died of his wounds, would have to wait a while longer for the financial remuneration.

The 1911 Census showed Robert Scougal, 53 years of age and a driller in a shipyard, living at 5 Bertha Street, West Hartlepool, with his wife Emma, and their five children, Florence, Arthur, Ethel, Nora, Norman and Robert. Arthur Scougal served during the war as a Private (DM2/169053) in the Army Service Corps. Unfortunately, neither his Army Service Record, nor his Army Pension Record, have survived so no further details are available.

Friday 15 June saw King George V and Queen Mary paying a visit to the North-East of England, the afternoon of which was spent in the Hartlepools. People turned out in their thousands to line the routes and welcome the royal couple to West Hartlepool. From the railway station and all the way down the High Street, they commandeered every vantage point, including the taking up of some extremely precarious-looking positions on the corners of tradesmen's shops. Every window was filled with an array of faces, eager to catch even just a fleeting glance at their king and queen. Having visitors of such high esteem was a rarity for the town, and accordingly the welcome they delivered was both spontaneous and warm hearted, as would be expected on such an important day, made even better by the warm and sunny weather.

Inside the busy yards of ship builders, William Gray and Co., it was even more manic. The premises consisted of two shipyards, the dock yard and the central yard. At the former there were four berths, and at the latter, a further five, which were capable of accommodating some large vessels. There were two dry docks and an extensive quay space, which allowed the company to provide a large repair service to its business. It was without doubt an extremely modern and up to date facility for its day, fitted out with some of the most expensive plant and machinery that money could buy.

By the time of the royal visit, William Gray & Co. had already built and launched an astonishing eighty-seven vessels. Their majesties were received by the chairman and owner of the company, Sir William Gray, who took great pride at showing them around. Part of their tour included seeing the building of a number of vessels, including a patrol boat, three cargo vessels and two oil carrying ships. As the royal guests were shown around they were introduced to some of the workers, including some of the ship yard foremen and departmental chiefs. One of them, Robert Brockett, was a retired Navy man, who had served in the Baltic as well as the Crimea War. Another was James Douglas, who had seven sons and a son-in-law serving in the Army.

The 1911 Census shows a Robert Brockett, who was a naval pensioner, living at 33 Reed Street, West Hartlepool. He was born in 1833, which meant that at the start of the Crimea War he would have been 20 years of age, but that would also have meant that if he was the same Robert Brockett who was introduced to the king in 1917, he would by then have been 84 years of age.

I found a John Douglas, who according to the 1901 Census was a married man, who lived at 9 Mildred Street, West Hartlepool, and was a ship yard worker. By the beginning of the First World War, all nine of his sons would have been old enough to have served in the military. He also had a daughter Dora.

By the time the king and queen had finished and had shaken so many welcoming hands, the queen's white gloves had become somewhat grimy from the oil and dirt covering the workers' hands. After leaving W. Gray & Co., the royal party went on to visit Irvine's Middleton ship building yard, as well as the Marine Engine Works of Messrs. Richardsons, Westgarth and Co.

A visit to a nearby Hartlepool National Shell Factory, which was part of the Central Marine Engine Works at West Hartlepool, turned out to be interesting for two reasons, firstly because the king and queen took a particular interest in a mechanism for lifting 8-inch howitzer shells, and secondly, the king recognized a chief petty officer who had served with him on both HMS *Inflexible* and HMS *Powerful*, but who now only had one arm. The officer explained that he had lost his arm three years earlier in an accident, when he had been hit by the back firing of a gun.

The factory, which had been equipped by the Ministry of Munitions, had begun operations in July 1916, to help support the nationwide need to produce more artillery shells for the war effort, before returning to making boilers for the Admiralty in December 1917. During its sixteen months of existence, its staff of 85 men and 365 women, turned out more than 81,000 8-inch shells, or just over 5,000 a month.

After an extremely busy and full day, where they visited many of the local businesses, which directly supported the war effort, the royal train finally left West Hartlepool railway station at five o'clock to make its way back to London.

Lieutenant Colonel Clive Wingham, who was serving assistant private secretary and equerry, wrote a letter of thanks on behalf of King George V to the then Managing Director of the Central Marine Engine Works, Mr Maurice Gibb.

> *Dear Mr Gibb,*
>
> *It was a great pleasure to the King and Queen to have an opportunity of visiting the Central Marine Engine Works, and I am commanded to thank you and those under you for the satisfactory arrangements for to-day's programme.*
>
> *His Majesty was impressed with the efficient manner in which all the shops were organized.*
>
> *The King and Queen much appreciated the warm welcome accorded them by the workers, in whose welfare and well being Their Majesties always take the greatest interest.*
>
> *Yours very truly,*
> *Clive Wigram.*

Friday 29 June saw the death by suicide of the well-known local businessman, Mr Charles Otto Trenchmann, who was the Chairman of Messrs Otto Trenchmann & Co., cement manufacturers, of Hartlepool. Mr Trenchmann was found shot dead at his home, Hudwork Towers, at Castle Eden. He had been unwell for some time and had undergone an operation of a serious nature at Leeds only a matter of weeks before his death.

An inquest into his death took place the same afternoon. Evidence was given that he had been found at around noon in the bedroom of his home, with a bullet wound to his forehead, and a small calibre rifle that he used to shoot rooks in his garden, lying by his side.

Dr Warner Cook, referring to the illness from which Mr Trenchmann had been suffering, said that he did not have that much longer to live. A verdict of 'suicide whilst temporarily insane' was returned by the jury. He was 66 years of age and had previously been a Justice of the Peace for both the county of Durham and the district of Hartlepool.

The afternoon of Sunday 8 July saw a meeting take place in West Hartlepool, where one of the intended speakers was the town's MP, Mr Tom Wing but, sadly for him, he did not receive the reception that he was hoping for. He stood up on the stage to give his address at the open-air meeting, on the subject of 'Bread or Beer: Which?', but amongst the large crowd that had gathered, there was a strong element of opposition, many of whom were local steel workers, who by the very nature of their work, were hardy men. As Mr Wing began to speak, he was heckled, the noise being so loud that what he had to say was inaudible, the verbal uproar against him being continuous.

What hadn't helped his cause was that, just prior to him being given the stage, a resolution had been put forward, which he agreed with and supported, urging the government to adopt a state of prohibition on sales of alcohol for the remainder of the war. This did not go down well with the steel workers who had turned out in large numbers and were a majority amongst the gathered crowd. Although they appreciated their country was at war and everybody needed to be fed, they worked long arduous hours, week in and week out, and a drink was not only something which they felt was well earned, but something that did no real harm. There was a belief by some that the government were using the 'Beer or Bread' campaign to surreptitiously get the drinking of alcohol banned, not because it would affect the production of much needed bread, but because the government felt that if men were drunk they either wouldn't turn up for work or if they did, their effectiveness and productivity would be greatly reduced.

The meeting ended in uproar as a number of men climbed on to the trolley-style stage and pushed it 20 to 30 yards with Mr Wing, Canon MacDonald, vicar of Christchurch, and others, still on it. Fortunately, nobody was injured.

Saturday 18 August 1917 saw the inquest take place into the death of two soldiers from the Yorkshire Regiment, Lance Corporal James Hetherington (32) from Bridlington and Private F.W. Reed, from Darlington, during a regimental bathing parade. I could find no entry on the Commonwealth War Graves Commission website in relation to either James Hetherington or F.W. Reed, which battalion they served with, their home addresses or where they were buried.

A number of soldiers were in the water at the time of the tragedy, when an un-named man got into difficulties due to a dangerously strong undercurrent. The man survived whilst Hetherington and Reed, who went to the rescue, sadly died. Lieutenant Barker, who was another of those who took part in the attempted rescue, also got into difficulties, but was recovered, albeit in an unconscious condition, after managing to keep himself afloat with the aid of a lifebuoy.

The coroner paid tribute to the heroism and self-sacrificing determination of all those who took part in the rescue of their stricken colleague and added that he was glad to hear that Major Ryan had taken steps for the recognition of their acts of bravery.

The jury returned a verdict of accidental drowning and recommended that warning notices of the dangerous underwater currents should be placed close to the spot where the two soldiers died.

Wednesday 22 August 1917 saw the report in some local northern-based newspapers, concerning the death at 81 years of age, at West Hartlepool of Mr William Metcalfe Meredith, an engineer by profession. Along with the late Sir William Gray, he had been instrumental in the founding of the North of England Waggon Company Ltd.

Although born in Hollinwood, Lancashire, on 2 December 1836, he later moved to West Hartlepool and in the 1860s started up in business with a partner under the name of Messrs. Dunlop and Meredith. The company was involved in the manufacture of iron works, such as gates and fences, and undertook the construction of the ironworks for the Crystal Palace and St Pancras Station in London.

He first became involved with local politics in 1869, when he was voted in as one of the West Hartlepool Town Commissioners. It was twenty-five years later in 1894, when he was returned to represent the South-West Ward of the West Hartlepool Town Council, that he really came to prominence. On winning the election he made a statement in relation to a contract that had been awarded for the corporation's concrete flags. Not happy with what Mr Meredith had said, and more importantly, what he had intimated in his comments, the then Mayor of West Hartlepool, Alderman John Suggitt, and the Borough Surveyor, Mr J.W. Brown, took out a libel action against him which was heard at the Durham Assizes in February 1895. The two men won their case, with Mr Brown being awarded £50 and the mayor being awarded £10 in damages, along with their legal costs. The consequence of the libel case against him was that Mr Meredith filed for bankruptcy, but then attended the next council meeting, which due to his petition for bankruptcy he was not allowed to do. He did not leave the meeting when requested to do so until a police officer was called and he was threatened with ejection.

It was just before this that his private life also took a bit of a battering in the form of a divorce, which in the reputational-driven society of the late 1800s, was not a step that was taken lightly. The case was heard at the Royal Courts of Justice in the Strand where on 17 December 1892, the Honourable Sir John Gorell Barnes pronounced that the marriage of William Metcalfe Meredith and Sarah Ann Meredith (née Dixon), which had been solemnized on 28 March 1888 at Hartlepool Parish Church, should be dissolved by reason of the fact that the respondent in the case, Sarah Ann Meredith, had been guilty of adultery. It was also decreed that two children, Sarah Elizabeth Meredith and George Meredith, should remain living with their father until further order of the court. It would appear that the divorce was not contested by William's wife. An interested aside to this case was that the record of divorce was closed to the public until 1993.

William had previously married on 30 December 1858. Mr Meredith was certainly a very interesting man as well as a determined individual, because rather than slip quietly away in to his twilight years of retirement, he once again decided to become a councillor, and in November 1902, when he was 66, he was duly elected as a member of West Hartlepool council. As had been the case on more than one occasion for Mr Meredith, nothing appeared to run exactly smoothly. A petition was raised to declare the election victory which had returned Mr Meredith to the council, void, on the grounds that he was an undischarged bankrupt. The petition was successful, but despite this he was again nominated in the re-run of the election, and was again returned victorious, taking his place in time for the next council meeting in May 1903. He remained as a councillor until 1911.

According to the 1911 Census, Mr Meredith, by now a widower, was living at 26 Burn Road, West Hartlepool, and had Mr James William Cann, and his wife, Christina Cann, living with him as lodgers.

Sunday 2 September saw one of West Hartlepool's own presented with the Distinguished Conduct Medal (DCM), by Lieutenant Colonel Robson CMG DSO. The man in question was Gunner (Acting Bombardier) 58530 John B. Fraser, who had enlisted in the Royal Field Artillery in 1909. He served with the 37th Battery, 8 Brigade, having first arrived in France on 19 August 1914, from the Battle of Mons in August 1914, up to and including the Battle of Vimy Ridge in April 1917.

He was mentioned in despatches by Sir John French for saving artillery pieces at Le Cateau, within 100 yards of hostile German infantry units and was awarded the French *Croix de Guerre*. The award of the DCM was as a result of working a gun on his battery, whilst under heavy and persistent shell fire at Ypres on 23 April 1915, when he was wounded. It was also for carrying wounded comrades away from danger and carrying much needed ammunition so that his battery could keep up their fight, both of these actions took place whilst under heavy enemy fire.

The citation for the award of his Distinguished Conduct Medal appeared in the *London Gazette* on 11 March 1916, and was worded as follows:

> *For conspicuous bravery and coolness on all occasions. Gunner Fraser was limber gunner of a detachment which went back to get away the last gun. Of the team of drivers, one was killed. Gunner Fraser limbered up the gun and rode on the limber. During subsequent operations he was wounded, but declined to have his wounds treated until ordered by an officer to do so.*

Some time after the award of his DCM, he transferred to the Royal Garrison Artillery, with the new service number of 225390.

A really interesting story appeared in the pages of the *Yorkshire Evening Post* dated Friday 28 September. It was in relation to women consuming alcohol in public houses. The decision was taken in Hartlepool to exclude women from drinking in public houses. This action attracted a great deal of attention across the country, although it is unclear if any other town ever followed suit. The decision had come about, not by the introduction of any restrictive power brought in by the Control Board or the Government, but by the mutual agreement of the town's licensed victuallers.

The move was a result of the Chief Constable, Mr A. Winterbottom, asking licensed victuallers to seriously consider the possibility of doing something to prevent women from congregating on their premises. Mr Winterbottom was greatly concerned as it was a practice that appeared to have drastically increased, especially amongst the wives of soldiers who were overseas serving their country. So the licensed victuallers held a meeting and decided unanimously that from a given date they would collectively prohibit women from drinking on their premises for the duration of the war. The decision appeared to have caused no major problems, and women were still able to purchase alcohol, in reasonable amounts, for consumption off licensed premises.

The majority of the community appeared to be in agreement with the decision. This was, after all, an age of high morality, when women did not generally enter pubs and consume alcoholic beverages, those who did were often referred to as being 'women of the night'.

On the evening of Thursday 4 October an accident took place in Hartlepool between two large tramcars that were travelling in opposite directions. Each of the cars was carrying a large number of passengers. It happened about 7pm in the evening, by which time it was already dark, on the West Hartlepool to Hartlepool line. Even though it was a heavy collision, and both cars were badly damaged, thankfully nobody was killed, although several people were injured.

The accident happened opposite the Queens Ice Rink, a very dark section of the line, where there is a loop in the track. It is believed that the driver of one of the cars thought that the other car was static in the loop and waiting for his car to pass, but what actually happened was the oncoming car had passed the junction with the loop. This misjudgement resulted in both the cars colliding with the other's driver platform.

The driver of one of the cars was seriously injured, sustaining injuries to his right leg, left ankle and the right side of his forehead. The man's name was Charles Collins, who lived at 15 Thomas Street. He had served in the Army earlier in the war, been wounded and then discharged on the grounds that he was no longer physically fit for wartime military service. Having such men as tram car drivers on their return to civvy street was normal practice during the war.

The driver of the other car, Fred Porrett, of 18 Cambridge Street, on realizing that the two cars were going to collide and that there was nothing that he could do to prevent it, jumped clear at the last moment, and sustained only minor injuries.

Dr Biggart attended the scene of the crash and treated several of the passengers, who were not seriously injured, all of whom were later conveyed to their homes in a VAD ambulance.

Saturday 13 October saw the inquest take place at West Hartlepool of Sergeant John V. Ashworth, of the Yorkshire Regiment whose home was in Chorley Road, Swinton, Manchester. He was an instructor in musketry, or as would be termed today, a firearms instructor. His sad death was somewhat unusual; he was lying down with a disc to his right eye, whilst instructing Private Gardener. In such training, actual rounds which had their cordite charge removed were used, this meant that they were inert and could not actually discharge, but could then be ejected from the standard British Army weapon, the Lee Enfield .303 rifle, and the next round loaded into the chamber. It was all part of the basic training of a soldier in the handling of his weapon.

Sergeant Ashworth instructed Private Gardiner to take aim at the disc that he had placed over his right eye, and fire. Private Gardiner did as he was told; he pulled the trigger, 'click', and then used the rifle's bolt action mechanism to eject the dud round, before reloading and taking aim for a second time. When he was happy with his point of aim he pulled the trigger for a second time, but there was no dull sound of a click this time. The round was a live one, and as the rifle's firing pin hit the percussion cap on the end of the .303 round, there was a flash, followed by a loud bang, and the round struck Sergeant Ashworth just under his right eye, travelled through his head, came out through his neck and entered the muscles at the top of his shoulder blade.

How there came to be a live round in amongst the inert ones in the magazine is unclear, and a subsequent examination of the remaining rounds in the magazine showed that they were all minus the cordite charge, as they should have been.

The coroner, in summing up, remarked that the evidence showed almost conclusively that the deceased had used misfire ammunition for the rapid fire drill, as was standard procedure, and would have had no reason to suspect that the rounds he was getting the men under his charge to use, were anything other than harmless training rounds. How the live round came to be in the magazines with the training rounds, was unclear. There was no evidence to suggest foul play, and no blame could or was attached to Private Gardiner.

Accordingly, the jury returned a verdict of 'death by misadventure'. They also expressed their deepest sympathy for the widow of Sergeant Ashworth, who was present at the inquest. Lieutenant Colonel Purnell passed on his own personal commiserations, along with those of the regiment to Mrs Ashworth, on her sad bereavement.

On Tuesday 6 November an article appeared in the *Newcastle Journal* newspaper, concerning the new mayor of West Hartlepool, Councillor William Edgar.

William Edgar was born in the town in 1870. He left school at 14 years of age, as was the norm in those days, and began working for Messrs. George Horsley & Co., who were shipbrokers and coal exporters. He stayed with them for eight years before moving on to work for Messrs. C H Ford & Co. A further eight years down the line and it was now 1901. By now William was a successful 31-year-old businessman as well as being happily married to Annie, and living at 169 Stockton Road, West Hartlepool, with their son Douglas. Ten years later, the family, which had increased with the birth of two more sons, William and Malcolm, had moved across town to Linden Grove.

It was at this time, having learnt his trade, made his contacts and having proved his worth, he took the difficult and decision to start up his own business as a shipbroker and coal exporter, before finally amalgamating with Messrs. E A Casper in 1912.

His time as a councillor began in 1910 when he was elected to represent the Park Ward of the town. He played an active and supportive role in corporation life, becoming the vice-chairman of the Finance Committee. He also sat on the Health Committee, the Electricity Committee, the Library Committee, and the General Purposes Committee. He was a member of the Hartlepools Port Sanitation Authority, and later went on to become the chairman of that particular group. He was a representative of the North Eastern Railway Co, on the Hartlepool Pilotage Board, and one of the Hartlepool Port and Harbour Commissioners.

He was a Presbyterian, who had for many years been a member of the congregation of the Park Road Church in West Hartlepool, and last but not least, he was also a Freemason of the Stranton Lodge, which had been formed in 1862. Thankfully for William and Annie, all three of their sons were too young to have served through the horrors of the First World War.

Four days later on Saturday 10 November 1917 a similar article appeared in another northern-based local newspaper, reporting on the election of the mayor of Hartlepool.

This honour had been bestowed upon Councillor Charles Thomas Watson, a Scotsman by birth, born in Mussleburgh, but somebody who had spent most of his life as a resident of Hartlepool, at Roslyn House, Henry Smiths Terrace, where he lived with his wife Mary, and their four daughters, Mary, Jane, Amy and Muriel.

He had, for many years, been a builder and contractor and had been involved in local politics as a Conservative, since first being elected on to the Hartlepool Town Council in 1905. He died on 17 April 1941 at 91 years of age. His wife Mary, was a native of the town, being from an old Hartlepool family, the Richardsons.

By December 1917 food rationing throughout the realm had become a real problem, a situation which resulted in representatives of trade unions, co-operatives, and other organisations, attending a conference at Hartlepool. The feeling of unrest and mistrust amongst the majority of workers had reached fever pitch and the threat of a national strike had become very real. The result of the meeting was the adoption of a resolution expressing the opinion that the only thing that would alleviate the food crisis which existed at the time would be direct government control of all foods, which would allow for its fair and equal distribution.

The adopted resolution also stated that if the government failed to adopt this policy by a deadline of 31 January 1918, that all workers, not just from Hartlepool, but from across the country, who were union members, would be called out on strike by their respective unions on 4 February 1918.

It was reported on Monday 10 December that Mrs Lawson, of 69 Percy Street, West Hartlepool, had received news from the War Office that her husband, Second Lieutenant W.E. Lawson, was in hospital in France, having been seriously wounded in action. Before enlisting he was employed by the Great Central Railway Company, Victoria Terrace, West Hartlepool.

According to the Commonwealth War Graves Commission website, there were 89 men with the name and initial Lawson, W, who were killed or died during the First World War, but none of them were a match for W.E. Lawson, so I assume that despite the injuries he received whilst serving in France, he survived. His parents lived at 49 Milton Street, West Hartlepool.

Sunday 16 December was the third anniversary of the bombardment of the Hartlepools and Scarborough and, as in the previous two years, the occasion was marked by fund raising events in an effort to raise money for the two local hospitals, the Cameron General which had first opened in 1905, and St Hilda's which opened in 1865.

Flags, medallions and brooches were all sold in an effort to make money for the two hospitals. Musical concerts of varying types were also a popular way of adding to the monies raised. Whilst the efforts of 1916 had helped raise just over £2,359, 1917, whilst still a good effort, fell just short of the previous year's amount at £2,048, but still enough to make sure 1917 finished on a high note for the people of the Hartlepools.

CHAPTER SIX

1918 – The Final Push

There were at least twenty-six battles which took place during the final eleven months of the war, which cost the lives of men from the Hartlepools. Here are just a few of them:

- 21 March was the start of the German Spring Offensive known as the *Kaiserschlacht* or Kaiser's Battle, as the German Army stormed the Allied lines in an attempt to finish the war before the arrival of American troops.
- 9 April – the start of the Battle of the Lys
- 23 April – the raid on Zeebrugge
- 27 May – the start of the Third Battle of the Aisne
- 1 June – the start of the Battle of Belleau Wood
- 4 July – the start of the Battle of Hamel
- 15 July – the start of the Second Battle of the Marne
- 18 July – the start of the Battle of Soissons
- 8 August – the start of the Battle of Amiens
- 31 August – the start of the Battle of Mont Saint-Quentin
- 12 September – the start of the Battle of Havrincourt
- 27 September – the start of the Battle of the Canal du Nord
- 8 October – the start of the Battle of Cambrai

As the new year began, and with the war in what would turn out to be its final year, everyday life was still going on throughout all communities across the country, and Hartlepool was no different. Couples married, babies were born, children went to school, people went out to work, crimes were committed, people passed away, and some, despite the potential social stigma attached to it, were divorced. Here's one such case.

On Wednesday, 16 January 1918 Mr Justice Coleridge sitting in the Divorce Court at Hartlepool, heard the undefended petition of Mrs Jane Constance Ropner, of Ingledene, Hutton Avenue, West Hartlepool, who was asking for a divorce on the grounds of cruelty and misconduct of her husband, Mr Walter Ropner, who did not defend the case.

The couple, whose families were both well known in the world of shipping, were married in April 1894 at the Congregational Church, in Hartlepool. According to Mrs Ropner the problems in the marriage started very early on, and she did her best to conceal the true state of their relationship from their friends and family, which subsequently made it difficult for some of her allegations against her husband to be corroborated, as the claims she was making in her application for a divorce were not necessarily ones that those close to her immediately recognized.

She alleged that from time to time her husband 'gave way to drink'. In 1914 after the outbreak of the First World War, Mr Ropner enlisted in the Army and joined the Sportsman's Battalion of the Royal Fusiliers, and it was soon after this that Mrs Ropner began to hear rumours of his association with another woman. She told the court that despite their problems, she lived with her husband quite happily for the first seven years, but it was when he drank that he changed and ill-treated her. She related the somewhat strange occasion when Mr Ropner went yachting, leaving a gentleman friend staying in the house. He returned home un-announced, evidently hoping that he would catch his wife and the male guest in a 'delicate situation'. Even though that was not the case, he still accused her of misconduct with the male guest. When the latter left, Mr Ropner apologized to his wife.

Mrs Ropner alleged that on one occasion her husband had even threatened to shoot her because she had dared write to his father, telling him of his son's conduct towards her.

After hearing further evidence from Dr Angus Macgregor and Margaret Fox, who was the Ropners' family cook, and Mr William Ropner, her husband's brother, Mr Justice Coleridge awarded a decree nisi with costs and custody of the youngest child to Mrs Ropner.

Mr Walter Ropner did in fact enlist in the Army during the war, at London on 6 October 1914, when he was 43 years of age, and became private 19805 in the 23rd (Sportsman's) Battalion, Royal Fusiliers. On 6 August 1915 he was posted to the 30th Battalion and on 16 March 1916, he was further posted to the 6th Battalion with whom he was promoted to the rank of lance corporal on 11 April 1916. On 5 September 1916 he was transferred to the 1st (Home Service Garrison) Battalion, East Kent Regiment, The Buffs, at the same rank. On 29 November 1916 he was appointed as an acting corporal, but just five days later he had the acting rank removed for being drunk on duty.

On 26 April 1917, Walter was discharged from the Army for no longer being physically fit for wartime military service, by which time he was 45 years of age. All of his war service was spent in the United Kingdom.

Correspondence on his Army Pension Record, shows that a Mrs Rose Eastman from Lanesborough in Guildford wrote a letter to the War Office dated 20 July 1921.

Dear Sir,

I should be very grateful if you could give me information as to the present whereabouts of a very old friend, a Mr Walter Ropner, Lance Corporal in the Sportsman's Battalion, Royal Fusiliers, when he was stationed at Hornchurch, Romford and Dover, in the late winter of years 1914, 15, and 16. I think I lost sight of him very abruptly in the winter of 1916, or the following summer. I can't remember which.

Yours sincerely

(Mrs) Rose Eastman.

The letter was passed on the Infantry Records Office at Hounslow, who in turn wrote to Walter Ropner, who by then was living at 27 Brackley Road, Chiswick, London, requesting that he contact Mrs Eastman direct. It is not known if he ever did. Is Mrs Eastman the same woman that Mrs Ropner referred to in her divorce petition, the same one that it had been rumoured Walter Ropner had been 'associating with'.

On Friday 15 February 1918 an unusual case was heard at the West Hartlepool court of the harbouring of escaped German prisoners by local residents. Mary Elizabeth Collins, Elizabeth Ann Mallon, and Mary Jane Fenby, were all charged with having failed to notify the authorities of the presence of aliens in their properties.

The evidence given by the police was that two German civilian prisoners of war, who had escaped from a camp somewhere in Wales, had ended up in Hartlepool and had at different times stayed at the homes of all three women, and were only ever seen to leave the houses after the hours of darkness. The two Germans were recaptured in Hartlepool and had been retuned under escort to their camp in Wales. All three women were found guilty. Collins, a married woman whose husband was a serving soldier, was sentenced to two month's imprisonment, Mallon was sentenced to one month, and Fenby also received a sentence of two months.

The 1911 Census showed Mrs Mary Jane Fenby, living at 28 Robinson Street, West Hartlepool, but her husband wasn't shown as living at the address, only a male lodger Alexander Gillis, who was eleven years younger that Mrs Fenby.

Alexander Gillis had enlisted in the Army on 14 December 1896 at Richmond in Yorkshire and became a private (5317) in the 2nd Battalion, Prince of Wales's Own (Yorkshire Regiment). During his twelve years of Army service, he found himself the subject of three courts of enquiry, due to minor injuries he had sustained. The first time was in relation to an incident when he was part of a working party who were engaged in moving artillery shells; he dropped one of them on his foot which resulted in him being treated in hospital at the South Barracks, Gibraltar. The subsequent court of enquiry took place on 11 May 1898. The findings were that it was nothing more than an accident, when a colleague passed a shell to him and let go of it before he had full control of it.

Whilst stationed in Sitapur in the Uttar Pradesh state of India, he was subject to not one but two courts of enquiry, due to injuries he had sustained. On both occasions he was admitted to the Station Hospital at Sitapur. On the first occasion, he sprained his right ankle when he slipped on some stairs on 28 December 1901. The subsequent Court of Enquiry which took place on 8 February 1902, found it was no more than an accident and that it would have no long term affect on his ability to remain a soldier in the British Army.

On the second occasion, he sprained his right knee whilst out in the town. He was admitted to the Station Hospital at Sitapur on 14 March 1902, and a court of enquiry was assembled at the hospital on 21 April 1902. The subsequent findings of the enquiry determined that Gillis had been off duty at the time that his injury occurred and that it was not likely to interfere with his future ability to perform his duties as a soldier.

The third and final Zeppelin attack on Hartlepool during the course of the First World War took place on the evening of 13 March 1918, some sixteen months after the previous attack. The German invader dropped its bombs from high up in the skies, which provided it with perfect cover, at a height which ensured that it could not be seen from the ground, and the longer it could not be seen, then the safer it would be. The problem with this scenario of course was that not being able to see their potential targets, the German aviators had absolutely no idea on which areas of the town they were dropping their bombs.

In the first batch that were dropped, one hit the Normandy Hotel, blowing a massive hole in its roof. Further bombs landed on the beach at Middleton and in the area of the old town. Some damage was caused to property owned by the North Eastern Railway Company, along with numerous other buildings across the town, including soldiers' billets. By the time the Zeppelin had made good its escape, it had left behind it a trail of damage and destruction across the town, with eight people having been killed and a further twenty-two injured, mainly by flying glass.

Although having a commercial purpose in civilian life, it has always been a topic of debate about the true value of the airship's deployment in a military sense during the First World War. Other than possibly affecting morale when they carried out their un-announced raids on civilian populations across Kent, London, and along the east coast from Essex all the way up to, and including, Hartlepool, they served very little actual military purpose. When taking into account the cost of building the airships, fuelling them and training young men who were brave enough to become part of their crews, they were not that effective. They very rarely, if at all, targeted military locations or personnel, which would have at least afforded them some kind of credence.

They were also extremely vulnerable once spotted. Their main form of defence was the height at which they could fly, to keep themselves safe from any British aircraft that were looking to attack them. The down side of this was that because of the upper levels at which they had to fly to ensure their safety, they were often blown off course because of the strong winds, and any accuracy they were hoping to achieve in dropping their bombs was greatly affected. In the early years of the war they kept their attacks to the hours of darkness for their own protection, but this tactic, understandable as it was, simply hampered their attempts to effectively navigate their way to their intended targets.

According to the Commonwealth War Graves Commission there were at least 300 men who had connections to either Hartlepool or West Hartlepool, who lost their lives between 1 January and 11 November 1918.

Perhaps the youngest was a 15-year-old boy, GEORGE SHEPHERD, who lived with his parents, William and Mary Elizabeth Shepherd, at 13 Brown Street, West Hartlepool. He was an Ordinary Seaman in the Mercantile Marine who died on 19 February 1918, whilst serving on SS *Barrowmore*, a British cargo ship. The vessel was attacked and sunk without warning by the German submarine *U-94* when she was 53 nautical miles north-west of the Bishop Rock in the English Channel, off the south-west coast of England. George was one of the twenty-five members of the crew who lost their lives, a tragic loss to his parents.

George's father William, who before the war had been a shipyard labourer, enlisted in the Army on 22 April 1915 at West Hartlepool, when he was 36 years and 8 months old, becoming a private (25315) in the Durham Light Infantry. He began his basic military training the next day at Newcastle-upon-Tyne, but just 16 days later on 7 May 1915, he was discharged from the army for not likely to become an efficient soldier, as per King's Army Regulations. No doubt one of the shortest lived military careers on record.

If I have read his Army Pension Record correctly, then it shows that he was not a well man, despite his age and previous employment as a shipyard labourer. He suffered with chronic interstitial nephritis or kidney problems; he had heart problems with his left ventrical; oedema, or fluid in tissue cells which caused swelling under his eyes and two other conditions which I simply could not read due to the poor quality of the writing. Even though William must have had some idea of his failing health, he still tried to do his bit and serve his King and country. It is amazing that he actually managed to pass his enlistment medical.

George and Mary had married on 9 May 1893 at the West Hartlepool Parish Church and by 1910 they had five children, three sons, Jonathon, George, and Charles and daughters Catherine and Mary.

Another West Hartlepool member of the crew who perished with George was 18-year-old Third Mate FREDERICK HUGHES. He lived with his mother Mary at 49 Lowthian Road in the town.

News reached Hartlepool on Monday 1 April, as reported in many local newspapers, of more local men who had been killed and wounded.

Jacob Kruse Muller and Christiane Johanne Hessler of 'Wyndcliffe', Seaton Carew, West Hartlepool, naturalized British citizens who were born in Norway, heard that their son JACOB KRUSE 'JACKIE' HESSSLER, 21 years of age and a captain in the 5th Battalion, Durham Light Infantry, had been killed in action in France on 23 March 1918. Commissioned as an officer in June 1914, he had also been Mentioned in Despatches for his bravery. He has no known grave but his name is commemoratcd on the Pozières Memorial.

He was the second youngest of five children. His two sisters were, Jane Daisy Hessler, and Sigrie Vera Hessler, as well as brothers, NORMAN ANDREW HESSLER and Charles Anderson Hessler. Before the war Jacob had been a student at the prestigious Haileybury College, Haileybury, Hertfordshire. Two months after Jacob's death, Mr and Mrs Hessler would receive bad news for a second time, when his brother, Norman, was also killed in action at the age of 25, whilst serving in France. He was also a captain in the 5th Battalion, Durham Light Infantry. He has no known grave and his name is commemorated on the Soissons Memorial in the Aisne region of France.

Mr Herbert Thornton, who was in the Merchant Navy, and Mrs Ann Elizabeth Thornton of 22 Lister Street, West Hartlepool, received the dreaded visit from a telegram boy. As was the case with such calls, the news was never good. His 21-year-old son, Second Lieutenant JOHN WILLIAM THORNTON of the 2nd/4th Battalion, York & Lancaster Regiment, who had enlisted in the Army on 1 February 1916, had been killed by an exploding German artillery shell on 27 March 1918 at Roclincourt.

Initially, he had enlisted as a private in the 21st (Service) Battalion, Durham Light Infantry. In April 1916 he was offered a commission with the same regiment but turned it down. Two months later on 28 June he transferred to the 9th Battalion, York and Lancaster Regiment and went with them to France as part of the British Expeditionary Force, taking part in the Battle of the Somme between 1 July and 25 September 1916. He was then appointed quartermaster sergeant to the 2nd Musketry School where he was recommended for a commission. He returned to England in March 1917 and was gazetted as a second lieutenant in the 4th Battalion, York and Lancaster Regiment, on 26 September. He returned to France in December 1917.

Initially wounded in the shell blast, he was admitted to No.6 Stationary Hospital but died there later that day. A comrade of his, Lieutenant Warr, wrote a letter to John's parents: *'We are all so grieved at your son's death, as he was a splendid soldier, and liked by everybody. Your son was a fine character and we feel his loss dreadfully.'*

The battalion's chaplain, the Rev. B.F. Hinds, wrote: *'Your son was held in high esteem by all the officers, men and myself, both as a friend, and also as an officer.'*

Before enlisting in the Army, John worked as a clerk in the North Eastern Railway Company's Carriage and Waggon Department at West Hartlepool. The 1911 Census showed John, his parents along his five brothers and sisters, living at 19 Olive Street, Hartlepool. He is buried at the St Hilaire Cemetery, Frevent, in the Pas de Calais region of France.

Captain John Laycock of the Royal Engineers, the eldest son of the late Mr B.C. Laycock, of West Hartlepool, was admitted to hospital with severe gunshot wounds to his chest. He had initially been commissioned as a second lieutenant in the 9th Battalion, Yorkshire Regiment, having twice previously been Mentioned in Despatches. His brother, Captain C. Laycock, a holder of the Military Cross, had been reported missing since 24 March 1918.

It would appear that both men survived the war, and in fact John Laycock, who first went out to France on 21 August 1915, went on to reach the rank of major, before he retired.

Mrs Thirkell of 69 Peroy Street, West Hartlepool, received news that her husband, Lieutenant H. Thirkell, of the Royal Marines Light Infantry, had been wounded with gas and a gun shot wound to the head. He had previously served as a lieutenant with the 3rd/5th Battalion, London Regiment.

Second Lieutenant ROBERT ANDREW TAIT, aged 19, was not born in the Hartlepools nor had he lived there, but before the war he had worked at the town's branch of Barclays Bank. He was 19 years of age and serving with the Loyal North Lancashire Regiment when he was killed on 22 March 1918. He is buried at Lebucquière Communal Cemetery Extension in the Pas de Calais region of France. His father had been a police inspector with the Newcastle Constabulary.

On Saturday 11 May a new club for girls opened at West Hartlepool, which for the time was unusual as most of the 'clubs' that were opened during the First World War were for servicemen. One of them was situated in Lynn Street, West Hartlepool. The aim of the clubs was to provide a place of relaxation and comfort for soldiers before they left for the front.

This particular one was for the Women's Army Auxiliary Corps (WAACs), so that they had somewhere local to go when they were enjoying some rest and relaxation. The club was known as a Tipperary Club and was located in a set of rooms rented and furnished by a committee of ladies, who ran three similar clubs for soldiers in the town throughout the war years. Mrs J.R. Fryer, the president of the lady's committee, conducted the club's opening ceremony.

In the clubs provided for soldiers, who were billeted in various different buildings across the Hartlepool district such as schools, workhouses, the town hall, hotels, as well as private houses, items such as writing materials, books and newspapers were provided for the troops. Different forms of entertainment were also put on. The men could purchase hot and cold drinks, although not alcohol, and cakes and sandwiches, all of which were reasonably priced.

On Wednesday 15 May, the theme of new clubs continued with the opening of the Trafalgar Club in the High Street, Hartlepool. This club was for the benefit of local members of the National Federation of Discharged Sailors and Soldiers. The official opening ceremony was performed by the mayor, Councillor C.T. Watson, with other councilors and members of the clergy, also in attendance. In declaring the new club open, the mayor referred to the sacrifices that had been made by the men of Hartlepool who had fought for their country in the various theatres of war, no matter what branch of the armed forces they had served in. He had no doubt that the full sympathy of members of the local community were with the discharged sailors and soldiers. In closing he promised to do his best to gain encouraging support for the club amongst his own friends, who had the privilege of becoming honorary members.

Mr James Wells, the honorary secretary of the new club, explained that club membership was already flourishing, with over a hundred members. The new premises were spacious and well equipped, and included two billiard rooms, recreation and reading rooms, bathroom and a canteen.

On Friday 31 May an article appeared in the *Hartlepool Northern Daily Mail* newspaper, which reported on the benefits of re-cycling newspaper. At the time there were between 18,000 and 19,000 homes in the Hartlepool area, and somebody realized that if each home saved just one pound of newspaper each week, this would allow the government to re-pulp it and make it reusable paper. It would provide more than eight tons every week, which would come in extremely useful, when realizing that the government alone required four tons per week for their own needs. It was a scheme that everybody could take part in, and the hope was that everybody would. Housewives in particular were requested to collect household waste paper of any kind and forward it on to the *Mail* office, or request that it might be collected. A payment was made for all paper received, and there was no charge for its collection.

Saturday 22 June saw history made in Hartlepool when two teams of American soldiers played a game of baseball against each other on the Friarage Field before a very interested if not very large crowd of spectators. Whether all of those who were present actually understood what they were watching, or understood the rules is not known. One reporter described the pitching and catching as being *'fascinating and good, and the running to bases at times, very thrilling'*, adding that baseball was *'a peerless game which cultivates quick thinking and decision making'*.

The two teams were provided with lunch at the Station Hotel on their arrival, and were addressed by Mr Edwin Birks JP, who apologized that their welcome by the local community wasn't more of a hearty and robust affair, explaining that knowledge of their attendance had only been passed on at very short notice, but that in his capacity as a local magistrate he tendered each and everyone of them a hearty and sincere welcome on behalf of the people of Hartlepool.

Mr Birks informed the visiting American soldiers that the town of Hartlepool was one of the most patriotic in the whole of the United Kingdom, and that its people had given more money per head of population to the nation's war funds than any other town or city in the country. He welcomed 'our brothers' from across the sea as comrades in the great struggle which was raging for liberty, honour and civilization, a great enterprise that was comparable to knights from centuries past.

The eulogies and platitudes were appreciated and well received by the American soldiers. Photographs followed before the men left for the Friarage Field and the historic match that saw one of the sides win by a score of 5 – 0. It was hoped that future matches would be arranged, but with more notice, so that the American visitors would see at first hand the true support and appreciation of the people of the Hartlepools.

Monday 24 June saw a sad and tragic case brought before the Hartlepool Police Court. The mayor Councillor William Edgar, sitting with Mr W.R. Owen, Mr William Brankston, Alderman Martin and Mr E. Birks, heard the case of Isabella Griffin, aged 22, facing a charge of unlawfully causing the death of her illegitimate child. Griffin, who was chaperoned by Police Matron Scott, stood passively whilst Superintendent McDonald of Hartlepool Police, read out the charge.

Detective Sergeant Dodsworth gave evidence to the court that he had attended the house where Griffin was employed as a domestic servant and was shown the body of her dead child which had been discovered in a box. Although the circumstances of how the infant had died were not apparent, and no admission was made by Griffin for the responsibility of her child's death, she was arrested and taken to Hartlepool police station where she was remanded in custody.

On 25 June an inquest was held into the child's death when the girl's employer, Master Mariner Christian Moller, said that his wife had noticed a strange smell on the landing and traced it to the girl's bedroom where the body of a child was found in a tin trunk. The police were called and when interviewed Isabella Griffin said: 'I put it in the box. It was born about three weeks ago, and a soldier from Bradford is the father.'

Dr Arnold Biggart, who examined the body, said it was that of a fully developed female child weighing about 9lb. A woman's undergarment was wrapped round the throat of the infant and a handkerchief stuffed in the corner of its mouth. The doctor said that death was due to asphyxia as a result of the mouth being stuffed with a handkerchief and the garment round the throat.

At Durham Assizes on 4 July Isabella pleaded guilty to the concealment of the birth of her child and was sentenced to two months imprisonment.

The Durham County Appeal Tribunal met on Wednesday 17 July, Judge Greenwell presiding, who was dealing with a National Service appeal in respect of the manager of a butcher's shop. The un-named man was married,

45 years of age and employed by the Argentine Meat Company, at their branch in Lynn Street, West Hartlepool.

Captain Roberts, the military representative, said that the appeal by the individual concerned was against the decision of the local tribunal, which granted an exemption until 4 January 1919.

The Argentine Meat Company owned three butcher's shops in West Hartlepool, each of which had a manager. Judge Greenwell proffered the suggestion that one of the shops could close without damaging the business. A representative of the company stated in response that each of the three shops had extensive numbers of customers, many of whom had shopped with them over many years. Also, the managers were all kept extremely busy, as they had to carry out a lot of the butchery work as they could not get sufficiently qualified staff to do it.

Captain Roberts thought that the firm should be able to manage all three shops with just two managers sharing the extra workload of the third.

On hearing all the arguments put forward by those concerned, Judge Greenwell determined that the six month's exemption should be reduced to three months.

In the case of another butcher, the National Representative appealed against the six-month exemption certificate which had been granted to the man in question. On having heard the arguments for both sides in the case, Judge Greenwell reduced the exemption by three months. The man then applied to be medically re-examined stating that there was something wrong with his heart. In response to the man's comments, Judge Greenwell said: *'It depends upon what there is wrong with your heart. A good many people come here and say there is something wrong with their hearts. It does not mean that they are physically wrong.'*

He granted permission for the man to be medically re-examined to determine his actual physical condition.

It was reported on Thursday 15 August 1918 that Sergeant William Parkes of the Royal Field Artillery had been awarded the French *Croix de Guerre*, second class, for good work done at the Battle of the Marne. He had already been awarded the Distinguished Conduct Medal and a Bar to his Military Medal which his previous brave actions had so rightly warranted.

The news came in the form of a letter which he had sent to his brother James Parkes, who lived at 7 Gill Street, West Hartlepool, with his wife Susan and their two sons, Edward and William. James had the uniquely titled job of a 'Shipyard Holder Up for a Riveter'.

Tuesday 20 August saw the opening of Hartlepool's third National Kitchen, opened and overseen by the town's corporation. The latest kitchen was situated on the Central Estate, at the corner of Hart Road and Stephenson Street. The other two, which were in Durham Street and the High Street, had proved highly successful, hence why the corporation had been encouraged to open a third.

The opening ceremony was performed by the mayoress, Mrs C.T. Watson. The mayor, along with other local dignitaries and clergymen, were also in attendance, the kitchens being a scheme which they fully supported. Councillor Turner, who was the Hartlepool Corporation's, chairman of the kitchens committee, gave a brief overview of the benefits of the kitchens, explaining that they were a way of conserving food, as well as a means of bringing about an economy in both light and fuel.

Sunday 8 September saw a company of Boy Scouts from the Central Estate of Hartlepool attending divine service at the town's St Hilda's Parish Church. Scoutmaster Rutherford was in attendance along with other Scout companies from West Hartlepool, and a band, who collectively made an impressive sight, as they marched their way through the streets, en route to the church. The choir was in good voice throughout the service and was expertly conducted by the rector. After the lengthy service all the Scouts lined up outside the church, every one of them impeccably turned out, resplendent in their uniforms. One of the young boys was then presented with the much sought after honour, but one that was rarely achieved, the King's Scout, which at the time was the second highest honour that it was possible for a Scout to achieve.

An inquest was held by the deputy coroner, Mr G. Newby on Friday 13 September into the death of a new-born female child, whose body had been discovered in an alley way, which ran between Wilton Avenue and Hutton Avenue. The sad discovery had been made by a school boy, who took the child's body to the police station.

Doctor Biggart carried out a post-mortem on the dead infant, and determined that the child, who was fully formed and developed, had lived after birth, rather than having been the result of a pre-term abortion. The cause of death was asphyxia, but it had not been possible to establish whether this had been as the result of an accident or had been carried out intentionally.

The inquest was then adjourned for a period of two weeks so that further enquiries could be carried out by the police to try and establish the identity of the mother of the dead infant. It was felt to be highly unlikely that the pregnancy had been that of a married woman. In today's society, having a child outside marriage has very little or no stigma attached to it. In 1918, the same moral standards did not prevail, living together without being married would have been unacceptable to most elements of society, let alone giving birth to a child outside of wedlock.

The edition of the *Hartlepool Northern Daily Mail* newspaper dated Friday 27 September included a list of local men who had become casualties of the war, both those who had been wounded and killed.

Mrs J. Wharton of 58 Hill Street, West Hartlepool, had received a post card informing her that her husband, Joshua Wharton, a shoeing smith with the Royal Field Artillery, had been wounded whilst serving in France and was now being treated in a Manchester hospital. He had enlisted in the Army in 1907 and been part of the initial British Expeditionary Force that crossed the English Channel, in an effort to stop the German advance into Belgium. Prior to his departure he had been stationed in Glasgow.

Private 42151 H. MORTON, who was 34 years of age and a married man, was serving with the 9th (North Irish Horse) Battalion, Royal Irish Fusiliers, was killed in action on 4 September and is buried at the Mont Noir Military Cemetery, in the village of St Jans-Cappel, which is situated 3 kilometres north of Baillieul, in the Nord region of France. Private Morton was called up for war service in 1916. Prior to this he had worked at the town's Expanded Metal Works and lived with his wife and five young children at 85 Westmoreland Street, West Hartlepool.

GEORGE HAROLD PAXTON was an Able Seaman (R/4855) in the Royal Naval Volunteer Reserve, when he was killed in action on 25 August 1918, whilst serving as part of the Hawke Battalion, Royal Navy Division. He has no known grave, but his name is commemorated on the Vis-en-Artois Memorial, which is situated about 6 miles south-east of Arras, in the Pas de Calais region of France. The rather impressive looking memorial commemorates the names of some 9,000 men from Australia, Canada, Great Britain, Ireland, New Zealand and South Africa, who fell during the advance to victory in Artois and Picardy, between the Somme and Loos areas, and who have no known grave.

Mr John and Mrs Alice Armin of 22 Darlington Terrace, West Hartlepool, had initially been informed that their 22-year-old son, Private S/4747 ALEXANDER ARMIN, who was serving with the 2nd Battalion, a signals section in the Gordon Highlanders, had been officially reported as missing since 5 October 1917. Nearly a year later, the grieving parents heard from the War Office, that their son was now being officially classified as missing presumed dead as from the initial date they had been given. He was the second son Mr and Mrs Armin had lost to the war, whilst their third and eldest son John, served in the Army in Mesopotamia during the latter stages of 1918 and survived.

Alexander has no known grave but his name is commemorated on the Tyne Cot Memorial in the West-Vlaanderen region of Belgium.

The 1901 Census shows John and Alice living at 18 Bailey Street, West Hartlepool, with their four children, John, Margaret, Willie and Alexander. But by the time of the 1911 Census, the family were at 17 Alexandra Street, West Hartlepool, with Alexander, by now 16 years of age, and the only child of the family still at home.

Willie or WILLIAM ARMIN, had served as an Able Seaman (J/4936) on board HMS *Clan McNaughton*, an armed merchant cruiser and was drowned when the ship foundered and sank in turbulent waters and inclement weather, on 3 February 1915, in the North Sea. There were no survivors from the

281 members of the crew. His name, along side those who died with him, is commemorated on the Chatham Naval Memorial.

Private 31536 ADAM GRAHAM TURNER, and a holder of the Military Medal, served with the 7ᵗʰ Battalion, Lincolnshire Regiment. He was 20 years of age when he was killed in action whilst serving in France, and was buried in the Hermies Hill British Cemetery, in the Pas de Calais region of France.

His widowed mother, who lived at 38 Maiton Street, Hartlepool, heard the tragic news in the form of a telegram, together with an expression of sympathy from the King and Queen. The chaplain of the Lincolnshire Regiment also wrote to Mrs Butler (she had re-married after the death of her son's father) expressing his sorrow at her son's death:

> *I am extremely sorry to have to tell you that we have just paid the last tribute of respect to your son. He was killed by a shell which burst in the place he was sleeping in. His principal wound was over the heart, and fortunately, his death was almost instantaneous, so that he could have suffered no pain. He had proved himself a thoroughly good soldier. That is shown by the fact that he was No.1 on a Lewis gun, and the Military Medal that he won bears witness to exceptionally fine work in the past. At his funeral this afternoon (September 6ᵗʰ) a number of his comrades were present and all his company officers. We had a full service. A rough cross has been put at his grave, and we hope soon to get a properly carved one made by the Pioneers of the battalion.*

He first arrived in France in November 1916 and between then and his death, he was lucky enough to have been able to go home on leave, and whilst there he made a point of visiting his old school, where he received a hearty reception.

Monday 21 October saw the annual general meeting of the 1ˢᵗ Hartlepool Company of the Boys Brigade and Old Boys Club. It took place at the club's premises in the High Street, Hartlepool. The club's president and founder, Dr A.E. Morison, chaired the meeting, and along with the honorary treasurer, Mr Armstrong, and the secretary, Mr Frank Hodgson, read out his yearly reports, all three of which painted an extremely positive picture of the club and all its members.

In his address Dr Morison urged the club members to keep in mind that whilst the club had a very strong social side, its main object was the promotion of Christ's Kingdom amongst boys, which it sought to do through both the Boys' Brigade as well as the Boys' Reserve, the latter of the two units being the training reserve of the former. Collectively they catered for boys from 9 years of age and upwards, until they were old enough to undertake military service.

After the business of the meeting had finished, the brigade's two local chaplains, the Rev. F.L. Ward and the Rev. J. Wadsworth, led the usual weekly concert, which helped provide entertainment for the local soldiers and sailors, those who were still serving as well as those who had already been discharged. Before the night was over, Dr Morison and his wife were presented with an ornate silver rose bowl and a flower stand, to mark their twenty-fifth wedding anniversary, by Mr Frank Horsley on behalf of the Boys' Brigade. Dr Morison responded by giving his thanks for the generosity which they had both been shown throughout the course of the evening. He finished by stating that it was his wish that when he eventually retired, he would devote his time to working with youngsters in an effort to help them choose the right path, which would provide them with better job opportunities and a more fulfilling life.

The early years of the twentieth century were difficult times for many in society, with the majority of people living on the wrong side of the haves and the have nots. Work was hard to come by, wages were predominantly low, housing and sanitation were of a very poor quality, and food wasn't so easily obtainable for the lower classes. All of these factors made life extremely harsh and stressful for most, as they struggled to make ends meet.

On the morning of Saturday 9 November, the deputy coroner of Hartlepool, Mr George Newby held an enquiry in to the death of 54-year-old Mrs Isabella Parr, who lived at 13 Beaconsfield Square, Hartlepool. She died at the town's General Hospital, the result of a self-inflicted wound.

A neighbour of Mrs Parr, Mrs Mary Ellen Newton, informed the enquiry that on 30 October about 8.30pm, she heard a hammering on her kitchen wall, which adjoined the property next door. She went round to see her neighbour and saw Mrs Parr standing in the middle of her kitchen, silent and looking shocked. She asked her if she was unwell and she pointed to her throat, which Mrs Newton could see was bleeding. Mrs Parr then ran off and Mrs Newton went to get assistance.

Mrs Parr was employed by Mr J.F. Johnson, as his house keeper, who was generally satisfied with the quality and standard of her work, but he had noticed in recent times that she seemed depressed, and not quite herself. After Mrs Newton had spoken to Mr Johnson, he went to Mrs Parr's room and found her in her bedroom, blood was coming from her throat, and there was a blood-stained razor lying by her side.

One of Mrs Parr's nieces, Christine Fuller, told the enquiry that her aunt was taken to Hartlepool Hospital on Friday 2 November, where she went to visit her. Mrs Parr, she said, was nearly always down in her spirits, and had been since her husband had died some seventeen years previously. When she asked her why she had cut her throat, she replied by saying that she didn't remember doing anything.

Dr Boswell gave evidence that he saw Mrs Parr at Mr Johnson's home on 1 November 1918, and that she was suffering with what he described as a severe laceration to her throat. Once she arrived at hospital she came under the care of both Dr Boswell and his colleague, Dr Pearson, but sadly passed away at 10.20am on 7 November 1918 from septic pneumonia as a direct result of the self-inflicted wound to her throat.

In conversation with Dr Boswell after she was admitted to hospital, she told him that she had been having some terrible dreams and reiterated what she had told her niece, in that she had no recollection of cutting her throat.

Mr Newby, the deputy coroner, said that he was satisfied that Mrs Parr's death came about for the reasons outlined by Dr Boswell, and as a direct result of the self-inflicted wound to her throat, whilst being of unsound mind.

The 1911 Census found Mrs Parr, shown as a dressmaker, living with her father-in-law, William Parr, who was 80 years of age at the time, at 61 Commercial Street, Middleton, Hartlepool. He lived until he was 93 years of age and passed away in 1922, so it is unclear, why Isabella Parr became the live-in house keeper of Mr Johnson.

Even though the war was just about to come to an end, Isabella Parr's tragic passing, highlighted the sadness of death that was still apparent for some of the people of Hartlepool, just as the celebrations of the end of the war were about to begin.

CHAPTER SEVEN

The Aftermath

With the fighting now over and normality, or what passed for it, slowly returning to everyday life for the people of the Hartlepools, sadly some of the town's young men were still falling victim to the war. Between 12 November 1918 and 31 December 1921, when official figures of post war deaths stopped being included in official figures, at least sixty-nine men died of their wounds, injuries or disease. This figure is taken from the Commonwealth War Graves Commission website.

1918 (from 12 November) – 19
1919 – 36
1920 – 9
1921 – 5

The first man with a connection to the Hartlepools to die the day after the signing of the Armistice was Sergeant 21/33 FREDERICK JAMES STAGEMAN, who was 28 years of age and born in West Hartlepool. He served with the 21st Battalion, West Yorkshire Regiment (Prince of Wales's Own). He had enlisted on 26 October 1915, when he was 25 years of age, and promoted to the rank of Sergeant on 16 June 1916. He died of pneumonia on 12 November 1918, at the Royal Army Medical Corps No.22 General Hospital at Camiers, which was part of the enormous complex of hospitals at Etaples, which is also where he is buried at the base's Military Cemetery.

His parents, Albert Simion and Mary Stageman, were residents of West Hartlepool, whilst Frederick lived with his wife Bertha Evelyn Stageman at Woodland View, Stanley Hill, Wakefield. They married on 20 December 1913 in Wakefield and their first child, also Frederick James Stageman, was born on 31 March 1914.

The last Hartlepool man to die as a result of his involvement in the First World War, was 39-year-old Corporal (67796) CECIL JAMES DERRY, of the Royal Army Medical Corps who died on 19 July 1921. He was a married man and lived with his wife Clara Derry at 22 Milton Road, West Hartlepool, although he wasn't a local man by birth. He was born in Hereford, and at the

General Ernest Dunlop Swinton.

time of the 1911 Census he and Clara were living at 1 Station Road, Maldon, Essex, with their three children, where he worked as a reporter. He is buried at the Hartlepool North Cemetery.

Throughout the war and in an effort to raise money to be able to continue fighting it, the government came up with the idea of War Bonds and War Certificates, that members of the public could purchase and then cash in after the war was over and hopefully have made a decent return on their investment. This was, of course, slightly risky because the whole concept was based on the premise that Britain and her Allies were going to win the war. However, the idea turned out to be a very successful one.

To raise as much money as possible the National War Savings Committee, came up with the idea that whichever town or city raised the most per head of population, would be presented with one of the tanks to erect in their community as a memorial for their wartime efforts. The idea was born out of the appearance at the Lord Mayor's Show in London, of two British tanks which had been nicknamed, Egbert and Nelson. It is worth pointing out at this stage, that tanks had only been used in a large-scale encounter for the first time during the Battle of Cambrai in France, which had taken place between 20 November and 7 December 1917, which meant that there was a lot of public interest in these new-fangled machines.

'Nelson' made a promotional visit to West Hartlepool on 4 February 1918, which resulted in members of the public from the town fully embracing the idea, collectively purchasing more than £2,360,000 worth of War Bonds and Certificates, which resulted in the town of West Hartlepool winning the competition and in June 1919, being presented with 'Egbert' by General Ernest Dunlop Swinton, Royal Engineers, in front of the town's Municipal Buildings, before being mounted on a permanent display at Stranton Bull Garth.

General Swinton, who later became Major General Sir Ernest Dunlop Swinton, was actively involved in the development and adoption of the tank by the British Army during the First World War. He was also the individual credited with having coined the name 'tank'. He had served as a captain during the Second Boer War and was awarded the Distinguished Service Order in November 1900.

General Swinton and Benjamin Holt.

His other claim to fame during the course of the First World War was the title of official British war correspondent, by Lord Kitchener, the Minister for War.

The original idea for the use of a tracked vehicle for military purposes had first been suggested in 1911 when David Roberts of Richard Hornsby & Sons approached British military officials, but the idea was not progressed. The patents relating to the 'chain track' tractor were purchased by Benjamin Holt of the Holt Manufacturing Company from Richard Hornsby & Sons in 1914.

Although the Armistice, which ended the fighting, was signed on 11 November 1918, the official end of the war was not confirmed until the signing of the Treaty of Versailles at the Paris Peace Conference, on 28 June 1919, so although many of Hartlepool's men had returned to their loved ones in the immediate weeks and months after the signing of the Armistice, there was always the possibility they might be called up from the Army Reserve to carry on the fight, if an agreement hadn't been reached in Paris. It was only after this date that people could once again re-start and in some cases rebuild their lives, to somewhere near where they had once been before they had enlisted to go off and join the fight.

Within a week of the signing of the Treaty of Versailles everything was suddenly not so agreeable back home in Hartlepool. On Friday, 4 July 1919, it was reported that 300-400 Members of the Amalgamated Society of Engineers, who were employed at the Hartlepool Engine Works, owned by Messrs. Richardson, Westgarth & Co. Ltd, were still out on strike. There wasn't absolute clarity as to what the strike was about. One claim was that it began after six ex-Army men were taken on by the company, at the behest of the Appointments Department at the Ministry of Labour. This supposedly angered the members of the Amalgamated Society of Engineers, because the six ex-Army men were only expected to serve an apprenticeship for a period of three years rather than the five years that those already employed at the works, had to endure before they became fully qualified.

The six ex-Army men, possibly realising the situation that their continued presence was causing, removed themselves from the company's employment, how they managed to achieve this without official sanction, is not clear. This did not, however, sate the appetite of the striking engineers. They also contested that to accommodate the six ex-Army men, others, some of them returned soldiers, had been discharged to make way for them.

The management of the company agreed that some staff were laid off at around the same time that the six ex-Army men were sent to them by the Ministry of Labour, but the two acts were not in any way connected, simply co-incidental. The company further stated that the cause of the temporary reduction in their staff numbers, was because the Ministry of Shipping had cancelled a large number of orders for the machinery which they produced, and it was an absurd suggestion that fully trained men would have been discharged only to be replaced with untrained men.

In addressing the point concerning apprenticeships, the company pointed out that the practice in Marine Engineering was that it lasted for a term of five years, whereas the Board of Trade regulations only stipulated a time period of four years, and in the case of men who had served in a mechanical unit of the Army, the requirement according to the Board of Trade had been reduced to three years.

At this time there was an urgent need in lots of industries for skilled men, many of whom had been lost during the war, and if the nation was to recover quickly in an economic sense, then it needed men, fully trained, as quickly as possible, which was one of the possible reasons for the reduction in the length of time it took to serve an apprenticeship.

On the evening of Wednesday 16 July, in the Olympic Rink, 160 past and present members of the Hartlepool Special Constabulary were recognized for their wartime service, with the presentation of specially minted silver medals – just another of the post war ceremonies which took place in the Hartlepools after the war.

With the signing of the Treaty of Versailles, the official peace celebrations could at long last get underway. It was decided that there would be a national day of celebration on Saturday 19 July. The celebrations in West Hartlepool included a procession, which started from outside the West Hartlepool

Football Ground and finished just over a mile away at the park. It was led by the mayor and members of the corporation and included an estimated 10,000 local children and military marching bands. On reaching the park, each of the children was presented with a commemorative medal and three new pennies, a gift from the mayor Councillor G.F. Thompson. For some reason the town council had passed a resolution to present each of the members and officials of the Corporation with a specially struck silver medal, rather than those that had been given to the local children.

After receiving their gifts the children took part in the singing of patriotic songs which included the National Anthem, after which the mayor planted a commemorative oak tree, before reading out the king's message which had been prepared for this most special of occasions.

In the afternoon some 2,000 demobilised, soldiers, sailors, men of the merchant services, volunteers and ambulance corps, paraded outside the football ground before marching the same route as the children had done earlier in the day. On their arrival at the park, a flag was unveiled and the National Anthem was sung with passion and vigour by all of those in attendance. The mayor then made an address to those present and the Last Post was sounded by a lone bugler to remember those who had fallen during the war.

After the service there was a free open-air concert in the park, with a chorus of some 400 voices. When darkness finally settled in on the day's events, the entire area was illuminated and flares were lit.

There were also celebrations in neighbouring Hartlepool where commemorative peace medals were also distributed and two new sixpences were given to each child whose father had fallen during war.

The Promenade was the focus of the day's events, where a civic service was held. The highlight of the day was undoubtedly a salvo fired from the artillery guns at the Heugh Battery, which had played a part during the German naval bombardment of the town on 16 December 1914. The streets were adorned with flags and colourful bunting, with the ships at anchor in the harbour being suitably bedecked.

It was reported in some of the North-Eastern local newspapers on Wednesday 23 July, that a scheme for the establishment of a home for the treatment and training of disabled soldiers and soldiers, in West Hartlepool, was being proceeded with immediately. The idea was initially made possible with the donation of £10,000 by Mr J.W. Crosby, which was followed by a further donation by Viscount Furness, of Tunstall Court, a property which enjoyed the luxury of extensive grounds, which was the home of the late Baron Furness.

The plan's progression to fruition had been delayed for various reasons, until the mayor of West Hartlepool, Councillor T.F. Thompson, had a meeting in London with Sir Worthington Evans, the Minister of Pensions, who was extremely keen that the idea should be progressed with all haste. He even made an undertaking that the Ministry of Pensions would pay to equip and maintain the premises, with the intention of making it one of the largest such homes of its kind yet established, and a model for similar establishments around the country.

The intention was to provide, for a period of at least ten years, accommodation and training for up to 200 men at any one time, along with full time residential medical staff. The men who would become residents of the home, would be drawn from the Hartlepools and surrounding districts. It was also hoped to build a hostel to accommodate the wives and families of the disabled men who were at the home. The idea was to provide suitable training for the men, which would eventually lead to their finding work in local trades and industries.

CHAPTER EIGHT

Hartlepool War Memorial

By the time the Armistice had been signed on 11 November 1918, and the fighting finally came to an end, the town of Hartlepool was left to reflect on the part its young men had played and the hefty price they had paid to help secure victory.

The number of Hartlepool men who were killed in action or died of their wounds, illness or disease is not always agreed upon, mainly because there was no laid down, official criteria as to who qualified to be commemorated on the memorial. It was left to the individuals and committee members who had come up with the idea of erecting a war memorial to commemorate the town's dead, to determine the names of those men who would be included on it. Sadly, there would always be some who would initially be missed off, only to subsequently come to light over time.

The memorial includes a total of 1,545 names which are recorded on twelve brass panels at the base of the memorial, and has the following inscription:

> THE GREAT WAR 1914 – 1919
> IN GRATEFUL REMEMBRANCE
> OF THE MEN OF THIS TOWN
> WHO AT THEIR COUNTRY'S
> CALL LEFT ALL THAT WAS
> DEAR TO THEM TO HAZARD
> THEIR LIVES THAT OTHERS
> MIGHT LIVE IN FREEDOM
> THEIR NAME LIVETH FOR EVERMORE

The Commonwealth War Graves Commission website records a total of 1,154 men who died in the First World War, who had a connection with Hartlepool. But these figures were taken from documents, which if were missing the next of kin's details and address, would not show up as having a connection with the town.

West Hartlepool War Memorial.

Durham Records Online includes a list of 1,747 men from Hartlepool who died as a result of the First World War. This list was amassed by Mr Bert Wilson.

The West Hartlepool War Memorial is situated in Victory Square, Victoria Road, Hartlepool. It was unveiled on 11 October 1923 by Brigadier General Charles Lambton, whilst the dedication was carried out by the Bishop of Durham.

The names below amount to 1,714 in total, and include men who lived in the town, were born in the town or whose parents lived in the town. I fully accept that this doesn't agree with those names recorded on the local war memorial, but as is normal in these circumstances, and with the passage of time, more names often come to light over the years that had not been initially included.

George E. ADAMS	15 Florence Street, Hartlepool
Gordon ADAMS	61 Sheriff Street, Hartlepool
James W. ADAMS	Bramley Street, Hartlepool
Robert ADDISON	6 Plevna Street, Hartlepool
Sydney ADDISON	17 Talbot Street, Hartlepool
William H. ADDISON	27 Middleton Road, Hartlepool
James AFFLECK	15 Bertha Street, Hartlepool
Banks AGAR	1A Alice Street, Hartlepool
H.M. AGAR	
James AGAR	21 Moore Street, Hartlepool
John Robert AGAR	1 Alice Street, Hartlepool
Ralph AGAR	
John AINSLEY	42 Rodney Street, Hartleppol
Samuel AINSLEY	10 Back Lumley Street, Hartlepool
William Dixon AINSLEY	4 South Raby Street, Hartlepool
George AIREY	17 Bellerby Terrace, Hartlepool
Thomas AITKEN	
Arthur W. ALDERSON	
C.G. ALDERSON	
James W. ALDERSON	23 Anthony Street, Hartlepool
T. ALDERSON	3 Bengal Street, Hartlepool
Robert ALDUS	19 Plevna Street, Hartlepool
Coltman ALLAN	
Ronald ALLAN	
A. ALLEN	
Frank ALLEN	8 Silver Street, Hartlepool

Ronald ALLEN	30 Houghton Street, Hartlepool
Francis R. ALLINSON	14 Freeman Street, Hartlepool
Charles F. ALLISON	125 Lynn Street, Hartlepool
T. ALLISON	15 Albert Street, Hartlepool
Thomas W. ALLISON	44 Harcourt Street, Hartlepool
W. ALLISTON	
Arthur ALTON	
George ALTON	
Alexander ANDERSON	17 Conyers Street, Hartlepool
Harold H. ANDERSON	Cliffe House Avenue Road, Hartlepool
Harold T. ANDERSON	32 Ellison Street, Hartlepool
John ANDERSON	24 Charlotte Street, Hartlepool
Simpson ANDERSON	
Walter L. ANDERSON	12 John Street, Hartlepool
John W. ANDREWS	15 Bowser Street, Hartlepool
David ANDREWS	4 Hereford Street, Hartlepool
Joseph S. ANDREWS	
James H. ANGEL	
John William ANGEL	39 Florence Street, Hartlepool
Richard ANGEL	46 Hill Street, Hartlepool
Robert ANGELS (MC)	27 Mulgrave Road, Hartlepool
Billie ANNISS	
Frederick W. ANSON	41 Redworth Street, Hartlepool
Arthur ANTON	38 Sussex Street, Hartlepool
William ARCHIBALD	83 Chester Road, Hartlepool
Alexander ARMIN	22 Darlington Terrace, Hartlepool
William ARMIN	
Alf ARMITAGE	58 Hart Road, Central Estate, Hartlepool
John H. ARMSTRONG	5 Helmsley Street, Hartlepool
Nathan ARMSTRONG	8 Anthony Street, Hartlepool
Thomas ARMSTRONG	18 Bedford Street, Hartlepool
James ARNOLD	63 Turnbull Street, Hartlepool
S. ARNOLD	49 Brougham Terrace, Hartlepool
S.B.C. ARNOLD	4 Laurence Street, Hartlepool
Thomas Henry ASHTON	54 Keswick Street, Hartlepool
Edwin G. ATKINSON	33 Cumberland Street, Hartlepool
Harold T. ATKINSON	16 South Parade, Hartlepool
Harold W. ATKINSON	
Harold ATKINSON	

Herbert ATKINSON	South Parade, Hartlepool
John ATKINSON	35 Alice Street, Hartlepool
John ATKINSON	28 Johnson Street, Hartlepool
Robert ATKINSON	17 Redworth Street, Hartlepool
Thomas AUCKLAND	41 Everard Street, Hartlepool
Allen Harvey BACON	
Horace BACON	103 Murray Street, Hartlepool
Albert Edwin BAINBRIDGE	5 Collingwood Road, Hartlepool
A.C. BAINES	66 Scarborough Street, Hartlepool
Albert BAKER	41 Charlotte Street, Hartlepool
Allen BAKER	
E.J. BAKER	15 Beechwood Road, Hartlepool
George E. BAKER	
John J. BAKER	
J.R. BALDRY	
John W. BALDWIN	76 Scarborough Street, Hartlepool
Laurence BALDWIN	16 Seamer Street, Hartlepool
J.R. BALDRY	
Charles R. BAMFORD	11 Burn Road, Hartlepool
John R. BAMLETT	151 Burbank Street, Hartlepool
George H. BANKS	3 Grace Street, Hartlepool
Horace BANKS	8 South Parade, Hartlepool
Robert C. BANKS	158 Alma Street, Hartlepool
Ernest J. BANWELL	
Edwin BARBER	
Thomas BARBER	80 Stephen Street, Hartlepool
Robert BARFF	43 Charlotte Street, Hartlepool
Allan BARKER	75 Scarborough Street, Hartlepool
Anthony BARKER	30 Albert Street, Hartlepool
Joseph J. BARKER	75 Scarborough Street, Hartlepool
Leonard BARKER	11 Ladysmith Street, Hartlepool
Septimus BARKER	16 Jersey Street, Hartlepool
Thomas BARKER	80 Stephen Street, Hartlepool
Thomas BARKER	
William P. BARNARD	
Oswald BARNETT	Sydenham Road, Hartlepool
J.W. BARR	13 Carr Street, Hartlepool
John W. BARR	
William G.J. BARRETT	44 Furness Street, Hartlepool

Herbert BARROWCLIFFE   59 Ouston Street, Hartlepool
G.E. BARTHOLOMEW   47 Lilley Street, Hartlepool
George BARTLEY
Charles E. BARTRAM   12 Helmsley Street, Hartlepool
Samuel Paul BASTOW   Hartlepool Hotel, Hartlepool
Alan W. BATCHELOR   7 Grange Road, Hartlepool
Albert W. BATE   8 Faulder Road, Hartlepool
H.R. BATES
Mark BATES   29 Henry Street, Hartlepool
Bertie BAXTER   24 Cromwell Street, Hartlepool
Albert G. BAYNES   66 Scarborough Street, Hartlepool
Albert BEACH   37 Dalton Street, Hartlepool
Thomas BEARDSORE   2 Water Street, West Hartlepool
George BEATTIE   71 Watson Street, Hartlepool
William BEATTIE   87 Union Road, Hartlepool
Albert BECK   1 Dene Street, Hartlepool
G.E. BECKETT   10 Penrhyn Street, Hartlepool
Francis W. BEEDLE   26 Devon Street, Hartlepool
Joseph BEHA   24 Hermit Street, Hartlepool
Claude L. BELCHER   6 Park Street, Hartlepool
Eric BELK
Christopher W. BELL   2 Commercial Terrace, Hartlepool
James BELL
John Thomas BELL   41 Lilley Street, Hartlepool
John W. BELL   83 Murray Street, Hartlepool
John William BELL   4 Dalton Street, Hartlepool
R. BELL   8 Peckett Street, Hartlepool
R.H. BELL   44 Everett Street, Hartlepool
Robert Norman BELL   27 Pera, Clifton Avenue, Hartlepool Samuel
William BELL
Wilson BELL
John BENNETT   26 Hutton Avenue, Hartlepool
Reginald BENNETT
Thomas W. BENSON   22 Colwyn Road, Hartlepool
Victor E.E. BENTLEY
Wilfred BENTLEY   7 Slake Terrace, Hartlepool
Robert BERE   19 Penzance Street, Hartlepool
Edmund BERRY   81 Milton Road, Hartlepool
George BERRY   12 Mozart Street, Hartlepool

George Henry BERRY	36 Winter Street, Hartlepool
Thomas W. BERRY	84 Murray Street, Hartlepool
Wilfred BERRY	12 Mozart Street, Hartlepool
A. BEXFIELD	
E.J. BILLER	1 Brougham Terrace, Hartlepool
Robert BILLSBORROW	Beacon House, Hartlepool
Joseph F. BILTON	
Edward BINNING	
T.S. BINNING	46 Ashgrove Avenue, Hartlepool
Alfred BIRCH	64 Suggitt Street, Hartlepool
J.H. BIRKBECK	46 Alliance Street, Hartlepool
Clarence BIRKENSHAW	12 Ashburn Street, Seaton Carew
George H. BIRKENSHAW	
Arthur Reginald BIRKS	20 Westbourne Road, Hartlepool
Harold Victor BIRKS	17 Southburn Terrace, Hartlepool
Harold Victor BIRKS	17 Southbourne Terrace, Hartlepool
Donald BIRSS	
Ralph BLACK	7 Durham Street, Hartlepool
John BLACKETT	11 Clyde Street, Hartlepool
Gerald D. BLACKWELL	
James M. BLACKWOOD	43 Gas Street, Hartlepool
Tom BLADES	
Alex BLAIR	
William BLAIR	
Harry BLAKELEY	19 Alderson Street, Hartlepool
Bert BLOOM	Granville Avenue, Hartlepool
Robert L. BLYTHE	
George BOAGEY	9 Grosvenor Street, Hartlepool
George W. BOAGEY	Turnbull Street, Hartlepool
Robert BOAGEY	23 Alliance Street, Hartlepool
Frederick W. BODDY	12 Wensledale Street, Hartlepool
Thomas BOLAM	2 Angus Street, Hartlepool
John W. BOLTON	37 Belk Street, Hartlepool
Tom BONNARD	39 Studley Road, Hartlepool
Joshua BOOSEFIELD	44 Hill Street, Hartlepool
Cecil BOOTH	5 Berwick Street, Seaton Carew
Edward BOOTH	10 Dover Street, Hartlepool
Francis C. BOOTH	
Frederick S. BOOTH	

Percy BOOTH   5 Berwick Street, Seaton Carew
Ralph P. BOOTH
Robert BOOTH
William BOOTH   10 Dover Street, Hartlepool
William BOOTHAM   6 Gloucester Street, Hartlepool
Percy BORRETT   20 Belmont Gardens, Hartlepool
John R. BORROWS   29 Pilot Street, Hartlepool
George BORTHWICK   19 Cleveland Road, Hartlepool
Matthew BORTHWICK
R. BORTHWICK
R. BOULT
H.W. BOULTON   Moorside, Hartlepool
John G. BOUMPHREY   55 Furness Street, Hartlepool
Joseph BOUSEFIELD
William H. BOWER   14 Dyke Street, Hartlepool
William E. BOWES   20 Mary Street, Hartlepool
James A. BOWLT   102 Cumberland Street, Hartlepool
Thomas BOWLT
T.S. BOWLT
Arthur E. BOWMAN   1 Grosvenor Street, Hartlepool
James A. BOWMAN
William H. BOYCE
Alex C. BOYD
James BOYD   4 William Street, Hartlepool
John BOYLAN   53 Burbank Street, Hartlepool
James O. BOYLE
Albert E. BRADLEY   24 Gainford Street, Hartlepool
James BRADLEY
Joseph BRADLEY   35 Howard Street, Hartlepool
Sydney BRADLEY   22 Church Row, Hartlepool
William BRADLEY
William BRADLEY   18 Back Harrison Street, Hartlepool
Robert BRAITHWAITE   10 Harrow Street, Hartlepool
George BRATTIE
James BRENNAN
Thomas BREADSMORE   2 Water Street, Hartlepool
Walter BREWARD   6 Adelaide Street, Hartlepool
Robert W. BRIGHTON   14 Blaydon Street, Hartlepool
James H. BRISCOE   19 Seamer Street, Hartlepool

J.J. BROADHEAD	102 Hart Road, Hartlepool
Edward P. BROGAN	216 York Road, Hartlepool
Thomas J. BROGAN	216 York Road, Hartlepool
J.J. BROOM	3 Stainton Street, Hartlepool
John T. BROOM	7 Alfred Street, Hartlepool
William BROOM	13 Hermit Street, Hartlepool
Bert BROUGHTON	
Edward BROWN	35 Plevna Street, Hartlepool
Edward BROWN	Northumberland Street, Hartlepool
George W. BROWN	42 Scarborough Street, Hartlepool
Henry W. BROWN	
Jacob BROWN	
James E. BROWN	21 Frederick Street, Hartlepool
James L. BROWN	Hart Road, Hartlepool
John BROWN	
Joseph BROWN	98 Northumberland Street, Hartlepool
J.C. BROWN	12 Victoria Place, Hartlepool
J.W.H. BROWN	5 Slater Street, Hartlepool
Thomas W. BROWN	Temperance Street, Hartlepool
Tom BROWN	
Walter BROWN	Longdale, Westbourne Road, Hartlepool
Walters Brown	
William H. BROWN	4 Lancelot Street, Hartlepool
Tom BROWNING	50 Hurworth, Hartlepool
James BRUCE	24 Northumberland Street, Hartlepool
Herbert BRUCE	36 Durham Street, West Hartlepool
Robert W BRUCE	
Jack BRUNTON	
Robert BRYAN	26 Faulder Road, Hartlepool
James Ormiston BRYSON	25 Hart Street, Hartlepool
Walter Thomas BUCHAN	36 Alfred Street, Hartlepool
Sydney BUCKLEY	92 Murray Street, Hartlepool
Tom BULMAN	
John BULMER	
Herbert BULMER	
James M. BUNKALL	39 Archer Street, Hartlepool
Charles F. BURC	9 Lumley Square, Hartlepool
Walter R. BURDON	16 Marlborough Street, Hartlepool
James BURKE	16 Mainforth Terrace, Hartlepool

John BURKE	24 Richmond Street, Hartlepool
Rupert BURKE	17 Corporation Road, Hartlepool
Frederick J. BURN	10 Bengal Street, Hartlepool
Henry BURN	
Ernest BURNHAM	21 Rossall Street, Hartlepool
Norman BURNHAM	121 Studley Road, Hartlepool
Thomas BURNS	25 St John Street, Hartlepool
Joseph BURNS	8 Bedford Street, Hartlepool
Peter BURNS	201 York Road, Hartlepool
Matthew BURRELL	4 Burbank Street, Hartlepool
Thomas BURRELL	15 Laurence Street, Hartlepool
Harold BURROUGHS	29 Gas Street, Hartlepool
Robert BURTON	32 Stockton Street, Hartlepool
Robert BURTON	61 Cumberland Street, Hartlepool
H.G. BURTON	16 Stockton Street, Hartlepool
Septimus BUSBY	
Samuel BUSFIELD	71 Alma Street, Hartlepool
G. BUTCHER	3 Lily Street, Hartlepool
James W. BUTCHER	1 Laurence Street, Hartlepool
Edward BUTLER	62 High Street, Hartlepool
George W. BUTLER	60 Frederick Street, Hartlepool
Harry BUTLER	11 John Street, Hartlepool
Thomas BUTLER	14 Bangor Street, Hartlepool
James BUTTERY	
Thomas BUTTERY	4 Rugby Terrace, Hartlepool
Thomas H. BUTTERY	
Samuel L. BUXTON	
Richard B. CABLE	8 Lamb Street, Hartlepool
Thomas CADEN	4 Conyers Street, Hartlepool
Henry CAIRNS	17 Charles Street, Hartlepool
Edward H. CALDERWOOD	10 Bower Street, Hartlepool
Jonathan CALVERT	44 Frederick Street, Hartlepool
Reuben G. CALVERT	35 Everett Street, Hartlepool
Leslie CAMBRIDGE	Sunnyside, Stockton Road, Hartlepool
Malcolm CAMERON	31 Waldon Street, Hartlepool
A. CAMMILL	
Peter CANNON	
Harold CAPPLEMAN	Scarborough Street, Hartlepool
William H. CAREY	46 Burbank Street, Hartlepool

Frank CARLIN

Harold CARLING — 19 Charles Street, Hartlepool

J .CARLING

Jonathan CARPENTER — 5 Union Place, West Hartlepool

Bernard CARR — 18 Albany Street, Hartlepool

Edward CARR

Julian CARR

Thomas CARR — 56 Wilson Street, Hartlepool

Arthur CARRIGAN — 16 Stephenson Street, Hartlepool

Charles CARRIGAN — 24 Warren Terrace, Hartlepool

Frank CARROLL — 17 Pimlico Street, Hartlepool

John W. CARROLL — 9 Anthony Street, Hartlepool

Fred CARTER

George CARTER — 39 Burbank Street, Hartlepool

George W. CARTER — 6 Stephenson Street, Hartlepool

James CARTER

Victor CARTER — 17 Charlotte Street, Hartlepool

W.H. CARTER — 12 Brunswick Street, Hartlepool

John R. CARTWRIGHT — 19 Darlington Terrace, Hartlepool

Rowland T. CASEBOURNE

A.R. CASKIE — Brenda Street, Hartlepool

Henry CASS — 18 Leyburn Street, Hartlepool

Percy CASS

Richard J. CASS

Samuel CASSELL — 1 High Sarah Street, Hartlepool

Edward J. CATO

Harold CATRLING — 19 Charles Street, Hartlepool

Cuthbert CATTERSON — 9 Hanover Street, Hartlepool

Henry CAVE

Joseph CAWLEY — 16 Beacon Street, Hartlepool

Charles G. CHAMBERS

William CHAMBERS — 12 Havelock Street, Hartlepool

Wilfred CHAMBERS

Allison CHAPMAN — 47 Mainsforth Terrace, Hartlepool

George CHAPMAN — 32 Catherine Street, Hartlepool

John CHAPMAN — 33 Hill Street, Hartlepool

Albert CHAPPELL — 33 Briar Street, Hartlepool

William CHAPPLE

J.W. CHARLES

A.C. CHARLTON   Northgate, Hartlepool
Louis CHARLTON   The Green, Seaton Carew
William CHARLTON   Bank House, Victoria Road, Hartlepool
Stephen H. CHENEY
Henry CHERRY   22 Darlington Terrace, Hartlepool
Frank D. CHESNEY   Sheriff Street, Hartlepool
William CHESSMAN   35 William Street, Hartlepool
William J.M. CHILD   27 Grosvenor Street, Hartlepool
Carl CHRISTENSEN
James E CHRISTISON   19 Hope Street, Hartlepool
J.W. CHRISTON   Alma Hotel, Hartlepool
John R. CHRISTOPHER   Cornwall Street, Hartlepool
Charles CLARE   63 Tower Street, Hartlepool
Edward T. CLARK
Frederick J. CLARK
George CLARK
J. CLARK   94 Northgate, Hartlepool
John A. CLARK   9 Walworth Terrace, Park Road, Hartlepool
Peter CLARK   19 Jersey Street, Hartlepool
Robert P. CLARK   7 Collingwood Road, Hartlepool
Thomas CLARK
Charles S. CLARKE   47 Sheriff Street, Hartlepool
Frederick J. CLARKE   3 Mildred Street, Hartlepool
George CLARKE   23 Briar Street, Hartlepool
John CLARKE   53 Pilgrim Street, Hartlepool
John E. CLARKE   5 Jesmond Gardens, Hartlepool
W.D. CLARKE   18 Lister Street, Hartlepool
D. CLEARY   Hart Street, Hartlepool
Robert R. CLEMENTS
Sidney CLEMENTS   29 Grayson Street, Hartlepool
R.S. CLEMENTSON   Harpey House, Russell Street, Hartlepool
R.H. CLEMITSON
Andrew L. CLOSE   49 Frederick Street, Hartlepool
Alfred COATES   27 Russell Street, Hartlepool
G.W. COATES   17 Studley Road, Hartlepool
John R. COCHRANE   38 Burbank Street, Hartlepool
Arthur COCKERILL
John COCKRILL   16 Freeman Street, Hartlepool
George COCKRILL   19 Stainton Street, Hartlepool

George H. COCKROFT	19 Marlborough Street, Hartlepool
Richard COLE	5 Tennant Street, Hartlepool
Matthew R. COLEMAN	104 Burbank Street, Hartlepool
T.W. COLEMAN	
A.W. COLLINWOOD	21 Snook Cottage. Seaton Carew
George COLLINS	14 Harrison Street, Hartlepool
Frederick COLLINS	4 Dover Street, Hartlepool
Harry COLLINS	39 Sheriff Street, Hartlepool
James COLLINS	44 Bramley Street, Hartlepool
Adamson COLTMAN	23 Osborne Road, Hartlepool
Thomas COLTMAN	
Harry CONLON	53 Grace Street, Hartlepool
Charles CONNELL	27 Durham Street, Hartlepool
A. CONNELLY	37 Rokeby Street, Hartlepool
Owen CONNELLY	14 Mozart Street, Hartlepool
Charles W. CONNON	27 Albert Street, Hartlepool
John W. CONNOR	
John CONWAY	11 Rowell Street, Hartlepool
William CONWAY	6 Well Street, Hartlepool
Henry W. COOK	
John COOK	139 Durham Street, Hartlepool
Walter COOMER	20 Marmion Road, Hartlepool
James COONEY	3 Garibaldi Street, Hartlepool
Ernest COOPER	21 South Casebourne Road, Hartlepool
John L. COOPER	33 Wood Street, Hartlepool
T. COOPER	
William COOPER	21 South Casebourne Road, Hartlepool
William COPELAND	38 Eden Street, Hartlepool
Alfred COPEMAN	40 Helmsley Street, Hartlepool
John W CORBETT	5 Windsor Street, Hartlepool
Robert CORBETT	
Joseph C. CORK	10 Henry Street, Hartlepool
Thomas W. CORNER	18 Moreland Street, Hartlepool
Thomas R. CORNLEY	69 Everard Street, Hartlepool
Thomas COSTELLO	48 Longmore Street, Hartlepool
Harry COTSON	8 Winter Street, Hartlepool
Charles COULSON	38 Milton Road, Hartlepool
John COULSON	25 Dover Street, West Hartlepool
Robert COULSON	61 Thornhill Gardens, Hartlepool

Frank COULTAS	Sheriff Street, Hartlepool
William COULTAS	60 Watson Street, Hartlepool
Arthur COVERDALE	22 Alma Street, Hartlepool
Ernest COVERDALE	4 Harbour Terrace, Hartlepool
Herbert COVERDALE	4 Mary Street, Hartlepool
Robert COVERDALE	70 Lister Street, Hartlepool
Robert COVERDALE	30 Eton Street, Hartlepool
Thomas COWAM	
Walker W. COWARD	18 Arch Street, Hartlepool
John J. COWLEY	7 Lee Place, Hartlepool
William COWLING	5 Ridley Street, Hartlepool
George COWTAM	31 Alfred Street, Hartlepool
Valentine COWTON	21 Adelaide Street, Hartlepool
Robert H. COX	10 Penrhyn Street, Hartlepool
John COXON	17 Beacon Street, Hartlepool
William COYLE	1 Lumley Square, Hartlepool
John R. CRAGGS	9 Park Street, Hartlepool
William CRAGGS	10 Queen Street, Hartlepool
Alex B. CRAWFORD	14 Roker Street, Hartlepool
Duncan B. CRAWFORD	14 Roker Street, Hartlepool
James CRILLEY	24 Ashburn Street, Seaton Carew
Joseph CROOKS	
Ernest CROSBY	16 Angus Street, Hartlepool
J. CROSBY	
John M. CROSBY	Hutton Avenue, Hartlepool
J.C. CROSSING	6 Warden Street, Hartlepool
James CROSSMAN	5 Houghton Street, Hartlepool
Sidney CROSTHWAITE	79 Cornwall Street, Hartlepool
John Thomas CROWTHER	
J.B. CUBEY	59 Arncliffe Gardens, Hartlepool
Valentine CUMMINS	35 Collingwood Road, Hartlepool
S.L. CUNNINGHAM	
William J. CUTTER	16 Wilson Street, Hartlepool
Ebenezer DABBS	86 Durham Street, Hartlepool
James W. DALE	21 Grace Street, Hartlepool
Joseph T. DALE	28 Southburn Terrace, Hartlepool
John DALKIN	26 Lansdowne Road, Hartlepool
Robert DALKIN	20 Alliance Street, Hartlepool
John W. DALTON	

James DARLING	31 Studley Road, Hartlepool
Robert DARLING (MC)	
William H. DARNELL	37 Slater Street, Hartlepool
Charles W. DAVIDSON	23 Bertha Street, Hartlepool
Hugh D. DAVIDSON	13 Raby Street, Hartlepool
James W. DAVIDSON	17 Barnard Street, Hartlepool
T.O. DAVIDSON	24 Streatham Street, Hartlepool
Vivian T. DAVIDSON	24 Streatham Street, Hartlepool
F. DAVIES	24 Hereford Street, Hartlepool
Frank DAVIES	
Joseph DAVIES	
Thomas DAVIES	
John DAVIS	
Albert DAVISON	
Benjamin DAVISON	5 York Place, Hartlepool
Edward DAVISON	11 Thomas Street, Hartlepool
George E. DAVISON	18 Chapel Street, Hartlepool
J. DAVISON	
J.T. DAVISON	
Mark DAVISON	12 Croft Street, Hartlepool
R.W. DAVISON	
William DAVISON	Burdons Court, Hartlepool
Harry DAWSON	42 Plevna Street, Hartlepool
Victor DAY	23 Albert Street, Hartlepool
Frederick G. DEARLOVE	47 Brenda Street, Hartlepool
Joseph DEIGHTON	20 Cromwell Street, Hartlepool
John W. DENNIS	54 Northumberland Street, Hartlepool
John W. DENNIS	26 Mozart Street, Hartlepool
William E. DENNISON	8 Albany Street, Hartlepool
Charles DESBOROUGH	21 Dundas Street, Hartlepool
Frederick DESBOROUGH	21 Dundas Street, Hartlepool
Herbert DESBOROUGH	45 South Parade, Hartlepool
Cornelius DEVINE	96 Burbank Street, Hartlepool
John DICKINSON	57 Charlotte Street, Hartlepool
James H. DICKSON	6 Leeds Street, Hartlepool
Albert H. DINSDALE	34 Reed Street, Hartlepool
Percy DINSDALE	20 Reed Street, Hartlepool
Thomas DINSDALE	3 Kenilworth Street, Hartlepool
Charles DIX	

Arthur E. DIXON	34 Durham Street, Hartlepool
Frank DIXON	11 Union Place, Hartlpool
H. DIXON	
Harold P. DIXON	75 Milton Road, Hartlepool
Joseph DIXON	13 William Street, Hartlepool
Thomas DIXON	9 Raby Street, Hartlepool
Willie DIXON	31 Topcliffe Street, Hartlepool
William R DOBSON (MM)	62 Rodney Street, Hartlepool
Harry DOCHERTY	Crown Inn, Hartlepool
Frederick DODD	2 Andrew Court, Hartlepool
James H. DODD	
Edmund DODGSON	
John W. DOLMAN	9 Mill Street, Hartlepool
William DOLPHIN	30 Ramsey Street, Hartlepool
Robert DONACHIE	14 Derwent Street, Hartlepool
Robert S. DONAGHEY	4 Howbeck Terrace, Hartlepool
Victor DONCASTER	58 Derwent Street, Hartlepool
John G. DONKIN	1 Sandside, Hartlepool
John J. DONLEY	1 Carlisle Place, Street, Hartlepool
William S. DONLEY	17 South Street, Hartlepool
William DONNISON	54 Beechwood Road, Hartlepool
John W. DOTMAN	9 Mill Street, Hartlepool
Arthur DOUGLAS	57 Grace Street, Hartlepool
John J. DOUGLAS	37 Sunderland Street, Hartlepool
Thomas DOUGLAS	28 Briar Street, Hartlepool
Roland DOVASTON	14 Cameron Road, Hartlepool
DOVE	15 Plevna Street, Hartlepool
T.J. DOWNES	
Mark K. DOWNES	15 Rugby Terrace, Hartlepool
S.J. DOWNES	
George A. DOWNING	21 Leyburn Street, Hartlepool
Harry T. DRAPER	
Frederick DREW	
Joseph DREW	46 Cameron Road, Hartlepool
Phillip DRYBURG	30 Percy Street, Hartlepool
Frank DUFFY	18 Back George Street, Hartlepool
James DUFFY	5 Winter Street, Hartlepool
T. DUFFY	95 High Street, Hartlepool
Hurbert DUNBAVAND	25 Hutton Avenue, Hartlepool

W.H. DUNCAN	36 Perth Street, Hartlepool
Alfred DUNN	37 Stephen Street, Hartlepool
Frederick DUNN	
Laurence DUNN	5 Seamer Street, Hartlepool
Joseph W. DUTHIE	27 William Street, Hartlepool
Horace DYER	115 Thornton Street, Hartlepool
Thomas DYER	
Walter DYER	115 Thornton Street, Hartlepool
William EDE	23 Freeman Street, Hartlepool
John C. EASBY	50 South Parade, Street, Hartlepool
H.W. EASBY	
W. EBDEN	
William EBB	
Tom EDMENSON	66 Florence Street, Hartlepool
Percy EDMUNDSON	5 Bright Street, Hartlepool
Edward EGGLESTONE	20 Bentley Street, Hartlepool
Joseph ELDER	25 Brunswick Street, Hartlepool
W ELENER	10 Norfolk Street, Hartlepool
William R. ELEY	66 Brougham Street, Hartlepool
John H. ELLERKER	
T. ELLIOTT	
George ELLISON	48 Moreland Street, Hartlepool
John R. ELSTOBB	74 Mainsforth Terrace, Hartlepool
Edward ELVIDGE	8 Warwick Place, Hartlepool
Arthur ELWIN	11 Hutton Street, Hartlepool
Alfred T. EMMERSON	
Mark EMMERSON	
Stanley EMERSON	20 Caroline Street, Hartlepool
T.R. EMERY	
Frederick ENGLISH	
James C. ENGLISH	
Wilfred ENGLISH	Burbank Street, Hartlepool
Tom ETHERINGTON	30 Topcliffe Street, Hartlepool
Frederick EVANS	13 Caroline Street, Hartlepool
Arthur FAIREY	3 Derwent Street, Hartlepool
George FAIRLEY	149 Alma Street, Hartlepool
Thomas E. FALKINGHAM	11 Jackson Street, Hartlepool
Frederick Charles FARMER	
Ernest FARNSWORTH	51 Wilson Street, Hartlepool

Joseph H.T. FARROW   5 Friar Terrace, Hartlepool
John W. FAWCETT
Ernest V. FEATHERSTONE   93 Stockton Road, Hartlepool
C.P. FELTHAM   27 Alfred Street, Hartlepool
Joseph FENNELLY   29 Tweed Street, Hartlepool
Jack FENTON
Charles FENWICK   14 Tower Street, Hartlepool
William FENWICK   14b Tower Street, Hartlepool
Ralph FERGUS   95 Dent Street, Hartlepool
Harry FERGUSON
John A. FERGUSON   27 Faulder Road, Hartlepool
Michael FERGUSON   38 Dene Street, Hartlepool
James FERRIS   15 Brook Street, Hartlepool
Joseph FIELDHOUSE   43 Gill Street, Hartlepool
John H. FILBY   16 Hawkride Street, Hartlepool
Luke FINCKEN   Blandford Street, Hartlepool
Joseph E.E. FLEETHAM   9 Dyke Street, Hartlepool
Thomas FLEMMING
Frank FLETCHER
Stanley FLETCHER   86 Scarborough Street, Hartlepool
Harry FLEWKER   3 Sheriff Street, Hartlepool
J.S .FLINTOFT
Robert FLUTE   9 Bolton Street, Hartlepool
James FORCER   73 Hermit Street, Hartlepool
Percy FORCER   23 Freeman Street, Hartlepool
Arthur L. FORD   Grovehurst, West Hartlepool
George FORDHAM   15 Baden Street, Hartlepool
Ernest FORREST
Arthur FORRESTER
James FORSYTH   6 William Street, Hartlepool
George FORTUNE   6 Wilson Street, Hartlepool
Stanley W. FORTUNE
Thomas P. FOSTER   53 Northumberland Street, Hartlepool
Tom FOSTER
Percy W. FOSTER   138 Colwyn Road, Hartlepool
William FOSTER   97 High Street, Hartlepool
Herbert FOTHERGILL
Fred FOWLER   1 Alice Street, Hartlepool
Richard W. FOWLER   1 Grace Street, Hartlepool

William FOWLER	6 Park Street, Hartlepool
Andrew S. FOX	14 Anson Street, Hartlepool
John FOX	4 Kenilworth Street, Hartlepool
Thomas H. FOX	22 Freville Street, Hartlepool
Anthony FRAIN	55 Alfred Street, Hartlepool
William FRAIN	51 Arch Street, Hartlepool
Ernest A. FRANK	
John G. FRANK	39 Water Street, Hartlepool
Ernest FRANKLAND	
Herbert K. FRANKLAND	
John P. FRANKLAND	27 Collingwood, Road, Hartlepool
Percy J. FRANKLAND	57 Collingwood Road, Street, Hartlepool
R.E. FRANKLAND	135 Burbank Walk, Hartlepool
R.D. FRASER	67 Grange Road, Hartlepool
Thomas E. FRETWELL	17 Marmion Road, Hartlepool
Harry FRIER	1 Powlett Street, Hartlepool
George S. FULLER	
Robert FULLER	
Henry FURLONGER	
R. FURLONGER	19 Bramley Street, Hartlepool
Robert GAIETY	18 Frederick Street, Hartlepool
Matthew GALES	27 Mosley Street, Hartlepool
R.H. GALES	
J.C.F. GAMBLE	14 Adelaide Street, Hartlepool
William J. GAMBLE	14 Adelaide Street, Hartlepool
John GARBUTT	47 Cambridge Street, Hartlepool
Mark GARBUTT	
Tom GARBUTT	11 Cleveland Road, Hartlepool
Arnold GARCIA	
Charles GARDNER	8 Everett Street, Hartlepool
David GARDINER	3 Slater Street, Hartlepool
Matthew GARDNER	2 Greatham Street, Hartlepool
Matthew GARDNER	8 Briar Street, Hartlepool
George W. GARGETT	
James GARLAND	
John GARLAND	
James GARRETT	
Philip GARRINGTON	
Tiplady GARTHWAITE	32 Belk Street, Hartlepool

John GATENBY	80 Studley Road, Hartlepool
Arthur F. GAYFORD	42 Thomas Street, Hartlepool
Hamilton GEDDES	7 Tower Terrace, Hartlepool
John W. GEDDES	21 Burbank Street, Hartlepool
William GEIPEL	Scarborough Street, Hartlepool
Valentine GENT	47 Caroline Street, Hartlepool
Frederick J. GEORGE	11 Slater Street, Hartlepool
Antonie GERALDIE	8 Warwick Place, Hartlepool
William GIBBIN	27 Alice Street, Hartlepool
John GIBBS	27 Baden Street, Hartlepool
Fred I. GIBSON	138 Lynn Street, Hartlepool
James GIBSON	7 Frederic Street, Hartlepool
J.W. GIBSON	34 Hermit Street, Hartlepool
Samuel T. GIBSON	
Gordon GILCHRIST	17 Croft Terrace, Hartlepool
Thomas GILFOYLE	
Ralph GILL	3 Derby Street, Hartlepool
Joseph GILLON	44 Coleridge Avenue, Hartlepool
J.W. GILLESPIE	28 Baden Street, Hartlepool
John S. GILLIES	
William GILLIES	
John GILMARTIN	26 Union Road, Hartlepool
Joseph GILMORE	24 Robinson Street, Hartlepool
William GLEESON	9 Ridley Street, Hartlepool
William GLEN	16 Angus Street, Hartlepool
John E. GLENN	29 Catherine Street, Hartlepool
George GLENNIE	40 Lancelot Street, Hartlepool
Thomas GLENNIE	
John GODDARD	73 Pilgrim Street, Hartlepool
John E. GOLDSBROUGH	14 Harrow Street, Hartlepool
James GOLLAGLEE	31 Reed Street, Hartlepool
John D. GOODE	19 Carr Street, Hartlepool
Charles E. GOODING	14 Thornton Street, Hartlepool
Thomas N. GOODWIN	20 Charles Street, Hartlepool
Walter M. GORDON	112 Northgate Hartlepool
John GORRIE	
Sidney G. GOUGH	35 Rokeby Street, Hartlepool
George H. GOULD (MM)	13 Kimberley Street, Hartlepool
John E. GOULDSBROUGH	35 Vincent Street, Hartlepool

William R. GOWEN	Durham Street, Hartlepool
Thomas GOWLAND	
W.H. GOWLER	24 Crossley Street, Harlepool
George GRAHAM	5 Clyde Terrace, Hartlepool
Robert GRAHAM	
John T. GRANGER	
Edward GRANT	
William GRAVES	64 Pilgrim Street, Hartlepool
James GRAY	38 Dene Street, Hartlepool
Samuel Charles GRAY	25 Rokeby Street, Hartlepool
Thomas W. GRAY	51 Everard Street, Hartlepool
William E GRAYLEY (DCM)	15 Carr Street, Hartlepool
Clarence R. GREATHEAD	
Herbert GREEN	16 Lilley Street, Hartlepool
Walter GREEN	33 Southburn Terrace, Hartlepool
Howard GREENLEES	20 York Road, Hartlepool
Henry GREENWELL	11 South Redworth Street, Hartlepool
Herbert H. GREENWELL	7 Streatham Street, Hartlepool
Percy GREIG	20 Johnson Street, Hartlepool
James E. GREY	
John GREY	17 Thomas Street, Hartlepool
Henry GRIFFITHS	
John H. GROVES	
Thomas GROVES	41 Ouston Street, Hartlepool
Thomas G. GROVES	
William GROVES	
Cecil R. GUTHE	
Thomas P. GUTHE	
Ernest GUTRIDGE	85 Northumberland Street, Hartlepool
George GUTRIDGE	87 Elwick Road, Hartlepool
Robert GUY	30 Mozart Street, Hartlepool
Carl A. GYLLENSPETZ	4 Wesley Street, Hartlepool
Ernest HADFIELD	71 Burbank Street, Hartlepool
John T. HADFIELD	
Christopher F.S. HAILS	
Bert HALL	47 Arch Street, Hartlepool
Bertram HALL	1 Derwent Street, Hartlepool
Charles HALL	
David HALL	

George HALL	2 Freeman Street, Hartlepool
John E. HALL	
John W. HALL	40 Marmion Road, Hartlepool
R. HALL	10 Frances Street, Hartlepool
Thomas HALL	29 Colenso Street, Hartlepool
Thomas Λ. HALL	1 Station Cottage, Street, Hartlepool
Thomas W. HALL	16 Osborne Road, Hartlepool
William HALL	
William E. HALL	18 Freeman Street, Hartlepool
David HAMER	13 Windermere Road, Hartlepool
Arthur HAMILTON	
A. HAMMILL	
E .HANCOCK	3 Hope Street, Hartlepool
William HAND	
Bert HANDISIDES	
Robert HANDLEY	20 George Street, Hartlepool
Albert HANSEN	
John J. HANSOM	25 Pelham Street, Hartlepool
Joseph HARDCASTLE	
Frederick W. HARDY	
George H. HARDY	Gainford Street, Hartlepool
C. HARGREAVES	
John HARKER	
Tom HARKER	
John HARLAND	
William HARNETT	19 George Street, Hartlepool
Harry HARPER	100 Burbank Street, Hartlepool
Thomas HARPER	
William HARPER	115 Whitby Street, Hartlepool
Jabez HARRIMAN	11 Rokeby Street, Hartlepool
Dennis HARRINGTON	3 High Sarah Street, Hartlepool
Joseph HARRIS	2 Mozart Street, Hartlepool
Alfred A. HARRISON	
Benjamin J.G. HARRISON	21 Seamer Street, Hartlepool
Charles H. HARRISON	19 Albany Street, Hartlepool
Ernest M. HARRISON	
George R. HARRISON	Red Lion Farm, Elwick, Hartlepool
Herbert F. HARRISON	54 Studley Road, Hartlepool
H.G. HARRISON	

James HARRISON
Robert W. HARRISON
Thomas R. HARRISON   12 Smith Street, Hartlepool
Will HARRISON
William HARRISON   30 Freeman Street, Hartlepool
William E. HARRISON   39 Bailey Street, Hartlepool
George HART   16 Scarborough Street, Hartlepool
John H. HART
William J. HART   42 Bailey Street, Hartlepool
John E. HARTLAND   27 Middlegate, Hartlepool
C.E. HARTLEY   4 Burbank Street, Hartlepool
Sam HARTLEY
Charles N. HARVEY
James HARVEY   Winter Street, Hartlepool
George HARWOOD
Edward HASKER   11 Yorks Street, Hartlepool
Matthew HASTINGS   17 Wells Yard, Hartlepool
William HATCH   4 Alma Street, Hartlepool
Bruce HAUXWELL   21 Grosvenor Street, Hartlepool
Stanley HAUXWELL
Cecil S. HAWKINS
Thomas H. HAYLOCK
Bertie J. HAYWOOD   39 Derwent Street, Hartlepool
Herbert G. HAYWOOD   5 Acclom Street, Hartlepool
Joseph HAZLEWOOD   18 Grace Street, Hartlepool
Edward HEAL   1 Beaumont Street, Hartlepool
John H. HEATH   69 Brenda Street, Hartlepool
John HEDLEY   19 Gas Street, Hartlepool
Richard HEGARTY   4 Longmore Street, Hartlepool
Ellis J. HENDERSON   25 Grosvenor Street, Hartlepool
George HENDERSON
John H. HENDERSON   15 Grosvenor Street, Hartlepool
Joseph HENDERSON
Robert HENDERSON
John HEPBURN
Ralph HEPPLEWHITE
James H. HERBERT
John G. HERBERT   18 Bedford Street, Hartlepool
Thomas HERBERT

John HERON
Robert HERON
Robert HERRING
John E. HESELTINE   5 Eamont Gardens, West Hartlepool
George R. HESELTON   30 York Road, Hartlepool
John W. HESLOP
Jackie K.M. HESSLER
Jacob A.N. HESSLER
John J. HESTER   46 Turnbull Street, Hartlepool
Robert HEWESON   68 Blandford Street, Hartlepool
George H. HEWITSON   30 Vincent House, Hartlepool
John HEWITSON
William HEWITSON   32 Stephen Street, Hartlepool
F. HEWITT
Charles HIGGINS   7 Chester Road, Hartlepool
J.E. HILDRICK   6 Bond Street Hartlepool
John T. HILL   6 Gordon Street, Hartlepool
William HILL
Francis G. HODGSON   8 Regents Place, Hartlepool
Frank HODGSON   37 Angus Street, Hartlepool
John HODGSON   20 Oxford Street, Hartlepool
John R. HODGSON
Jonathan HODGSON   28 Colenso Street, Hartlepool
Joseph W. HODGSON   48 Lowthian Road, Hartlepool
Philip HODGSON   1 Harrison Street, Hartlepool
Thomas HODGSON   3 Pease Street, Hartlepool
William HODGSON   36 Baden Street, Hartlepool
David M. HOEY
James P. HOEY   9 Cleveland Road, Hartlepool
John HOGAN   25 Blake Street, Hartlepool
James S. HOGARTH   19 Henry Street, Hartlepool
Andrew HOGG   23 Albert Street, Hartlepool
Martin HOGG   6 Raeburn Street, Hartlepool
Harry HOLBORN   27 Northumberland Street, Hartlepool
Raymond HOLBURN
Alderman O. HOLDEN   66 Grosvenor Street, Hartlepool
Barton G. HOLDFORTH   8 Gill Street, Hartlepool
Thomas HOLLENDER
Henry HOLMES   70 Burbank Street, Hartlepool

James HOLMES	92 Sandringham Road, Hartlepool
Samuel HOLMES	4 Bath Passage, High Street, Hartlepool
Isaac W HOLROYD	28 Sheriff Street, Hartlepool
Joseph HOLROYD	12 St Oswalds Terrace, Hartlepool
T. HOLROYD	
R.W H. HOOPER	
Jerry HOPE	19 Olive Street, Hartlepool
William HOPE	14 Melrose Street, Hartlepool
Frank HOPPS	34 Thorpville, Granville Avenue, Hartlepool
John F.H. HOPPS	Howbeck House, West Hartlepool
G.H. HORNSEY	7 Bramley Street, Hartlepool
Charles H. HORSEMAN	
John HORSLEY	
J.E. HORSLEY	3 Blaydon Street, Hartlepool
J.W. HORSLEY	15 Clayton Street, Hartlepool
John W. HORSPOLE	45 Everard Street, Hartlepool
Albert B. HORSWELL	
George N.W. HOTHAM	Sydenham Road, Hartlepool
R.D. HOUSE	31 George Street, Hartlepool
John HOWE	14 Wards Terrace, Hartlepool
David J. HOWELLS	6 Sarah Street, Hartlepool
Robert D. HOWSE	
J.R. HUDSON	
Thomas HUDSON	7 Lilly Street, Hartlepool
Michael T. HUGHES	51 High Sarah Street, Hartlepool
Peter HUGHES	51 High Sarah Street, Hartlepool
Leo J. HUGILL	
Harry HUMPHREY	
Taylor HUMPHREY	47 Collingwood Road, Hartlepool
J.W. HUNT	
Frederick G. HUNTER	Queen Street, Hartlepool
George F. HUNTER	36 Thirlmere Street, Hartlepool
John HUNTER	1 Sheriff Street, Hartlepool
John E. HUNTER	11 Albion Terrace, Hartlepool
Walter HUNTER	
James L. HUNTLEY	17 Cromwell Street, Hartlepool
Joseph HUNTON	
Frank H. HURWORTH	Granville Avenue, Hartlepool

Henry S. HURWORTH
John J. HUSBAND   28 Mainsforth Terrace, Hartlepool
James N. HUSSEY
Alfred HUTCHINSON
Arnold HUTCHINSON   1 Thornville Road, Hartlepool
Bert HUTCHINSON   45 Turnbull Street, Hartlepool
Herbert HUTCHINSON   11 Turnbull Street, Hartlepool
John HUTCHINSON   28 Casebourne Road, Hartlepool
Thomas HUTCHINSON   14 Stranton Green, Hartlepool
Robert HUTLEY
Harold HUTSON
Oswald HUTTON   55 Brougham Terrace, Hartlepool
Arthur HYDE   9 Oakley Gardens, Hartlepool
Henry M. HYDE   40 Winter Street, Hartlepool
Albert G. ILDERTON
John INGLE
John H. INGRAM   16 Brook Street, Hartlepool
Harry INGRIM
Luke B. IRVIN
Chas K. IRVINE
Malcolm JACK   145 Alma Street, Hartlepool
Albert W JACKSON   11 Trimdon Street, Hartlepool
E.W. JACKSON   32 Moor Street, Hartlepool
Frank JACKSON   59 Ouston Street, Hartlepool
Frederick JACKSON   52 Angus Street, Hartlepool
Henry JACKSON   8 Watt Street, Hartlepool
Herbert W. JACKSON   30 Percy Street, Hartlepool
John R. JACKSON   1 Grace Street, Hartlepool
J.W. JACKSON
Thomas JACKSON   84 Stephen Street, Hartlepool
William L. JACQUES   13 Middleton Road, Hartlepool
Bertram JAMES   30 Park Street, Hartlepool
David W. JAMES   5 Claydon Street, Hartlepool
Thomas R. JAMES   44 Wensleydale Street, Hartlepool
Charles JARMAN   71 Wansbeck Gardens, Hartlepool
Walter JARMAN   71 Wansbeck Gardens, Hartlepool
Reginald S. JARRETT   36 Warden Street, Hartlepool
R. JAYES   1 Colenso Street, Hartlepool
George T. JEFFERSON   21 Kimberley Street, Hartlepool

Thomas H. JEFFERSON	19 Dover Street, Hartlepool
Frederick JEFFRIES	
William JEFFRIES	9 Albion Street, Hartlepool
Christopher J. JELLY	84 High Street, Hartlepool
F.M. JENISON	10 Jackson Street, Hartlepool
Bertram H. JENKINS	Brooklands Hutton Ave, Hartlepool
David JENKINS	42 Longmore Street, Hartlepool
John JENKINS	
Matthew JENKINS	51 Blake Street, Hartlepool
Herbert JENKINSON	12 Coverdale Street, Hartlepool
Matthew JENNINGS	5 Friar Street, Hartlepool
Harry JENSON	10 Jackson Street, Hartlepool
Fred JOBLING	25 Derwent Street, Hartlepool
Harold JOBLING	38 Colenso Street, Hartlepool
Joseph W. JOBLING	68 Wansbeck Gardens, Hartlepool
Charles JOHNSON	3 Carlisle Place, Hartlepool
Charlie JOHNSON	30 Whitburn Street, Hartlepool
Frank JOHNSON	59 Ouston Street, Hartlepool
Fred JOHNSON	
Joseph H. JOHNSON	27 Alexander Street, Hartlepool
Reginald C. JOHNSON	75 Chester Road, Hartlepool
Robert E. JOHNSON	20 Duke Street, Hartlepool
Thomas JOHNSON	14 Low Burbank Street, Hartlepool
Tom JOHNSON	
William JOHNSON	24 Andrew Street, Hartlepool
William JOHNSON	4 Wharton Terrace, Hartlepool
William T. JOHNSON	22 Furness Street, Hartlepool
Arthur JOLLY	
Alfred JONES	44 Ashgrove Avenue, Street, Hartlepool
Arthur JONES	4 Abbotsford Road, Hartlepool
Arthur JONES	19 Thomas Street, Hartlepool
Bertram JONES	
Ernest JONES	
Frederick JONES	14 Portland Street, Hartlepool
Herbert JONES (DCM)	44 Ashgrove Avenue, Hartlepool
James JONES	10 Thorne Street, Hartlepool
John JONES	20 Middlegate, Hartlepool
John I. JONES	48 Hill Street, Hartlepool
Joseph JONES	16 Bramley Street, Hartlepool

Matthew J. JONES	22 Albert Street, Hartlepool
Reuben JONES	4 Wensleydale Street, Hartlepool
Theo JONES	44 Ashgrove Ave, Hartlepool
Vivian G. JONES	
William JOWSEY	68 Collingwood Road, Hartlepool
John J. JOYCE	16 Ladysmith Street, Hartlepool
John W. JUDSON	28 Princess Street, Hartlepool
Jack KEADY	23 Straker Street, Hartlepool
Cuthbert KEAN	
Thomas KEEGAN	
Robert KEELEY	86 Burbank Street, Hartlepool
Thomas R. KEENAN	6 Lawrence Street, Hartlepool
Joseph KEELEY	
James KELLY	
James M. KELLY	
John KELLY	
Joseph P. KELLY	16 Wood Street, Hartlepool
Martin KELLY	1 Hill Street, Hartlepool
Samuel KELLY	18 Frederick Street, Hartlepool
Thomas F. KELLY	
Charles KELSEY	36 Benson Street, Hartlepool
George KENDALL	9 Mitchell Street, Hartlepool
Arthur KENMIRE	51 Grace Street, Hartlepool
Albert E. KENNEDY	
George H. KENT	
S.A. KIDDELL	14 Arthur Street, Hartlepool
James KILPATRICK	
Edward KILRAIN	2 Seamer Street, Hartlepool
E.W. KING	24 Angus Street, Hartlepool
John J. KING	4 Lawrence Street, Hartlepool
Robert KING	48 Stephenson Street, Hartlepool
William KING	31 Windsor Street, Hartlepool
William KING	26 Furness Street, Hartlepool
Joseph KINGSTON	45 Albert Street, Hartlepool
Robert KINGSTON	50 Lansdowne Road, Hartlepool
Will J KINGSTON	94 High Street, Hartlepool
A. KIRKBY	12 Sheriff Street, Hartlepool
James W. KIRTLEY	
Charles R. KITCHING	69 Brenda Street, Hartlepool

Miles KNIGHT	15 Sydney Street, Hartlepool
William KNOWLSON	5 Grace Street, Hartlepool
T. LAFFIN	
Robert LAIDLER	40 Colenso Street, Hartlepool
Thomas LAKE	Surtees Street, Hartlepool
William Robert LAKE	19 Moore Street, Hartlepool
Cecil LAMBERT	70 Clifton Avenue, Hartlepool
Thomas LAMBERT	
William LANCASTER	32 Claydon Street, Hartlepool
F. LANGDALE	18 Claydon Street, Hartlepool
Frank LARGE	
Alexander G. LARKIN	
John LARKIN	32 Stainton Street, Hartlepool
Peter LARKIN	39 Bramley Street, Hartlepool
Thomas M. LAUGHLIN	10 Exeter Street, Hartlepool
William LAURIE	57 Bramley Street, Hartlepool
George H. LAVERICK	100 Frederick Street, Hartlepool
George F. LAWN	28 Shrewsbury Street, Hartlepool
Fred LAWRENCE	30 Jersey Street, Hartlepool
Ralph Herbert LAWSON	
John LAYBOURN	Everard Street, Hartlepool
Andrew LAYDON	1 Thorne Street, Hartlepool
Albert LEACH	
William LEADLEY	45 Durham Street, Hartlepool
James L. LEAVEN	Angus Street, Hartlepool
D'Arcy LEE	18 Back Lumley Street, Hartlepool
Edward W. LEE	9 Blaydon Street, Hartlepool
George R. LEE	South Crescent, Hartlepool
Matthew H. LEE	17 Acclom Street, Hartlepool
Thomas W. LEE	43 Chester Road, Street, Hartlepool
Frederick G. LEEMING	35 Archer Street, Hartlepool
Sydney LEEMING	17 Lamb Street, Hartlepool
Michael LEHENEY	1 Johnson Square Hartlepool
Thomas LEMON	
Henry LEONARD	19 Mozart Street, Hartlepool
Stanley LEVELL	28 Keswick Street, Hartlepool
F. Patrick LEWIS	
George W. LEWIS	
Charles B. LINCOLN	

William T. LINDRIDGE	3 Bentick Street, Hartlepool
William L. LINDSAY	7A Oxford Street, Hartlepool
C.L. LINES	37 Baden Street, Hartlepool
Harry W. LINNEY	
George W. LION	40 Gainford Street, Hartlepool
Sam LIPMAN	
Curzon G. LITHGO	
Arthur LITTLE	17 Arch Street, Hartlepool
John LITTLEWOOD	4 Florence Street, Hartlepool
Donald LIVINGSTONE	2 Watt Street, Hartlepool
John H LOACH	4 Queen Street, Hartlepool
Harry LOCKEY	8 Charles Street, Hartlepool
John LOCKWOOD	172 Burbank Street, Hartlepool
Joseph V. LOMASNEY	14 Alderson Street, Hartlepool
Benjamin H. LONDON	
T.M. LONGMORE	37 Back Street, Hildas Cottages, Hartlepool
John R. LORD	16 Richmond Street, Hartlepool
Herbert LORDS	5 Hermit Street, Hartlepool
Edward LOUGHBOROUGH	29 Brougham Street, Hartlepool
Harry LOUIS	
Herbert LOVELL	15A Watt Street, Hartlepool
William J. LOWCOCK	
Herbert LOWE	18 Mary Street, Hartlepool
Thomas B. LOWE	28 Baden Street, Hartlepool
R.H. LOWE	28 Henry Street, Hartlepool
Thomas W. LOWES	
Alfred H LOWDEN	2 Elliott Street, Hartlepool
Thomas LOWERY	7 Middlegate Street, Hartlepool
Joseph H. LOWTHER	8 Charles Street, Hartlepool
George A. LUCAS	23 Cumberland Street, Hartlepool
Joseph LUCAS	41 Durham Street, Hartlepool
Thomas H. LUND	68 Burbank Street, Hartlepool
Benjamin LUPTON	35 Acclom Street, Hartlepool
Stephen LUPTON	27 Bond Street, Hartlepool
Francis LYNCH (CSM)	8 Beacon Street, Hartlepool
Frank W. LYNCH	15 Duke Street, Hartlepool
Gilbert E. LYNCH	
Henry LYNCH	1 Tees Street, Hartlepool
James LYNCH	13 Ladysmith Street, Hartlepool

John J. LYNN	33 Kilwick Street, Hartlepool
Harry LYTH	25 Prissick Street, Hartlepool
John LYTH	29 Baden Street, Hartlepool
Ian C MACFARLANE	20 Hutton Avenue, Hartlepool
T.P. MACK	
Angus M. MACKINTOSH	12 York Road, Hartlepool
Albert MACLEAN	15 Sarah Street, Hartlepool
John K. MADDISON	33 Brook Street, Hartlepool
John F. MADGE	8 Bridge Street, Hartlepool
James MAHER	33 Bramley Street, Hartlepool
John T. MALLABAR	5 Frances Street, Hartlepool
James MALONE	16 Cleveland Street, Hartlepool
Wardle MANKIN	
Thomas B. MANN	3 Harte Street, Hartlepool
C. MANSEN	36 Moreland Street, Hartlepool
William MARINE	9 Raby Street, Hartlepool
James F. MARKWELL	
J.B. MARLEY	16 Temperance Street, Hartlepool
Joseph MARR	
Charles MARSH	52 Reed Street, Hartlepool
Ernest MARTIN	95 Milton Road, Hartlepool
William MARTIN	
William J. MARTIN	
Robert MARTINDALE	23 Raby Road, Hartlepool
Ernest C. MASON	
Frank E. MASON	
Frederick MASON	18 Stockton Street, Hartlepool
George H. MASON	69 Northumberland Street, Hartlepool
Harry L. MASON	
Heseltine MASON	25 Mayfair Street, Hartlepool
John G. MASON	28 Jersey Street, Hartlepool
Richard MASON	36 Duke Street, Hartlepool
Samuel MASSAM	
Harold V. MASSEY	2 Laburnam Street, Hartlepool
J. Henry MASSEY	William Street, Hartlepool
George MATHER	1 Alfred Street, Hartlepool
James MATTERSON	24 Water Street, Hartlepool
James MATTHEWS	30 Rokeby Street, Hartlepool
John R.L. MATTHEWS	

Leslie MATTHEWS   16 Lowthian Road, Hartlepool
William MATTHEWS   209 Stockton Road, Hartlepool
Joseph MAUGHAN   5 South Casebourne Road, Hartlepool
Charles MAUNDER   23 Russell Street, Hartlepool
Victor MAUNDER
Jack MAWHINNEY   15 Gas Street, Hartlepool
Joseph MAWSON   18 Colenso Street, Hartlepool
Ernest MAYES   21 Watt Street, Hartlepool
Richard W. MAYES   26 Milton Street, Hartlepool
Francis E.H. MAYSON
Frank McANDREW
Patrick McANDREW   13 Bridge Street, Hartlepool
Richard McANDREW   13 Bridge Street, Hartlepool
Robert William McBAY   68 Pilgrim Street, Hartlepool
John W. McBEAN
Charles H. McCARTHY
Frederick B. McCARTHY   72 Suggitt Street, Hartlepool
Frederick C. McCARTHY
James McCARTHY   15 Hermit Street, Hartlepool
K. McCLEAN   46 Kimberley Street, Hartlepool
O. McCLELLAND   26 Union Road, Hartlepool
Henry McCORMACK
Thomas McCORMACK
Thomas McCORMACK
William McCORMACK   33 Ellison Street, Hartlepool
Robert McCREEDY
Samuel McCREEDY   18 Portland Street, Hartlepool
William McCULLOCH   6 Stephen Street, Hartlepool
Edward McDONALD
H. McDONALD   140 Lynn Street, Hartlepool
Thomas McDONOUGH   42 Sarah Street, Hartlepool
Michael McDONNELL   4 Back Alfred Street, Hartlepool
Joseph McFADDEN
Joseph McGILL   16 Stainton Street, Hartlepool
Francis McGREGOR
J.A. McGREGOR   8 John Street, Hartlepool
Michael McGRORY   18 Wood Street, Hartlepool
William McGRORY   5 Thorn Street, Hartlepool
Niel McHUGH   3 Princess Street, Hartlepool

William McHUGH
James McINTOSH   21 Town Wall, Hartlepool
John McKIE
William McLAREN   10 Church Street, Seaton Carew
James McLAUGHLIN   16 Hermit Street, Hartlepool
Alfred McLEAN   7 Acclom Street, Hartlepool
Richard McLEAN
Thomas McLEAN   7 Acclom Street, Hartlepool
George McLELLAND   3 Greenside Court, Hartlepool
John McLOUGHLIN   33 Marmion Road, Hartlepool
John McMAHON   69 Cleveland Road, Hartlepool
Martin MCMANUS   31 South Street, Hartlepool
James McMORRIS   8 West St, Old Town, Hartlepool
John J. McNALLY   59 Everard Street, Hartlepool
Miles McPARTLIN   17 Brown Street, Hartlepool
Charles MEAD   38 Briar Street, Hartlepool
Edward MEAD   3 Arthur Street, Hartlepool
George MEGSON   13 Durham Street, Hartlepool
Thomas MELDRUM   13 Town Wall, Hartlepool
David MELLOR   22 Coleridge Avenue, Hartlepool
John MELVILLE   12 Moseley Street, Hartlepool
Alfred C MERLIN   7 Alma Street, Hartlepool
Edmund METCALFE   4 Cumberland Street, Hartlepool
Edward H. METCALFE   23 Westmoreland Street, Hartlepool
George METCALFE   41 South Parade, Hartlepool
John C. METCALFE
Laurence METCALFE   105 Musgrave Street, Hartlepool
John G. MIDDLEMASS   11 Bentick Street, Hartlepool
Thomas MIDDLEMISS   31 Pelham Street, Hartlepool
David MIDDLETON   9 Sunderland Street, Hartlepool
George E. MIDDLETON   25 Beechwood Road, Hartlepool
James MIDDLETON   5 Suggitt Street, Hartlepool
James W. MIDDLETON
Thomas MIDDLESTON
John M. MIDGLEY   24 Park Road, Hartlepool
Matthew MILBER   13 Brougham Street, Hartlepool
Henry MILLER   3 Angel Inn Yard, Hartlepool
Isaac MILLER
Robert MILLER   48 Montague Street, Hartlepool

Robert MILLER   Easeby House, Groves Street, Hartlepool
David MILLS   60 Burbank Street, Hartlepool
John MILLS   22 Milton Street, Hartlepool
Norman E. MILNE   St. Hilda Street, Hartlepool
Alex MILNE   1 Blandford Street, Hartlepool
William MINTO   South Scarborough Street, Hartlepool
C.E.D. MITCHELL
John MITCHELL   3 Collingwood Road, Hartlepool
John MITCHELL
John R. MITCHELL   3 Darlington Terrace, Hartlepool
R.S. MITCHELL   8 Conyers Street, Hartlepool
William MITCHELL
George T. MOFFITT   9 Penrith Street, Hartlepool
George MOFFITT   22 Harrow Street, Hartlepool
Hugh MONTGOMERY   15 Dover Street, Hartlepool
Arthur MONUMENT   Errol Street, Hartlepool
J. MOODY
Ernest MOON   17 Alma Place Street, Hartlepool
Thomas A. MOON   27 Seaton Lane, Seaton Carew
John R. MOONEY   49 Commercial Street, Middleton
William W. MOOR   34 Raby Road, Hartlepool
Charles H. MOORE   41 Keswick Street, Hartlepool
Coulson MOORE
Frank MOORE   94 Frederick Street, Hartlepool
John T. MOORE
James H. MOORE   1 Richmond Street, Hartlepool
Ralph MOORE   67 Hermit Street, Hartlepool
Wilfred H. MOORE   96 Dent Street, Hartlepool
George MOORSOM
William MORALEE   20 Stephenson Street, Hartlepool
John MORAN   Union Inn, Bridge Street, Hartlepool
Patrick MORAN   8 Cleveland Road, Hartlepool
Peter MORAN   2 High Winter Street, Hartlepool
Thomas MORAN
Charles MORDAUNT
Arthur MORGAN   143 Stockton Road, Hartlepool
David MORGAN   5 Casebourne Road, Hartlepool
Walter MORGAN   44 Brougham Street, Hartlepool Arthur
Arthur MORRELL

Robert MORRELL	10 Briar Street, Hartlepool
Edward MORRIGAN	39 Caroline Street, Hartlepool
Sydney K. MORRIS	15 Benson Street, Hartlepool
George MORRIS	7 Prissick Street, Hartlepool
George Lewis MORRIS	33 Jackson Street, Hartlepool
John K. MORRIS	15 Benson Street, Hartlepool
Sydney K. MORRIS	15 Benson Street, Hartlepool
Albert L. MORRISON	
Joseph MORRISON	
William MORRISON	36 Grey Street, Hartlepool
Sydney MORRISS	
Joseph E. MORTON	Golden Flats Farm Seaton Carew
Harry MORTON	85 Westmoreland Street, Hartlepool
Albert MOTT	
Charles De MOUILPIED	11 Water Street, Hartlepool
Mark A. MOULT	8 Mildred Street, Hartlepool
D. MUDD	24 York Street, Hartlepool
George L.B. MUDD	
John G. MUIR	
William MUIR	51 Charlotte Street, Hartlepool
Thomas MULLON	36 Moreland Street, Hartlepool
Thomas MULLON	Silver Street, Hartlepool
William MULLENDER	13 Longmore Street, Hartlepool
Sidney MULVEY	61 Howard Street, Hartlepool
Francis J. MURPHY	
John T MURPHY	9 Well Street, Hartlepool
George F. MURRAY	
George MURRAY	9 Frederick Street, Hartlepool
James MURRAY	30 Sarah Street, Hartlepool
Percival W. MURRAY	
Phillip E. MURRAY	50 Osborne Road, Hartlepool
Thomas MURRAY	7 Pimlico Street, Hartlepool
Ralph MUSGRAVE	45 Reed Street, Hartlepool
Bertram MUTIMER	
Henry MUTIMER	20 Temperance Street, West Hartlepool
George MAWHINNEY	15 Gas Street, Hartlepool
W.G. NEAVE	
Herbert W. NEEDHAM	Thrislington, Park Road, Hartlepool
John R. NEILSON	13 Grace Street, Hartlepool

Andrew NELSON	39 Catherine Street, Hartlepool
David NELSON	118 Alma Street, Hartlepool
Oswald A. NEWCOMBE	211 Stockton Road, Hartlepool
George R. NEWLOVE	41 Durham Street, Hartlepool
Joseph W. NEWLOVE	41 Durham Street, Hartlepool
Richmond H. NEWSHAM	22 Mitchell Street, Hartlepool
George W. NEWTON	4 Cundall Road, Hartlepool
Isaac S. NEWTON	16 Bengal Street, Hartlepool
Robert NEWTON	
William H. NEWTON	48 Sandringham Road, Hartlepool
Daniel NICHOL	7 Middlegate, Hartlepool
J.E. NICHOLLS	20 Swainson Street, Hartlepool
J.W. NICHOLLS	19 Houghton Street, Hartlepool
John F. NICHOLSON	82 York Road Street, Hartlepool
George A. NICHOLSON	Baltic Sawmills, West Hartlepool
George W. NICHOLSON	27 Dent Street, Hartlepool
John F. NICHOLSON	
James NICOL	6 Morton Street, Hartlepool
John NIELSON	
Geoffrey B. NILSSON	Leaholme, Clifton Avenue, Hartlepool
John NISBET	
John T. NIXON	Catherine Street, Hartlepool
Albert NOBLE	Angel Inn, West Hartlepool
Charles James NOBLE	20 Hart Street, Hartlepool
Ernest NOBLE	16 Powell Street, Hartlepool
J.T. NOBLE	
Rutherford J. NOLAN	25 Dundas Street, Hartlepool
Robert C. NORMAN	
Robert H. NORRIS	91 Cumberland Street, Hartlepool
Joseph NORTH	50 Everett Street, Hartlepool
Joseph NORTON	22 Charles Street, Hartlepool
George NOSSITER	1 Dock Gate Cottages, Hartlepool
Michael NUGENT	71 Brenda Street, Hartlepool
George NUTTALL	18 Pilgrim Street, Hartlepool
James O'BOYLE	24 Charlotte Street, Hartlepool
John O'BRIEN	10 Silver Street, Hartlepool
Patrick O'DONOVAN	2 Hampshire Street, Hartlepool
John H. OLDFIELD	
William P. OLDFIELD	28 Park Road, Hartlepool

Fred OLIVER	156 Burbank Street, Hartlepool
John OLIVER	
John H OLLIVER	31 Albert Street, Hartlepool
John O OLSSON	78 Osborne Road, Hartlepoo
James O'NIEEIL	3 Plevna Place, Hartlepool
Joseph O'NEILL	46 Grace Street, Hartlepool
William O'NEIL	3 Plevna Place, Hartlepool
George ORAM	
Gregory O'RORKE	12 Rodney Street, Hartlepool
Herbert O'RORKE	12 Rodney Street, Hartlepool
Bernard O'ROURKE	Blandford Street, Hartlepool
Constantine O'ROURKE	55 Florence Street, Hartlepool
John O'ROURKE	79 Hermit Street, Hartlepool
Henry ORD	6 Hart Lane, Hartlepool
James G. ORD	Sea View Terrace, Hartlepool
William ORLEY	14 Scarborough Street, Hartlepool
George ORWIN	25 Jersey Street, Hartlepool
H. OSBON	87 Thornton Street, Hartlepool
Edward OSBORNE	6 Temperance Street, Hartlepool
James OUTHWAITE	19 Bell Street, Hartlepool
James OUTHWAITE	31 Arch Street, Hartlepool
W.R. OUTHWAITE	
George A. OWBRIDGE	30 Bailey Street, Hartlepool
George C. OWEN	
William R. OWEN	
P. William OWH	
Henry A. OXLEY	30 Bedford Street, Hartlepool
Matthew S. PALLETT	
Charles H. PALMER	38 Moore Street, Hartlepool
Charles F. PARKER	
David W. PARKER	5 Burn Road, Hartlepool
George PARKER	
Jack PARKER	37 Gainford Street, Hartlepool
Sydney G. PARKER	32 Bentley Street, Hartlepool
Aaron PARKES	33 Edgar Street, Hartlepool
John J.A. PARKES	67 Percy Street, Hartlepool
Joseph PARKES	4 Shires Court, High Street, Hartlepool
Joseph PARKIN	
James A. PARKINSON	108 Alma Street, Hartlepool

John W. PARKINSON	59 South Parade, Hartlepool
Oswald PARKINSON	7 Gainford Street, Hartlepool
H.A. PARNABY	
Andrew PARR	40 Stephen Street, Hartlepool
Noel G. PARR	88 Milton Rd, Street, Hartlepool
Norman E. PARR	
T. PARR	35 Arthur Street, Hartlepool
J.R. PARSELL	36 Frederick Street, Hartlepool
Luke PATCHCROFT	46 McDonald Terrace, Seaton Carew
Frederick PATERSON	12 Beacon Street, Hartlepool
Frank PATERSON	54 Grosvenor Street, Hartlepool
Henry PATTERSON	
Robert PATTISON	9 Jersey Street, Hartlepool
Edward J PATTEN	
James PATTON	9 Darlington Terrace, Hartlepool
Cecil PAXTON	
George H. PAXTON	88 Suggitt Street, Hartlepool
F.W. PEACH	
Tom PEARCE	
Ernest PEACOCK	Joicey Street, Hartlepool
John G. PEACOCK	14 Uppingham Street, Hartlepool
A.E. PEARSON	29 Robinson Street, Hartlepool
Charles E. PEARSON	60 Commercial Street, Middleton
Ernest W. PEARSON	82 Elwick Road, Hartlepool
George PEARSON	31 Alexandra Street, Hartlepool
J.F. PEARSON	29 Everard Street, Hartlepool
R.W. PEARSON	2 Princess Street, Hartlepool
William C. PEARSON	
Edward PEART	10 Nursery Gardens, Hartlepool
Harry PEAT	12 Alderson Street, Hartlepool
Joseph PEAT	19 Uppingham Street, Hartlepool
Thomas W. PEAT	14 Uppingham Street, Hartlepool
William PEAT	19 Uppingham Street, Hartlepool
Harry PEEL	59 South Parade, Hartlepool
James F. PEET	Front Street, Seaton Carew
Richard PENDLINGTON	
Robert A. PENDLINGTON	46 Montague Street, Hartlepool
Frederick PERCIVAL	11 South Street, Hartlepool
John G. PERKINS	

John PERRY	Park Road, West Hartlepool
William PETERS	9 Watson Street, Hartlepool
John S. PETTY	12 Baltic Street, Hartlepool
Edward PEVERELL	43 Rokeby Street, Hartlepool
John PHILLIP	26 Seamer Street, Hartlepool
William PHILLIP	26 Seamer Street, Hartlepool
Robert H. PICKEN	36 Burn Road, Hartlepool
Arthur PICKERING	2 Girvan Street, Hartlepool
Francis PICKERING	
Richard PICKERING	101 Whitby Street, Hartlepool
William V. PIKE	10 Wansbeck Gardens, Hartlepool
Fred T. PILCHER	40 Town Wall, Hartlepool
John PINDER	Mozart Street, Hartlepool
Charles PINKNEY	
William M. PITT	76 Church Street, Hartlepool
Herbert PLAICE	22 Roker Street, Hartlepool
James PLUMPTON	17 Pelham Street, Hartlepool
Joseph H. POLLARD	19 Duke Street, Hartlepool
Henry PORRITT	
Thomas E. PORRITT	7 Kenilworth Street, Hartlepool
Edward PORTER	27 Mayfair Street, Hartlepool
Thomas PORTER	22 Thornville Road, Hartlepool
Fred T. POTTS	18 Corporation Road, Hartlepool
Frederick POUNDER	32 Jersey Street, Hartlepool
William POUNDER	4 Back Lumley Street, Hartlepool
A.E. POWELL	24 Alma Street, Hartlepool
John G. POWELL	31 Howard Street, Hartlepool
Edwin S. POWELL	99 Lynn Street, Hartlepool
William H. PRENTICE	
William Henry PRENTICE	
A.E. PRIOR	96 Durham Street, Hartlepool
Walter R. PRITCHARD	67 Weatherby Terrace, Hartlepool
Mowbray PROCTOR	
Robert PROCTOR	75 Cumberland Street, Hartlepool
Archibald PROUD (DCM)	10 Watson Street, Hartlepool
Fred PROUD	5 Victoria Street, Hartlepool
James PROUD	10 Watson Street, Hartlepool
J.J. PROVERBS	25 Havelock Street, Hartlepool
George PUGH	30 Brook Street, Hartlepool

William J. PUGH	32 Mainsforth Terrace, Hartlepool
Richard P. PURVES	18 Rowell Street, Hartlepool
H.S. PURVIS	24 Trinity Street, Hartlepool
Allan PYMAN	
Edward RAFFERTY	1 Borrowdale Street, Hartlepool
William J. RAINE	5 Murray Street, Hartlepool
E. RAMSAY	
James RAMSBOTTOM	7 William Street, Hartlepool
Percival RAMSEY	7 Bolton Street, Hartlepool
Joseph RAMSHAW	
John W. RANDALL	
William RANKIN	26 South Street, Hartlepool
Charles RANSOME	56 Mooreland Street, Hartlepool
Joseph RANSON	
Albert RATCLIFFE	17 Throston Street, Hartlepool
John RAYMENT	41 Bramley Street, Hartlepool
Richard RAYMENT	41 Bramley Street, Hartlepool
T.H. RAYNOR	
George H. READ	48 Milton Road, Hartlepool
Guy S. READMAN	
James H. REDPATH	46 Alfred Street, Hartlepool
William REDPATH	29 Ladysmith Street, Hartlepool
Charles H. REDSHAW	14 Hope Street, Hartlepool
Albert H. REED	12 Alma Place Street, Hartlepool
Joseph REED	
Walter REED	26 High Street, Hartlepool
William REED	7 Portland Street, Hartlepool
R. REEVES	140 Cornwall Street, Hartlepool
Alexander REID	
Frank REINECKER	37 Tower Street, Hartlepool
John REINECHER	
Edmund REVELY	
L. RHODES	
Stanley C. RHODES	
Ernest RICHARDS	
John H. RICHARDS	
George RICHARDSON	42 Belmont Gardens, Hartlepool
Jack RICHARDSON	75 Dent Street, Hartlepool
John A. RICHARDSON	51 Grace Street, Hartlepool

John N. RICHARDSON	
John R.U. RICHARDSON	5 Christopher Street, Hartlepool
William RICHARDSON	4 Dyke Street, Hartlepool
Charles RICHMOND	33 Freville Street, Hartlepool
John H. RICHMOND	48 Bramley Street, Hartlepool
William RICHMOND	193 Burbank Street, Hartlepool
Harry RIDLEY	
F. RIDSDALE	18 Hart Road, Central Estate, Hartlepool
Philip RILEY	
Albert RISLEY	
Thomas ROACH	109 Murray Street, Hartlepool
Henry ROBERTS	28 Brook Street, Hartlepool
John ROBERTS	
Robert R. ROBERTS	28 Brooke Street, Hartlepool
William ROBERTS	17 Colenso Street, Hartlepool
Robert ROBERTSON	12 Chester Road, Hartlepool
Arthur J. ROBINSON	11 James Street, Hartlepool
Eustace D.S. ROBINSON	
George ROBINSON	9 Fawcett Street, Hartlepool
H. ROBINSON	11 Catherine Street, Hartlepool
Jasper ROBINSON	6 Everard Street, Hartlepool
John J. ROBINSON	23 Cobden Street, Hartlepool
John H. ROBINSON	21 Regent Street, Hartlepool
Richard ROBINSON	45 Dene Street, Hartlepool
Roland ROBINSON	1 Water Street, Hartlepool
Thomas F. ROBINSON	11 Hart Street, Hartlepool
Thomas R. ROBINSON	6 Back Lumley Street, Hartlepool
Charles ROBSON	28 Eden Street, Hartlepool
Fred ROBSON	72 Blandford Street, Hartlepool
Newby ROBSON	29 Percy Street, Hartlepool
Robert H. ROBSON	51 Thornton Street, Hartlepool
Robert H. ROBSON	
Reginald ROBSON	8 South Crescent, Hartlepool
Thomas E.S. ROBSON	5 Olive Street, Hartlepool
W. ROBSON	
William ROBSON	52 Everett Street, Hartlepool
Edward ROLPH	116 Durham Street, Hartlepool
Clarence ROPER	3 Princess Street, Hartlepool
Donald O. ROSS	Burnside, Stockton Road, Hartlepool

Thomas ROWBOTHAM	36 Helmsley Street, Hartlepool
Nicholas ROWE	35 Caroline Street, Hartlepool
George ROWLAND	10 Watt Street, Hartlepool
John T. ROWLAND	12 Freeman Street, Hartlepool
Thomas L. ROWLAND	Mere House, West Hartlepool
Harold ROWLANDS	
William ROWLANDS	
Frank ROWLEY	19 Devon Street, Hartlepool
Edward H. ROWNTREE	
James H.V. ROWNTREE	32 Devon Street, Hartlepool
Alfred RUMBLE	15 Brook Street, Hartlepool
E. RUMSAY	
Alfred J.B. RUNDLE	
John RUSH	39 Milton Street, Hartlepool
A RUSSELL	
Matthew RUSSELL	4 Burbank Street, Hartlepool
Edward RUTHERFORD	1 Pease Street, Hartlepool
Henry RYAN	
J.W. RYAN	35 Brunswick Street, Hartlepool
Richard RYAN	58 Florence Street, Hartlepool
John L F SAGE	
George SALTHOUSE	54 Blandford Street, Hartlepool
William K. SALTON	
George E. SANDERS	
Richard W. SANDERS	28 Gordon Street, Hartlepool
Charles SANDERSON	10 Rokeby Street, Hartlepool
George SANDERSON	John Street, Hartlepool
Henry H. SANDERSON	25 Brook Street, Hartlepool
John SANDERSONN	Henry Street, Hartlepool
G.H. SAWDON	Sunderland Street, Hartlepool
Walter SCALING	10 Houghton Street, Hartlepool
Albert SCOTT	7 Bower Street, Hartlepool
Arthur SCOTT	72 Westmoreland Street, Hartlepool
Benjamin SCOTT	
Bert SCOTT	
Henry A. SCOTT	18 Olive Street, Hartlepool
Frederick C. SCOTT	89 High Street, Hartlepool
James Thomas SCOTT	
John R. SCOTT	45 Howard Street, Hartlepool

John SCOTT	15 Brook Street, Hartlepool
Jack SCRIMSHAW	
Walter J. SCURRAH	24 Holt Street, Hartlepool
Albert SELBY	
Frederick W. SELCH	Stockton Road, Hartlepool
Harold SENGELOW	
Christopher SEWELL	24 South Parade, Hartlepool
John J. SEWELL	51 Thomas Street, Hartlepool
William SEWELL	74 Cumberland Street, Hartlepool
Alexander SHARP	Longmore Street, Hartlepool
Robert SHARP	17 Sarah Street, Hartlepool
Herbert SHARPE	27 Perth Street, Hartlepool
Walter T. SHAUL	5 Ouston Street, Hartlepool
J. Arnold SHAW	1 Waldon Street, Hartlepool
George Albert SHAW	21 Briar Street, Hartlepool
Joseph Miller SHAW	48 Gas Street, Hartlepool
William P. SHEEHAM	
James SHELLHORN	48 Murray Street, Hartlepool
Thomas P SHENTON	32 Richard Street, Hartlepool
George SHEPHEARD	30 Holt Street, Hartlepool
Ernest SHEPHERD	
John J SHEPHERD	17 Brunswick Street, Hartlepool
Henry SHERRY	69 Pilgrim Street, Hartlepool
Robert SHIELD	
John W. SHIELDS	50 Sarah Street, Hartlepool
Harry SHINGLE	6 Brunswick Street, Hartlepool
George SHINTON	48 Northumberland Street, Hartlepool
William SHIPPIN	5 Wilson Street, Hartlepool
Arthur SHIRES	
James SHIRES	25 Thornton Street, Hartlepool
Arthur SHORT	
Frank SHORT	17 Everett Street, Hartlepool
George H. SHORT	
James W. SHORT	8 Bedford Street, Hartlepool
John SHREEVE	
Thomas R. SHREEVE	158 Alma Street, Hartlepool
Ashley SHUTE	139 York Road, Hartlepool
Thomas SIDDLE	
Harold SIMM	34 Lister Street, Hartlepool

Alexander R. SIMPSON   59 Wilson Street, West Hartlepool
Herbert W. SIMPSON   Duke Street, Hartlepool
John L. SIMPSON   18 Back Henry Street, Hartlepool
Preston SIMPSON   54 Church Street, West Hartlepool
Robert SIMPSON   45 Dene Street, Hartlepool
Samuel SIMPSON   5 Ridley Street, West Hartlepool
Thomas L. SIMPSON   31 Alice Street, Hartlepool
William T. SINDEN
Edward SINGLETON   3 Bolton Street, Hartlepool
James SKELLHORN
George Dunlop SKELLY   23 Dundas Street, Hartlepool
William D. SKIDMORE   3 Sarah Street, Hartlepool
John Robert SKINNER   19 Sarah Street, Hartlepool
George SKINNER   48 Northumberland Street, Hartlepool
William R. SKIRVING   86 Whitby Street, Hartlepool
Walter SKIRVING   86 Whitby Street, Hartlepool
Alfred SLACK   25 Vincent Street, Hartlepool
Herbert W. SLATER
Oscar SMIRTHWAITE   Grange Road, Hartlepool
A.B. SMITH   12 Nursery Garden Terrace, Hartlepool
Charles E. SMITH   Back Frederick Street, Hartlepool
Edwin SMITH   9 Walworth Terrace, Park Road, Hartlepool
Gilbert P. SMITH   20 Clifton Avenue, Hartlepool
Hilton A. SMITH   44 Hurworth Street, Hartlepool
John H. SMITH   22 Eden Street, Hartlepool
John J. SMITH   10 Scarborough Street, Hartlepool
Joseph A. SMITH   7 Wells Yard, Hartlepool
Joseph H. SMITH   37 Bailey Street, Hartlepool
Robert W. SMITH   20 Sarah Street, Hartlepool
Sydney SMITH   10 Poplar Grove, Hartlepool
Thomas SMITH   9 Charterhouse Street, Hartlepool
Tom SMITH   12 Ramsey Street, Hartlepool
William SMITH   13 Hunter Street, Hartlepool
Ralph SMITHWHITE
Oscar SMURTHWAITE
Ralph SMURTHWAITE   19 Arthur Street, Hartlepool
Thomas R. SMURTHWAITE   2 South Road, Hartlepool
Robert SMYTH
Edward SNAITH

George SNAITH	
Herbert S. SNOWBALL	Caledonian Road, Hartlepool
Henry SNOWDON	56 Montague Street, Hartlepool
Herbert SNOWDON	68 Mainsforth Terrace, Hartlepool
William H. SNOWDON	35 Winter Street, Hartlepool
George B. SOLLORY	Bank House, Church Street, Hartlepool
W. SOURNAL	
James SOUTER	
Albert E. SPALDIN	10 Sheriff Street, Hartlepool
Harry SPALDING	
Henry SPALDING	10 Havelock Street, Hartlepool
Charles B. SPARKE	
James SPARKE	
William SPARKE	49 Thornton Street, Hartlepool
John SPARSHOTT	
Thomas SPEEDY	
R. SPENCE	4 Alfred Street, Hartlepool
Alexander SPENCE	Lord Clyde Hotel, Hartlepool
John SPENCE	20 Charles Street, Hartlepool
John J SPENCE	21 Francis Street, Hartlepool
William SPENCE	41 Bailey Street, Hartlepool
William G. SPENCE	3 Bell Street, Hartlepool
John Edward SPENCER	13 Hope Street, Hartlepool
Cantley SPILMAN	
Frederick H. SPINDLOE	
T.H. SPINDLOE	57 Clarendon Road, Hartlepool
Walter A. SPINDLOE	
William L. SPINK	29 Thirlmere Street, Hartlepool
J SPOUSE	
Mark SPOUSE	Gwendene, 87 Stockton Road, Hartlepool
Frank SQUIRES	Mitchell Street, Hartlepool
Charles A. STAINCLIFFE	37 Arncliffe Gardens, Hartlepool
J.H. STANGER	
James STATHER	5 Charterhouse, Hartlepool
John STEAD	5 Beacon Street, Hartlepool
William STEEL	7 Gas Street, Hartlepool
John W. STEEL	8 Middleton Road, Hartlepool
William STEEL	
William STEEL	

David STEERMAN	72 Mainsforth Terrace, Hartlepool
John W. STEERMAM	14 Alexandra Street, Hartlepool
William J. STEGGAR	11 Ashley Gardens, Hartlepool
Albert V. STELLING	50 Briar Street, Hartlepool
Thomas P. STENTON	
William STEPHEN	8 Florence Street, Hartlepool
Robert STEPHENS	79 Lister Street, Hartlepool
William STEPHENS	
John W. STEPHENSON	
George A. STEVENSON	
STEWARD	35 Winter Street, Hartlepool
Allan STEWART	27 Wansbeck Gardens, Hartlepool
James STEWART	42 Tweed Street, Hartlepool
James C. STEWART	13 Everard Street, Hartlepool
Arthur STOCKBURN	
Frederick STOCKBURN	
C.W. STOCKTON	
William STODDART	
Robert W. STOKER	5 Watson Street, Hartlepool
Tom STOKER	26 Studley Road, Hartlepool
William H. STONE	
Wilson B. STONEHOUSE	
Taylor STOREY	173 Burbank Street, Hartlepool
William J. STORR	12 Collingwood Road, Hartlepool
Henry J. STREET	28 Windsor Street, Hartlepool
G.A. STREETS	33 Stephenson Street, Hartlepool
George C. STRUGNELL	16 Exeter Street, Hartlepool
James STUART	42 Tweed Street, Hartlepool
D. STUART	12 Mozart Street, Hartlepool
Wilfred STUBBS	19 Moreland Street, Hartlepool
Albert SUDRON (DCM)	22 Portland Street, Hartlepool
John J. SUDRON	22 Portland Street, Hartlepool
Fred SUGGITT	40 Dent Street, Hartlepool
Thomas W. SUGGITT	4 Christopher Street, Hartlepool
Alexander SUMMERBELL	17 Kilwick Street, Hartlepool
John SUMMERFIELD	8 Eden Street, Hartlepool
Jonathan W. SUMMERHILL	39 Stockton Road, Hartlepool
Albert SUMMERSGILL	195 Burbank Street, Hartlepool
John F. SUMMERSGILL	195 Burbank Street, Hartlepool

T.W. SUMMERSGILL	6 Elliott Street, Hartlepool
Harold SUNDERLAND	11 Catherine Street, Hartlepool
Percy V. SUTTON	
J.R. SWAIN	
William SWALES	
Joseph SWALWELL	27 Dorset Street, Hartlepool
Eustace H. SWANWICK	
James SWEETING	37 Corporation Road, Hartlepool
John SWIFT	21 Arthur Street, Hartlepool
Albert SWINDEN	22 Albion Street, Hartlepool
William H. SWINDEN	21 Waldon Street, Hartlepool
W.T. SWINDON	50 Middleton Road, Hartlepool
Robert SWORD	
Henry SYKES	
Arthur SYMONDS	
Thomas G. TAITE	2 Durham Street, Hartlepool
Robert TAYLERSON	23 Chester Road, Hartlepool
Albert V. TAYLOR	41 George Street, Hartlepool
Robert B. TAYLOR	
Roy TAYLOR	25 Sheriff Street, Hartlepool
William TAYLOR	30 Cromwell Street, Hartlepool
William TAYLOR	
W. TEECE	38 Dene Street, Hartlepool
George G. TEMPLE	39 Silver Street, Hartlepool
Herbert TEMPLE	1 Durham Street, Hartlepool
George E. TEMPLEMAN	11 Northumberland, Hartlepool
John J. TEMPLEMAN	101 Studley Road, Hartlepool
Harry TERRING	
W.H. TERRING	36 Gainford Street, Hartlepool
Robert B. THEAKER	14 Wesley Street, Hartlepool
Robert W. THOMAS	
William THOMAS	63 Florence Street, Hartlepool
William U. THOMAS	146 Studley Road, Hartlepool
Edwin THOMPSON	25 Gill Street, Hartlepool
F.M. THOMPSON	
Harold J. THOMPSON	31 Hampshire Street, Hartlepool
Herbert THOMPSON	59 Osborne Road, Hartlepool
Hugh M. THOMPSON	89 Lister Street, Hartlepool
James THOMPSON	37 Briar Street, Hartlepool

John THOMPSON
John R. THOMPSON   10 Stranton Green, Hartlepool
J.T. THOMPSON   28 Everard Street, Hartlepool
P. THOMPSON   16 Longmore Street, Hartlepool
Ralph THOMPSON
Richard THOMPSON   11 Croft Street, Hartlepool
Thomas M. THOMPSON   3 Ridley Street, Hartlepool
Walter THOMPSON
Wilfred J. THOMPSON   42 Mayfair Street, Hartlepool
Ivar THOREN   38 Milton Road, Hartlepool
Albert C. THORNTON   Sydney Lodge, Stockton Rd, Hartlepool
E. THORNTON
John W. THORNTON   22 Lister Street, Hartlepool
Thomas TIERNEY   9 Thorn Street, Hartlepool
Charles W. TILLY
John TILLY (MC)
Oswald TINDALE   64 Alma Street, Hartlepool
William TINDALL   18 Kilwick Street, Hartlepool
William R. TIPLADY   32 Eden Street, Hartlepool
Thomas W. TIPP   Brook Street, Hartlepool
Alfred E. TODD   19 Farndale Terrace, Hartlepool
George H. TODD
William TOLCHORD   34 Wansbeck Gardens, Hartlepool
Edward F. TOLPUTT   18 Blandford Street, Hartlepool
Mark TOSE
Robert TOSE   12 Streatham Street, Hartlepool
William TRAIN   51 Arch Street, Hartlepool
John H. TRUBRIDGE   4 Sarah Street, Hartlepool
Wilfrid TUCKER   4 Corporation Road, Hartlepool
Benjamin TUMILTY   10 John Street, Hartlepool
Oliver TUNNELL   27 Eamont Gardens, Hartlepool
A.C. TURNBULL   12 Wharton Street, Hartlepool
Cuthbert R. TURNBULL   5 Powlett Street, Hartlepool
David E. TURNBULL   30 Back Slake Street, Middleton
Francis E. TURNBULL   62 Wansbeck Gardens, Hartlepool
George C. TURNBULL   10 Pilgrim Street, Hartlepool
James L. TURNBULL   47 Thornville Road, Hartlepool
Robert A. TURNBULL   37 Fredrick Street, Hartlepool
Thomas TURNBULL   6 Briar Street, Hartlepool

Thomas E. TURNBULL	
W. TURNBULL	
William S.L. TURNBULL	10 Pilgrim Street, Hartlepool
A.B. TURNER	37 Water Street, Hartlepool
Adam G. TURNER (MM)	38 Malton Street, Hartlepool
Herbert D. TURNER	32 Stanhope Street, Hartlepool
J.J. TURNER	
Thomas TWEDDLE	Greenhow, Belle Vue, West Hartlepool
Ralph W TWIZELL	73 Cornwall Street, Hartlepool
E.S. TYE	
Arthur TYREMAN	
C. UNDERHILL	Westfield House, Sydenham Rd, Hartlepool
Barnes UNDERWOOD	
Robert O. UPTON	103 York Road, Hartlepool
J. USHER	
Alfred VALKS	
Albert VARLE	
Alfred VASEY	3 Bower Street, Hartlepool
George VASEY	Cemetery Lodge, Hartlepool
Robert N. VASEY	4 Clarence Street, Hartlepool
Thomas VASEY	13 Brunswick Street, Hartlepool
Alfred VALKS	39 Dalton Street, Hartlepool
Alfred E. VAWER	15 Alston Street, Hartlepool
Arnold O. VICK	
John W. WADDINGTON	17 Albert Street, Hartlepool
G.N. WAITE	
George WAKE	140 Sheriff Street, Hartlepool
Joe WALE	62 Alfred Street, Hartlepool
David WALKER	Born at Hartlepool
Granville WALKER	44 Tower Street, Hartlepool
John R. WALKER	17 Croft Terrace, Hartlepool
John W. WALKER	Born at Hartlepool
William B. WALKER	
William R. WALKER	14 Sea View Terrace, Hartlepool
Edward WALLACE	22 Streatham Street, Hartlepool
Joseph W WALLACE	33 Victoria Road, Hartlepool
Samuel WALLACE	
Samuel S. WALLACE	11 Crossley Street, Hartlepool
Thomas W. WALLER	16 Carr Street, Hartlepool

Harold W. WALTON	91 Grange Road, Hartlepool
William WALTON	
Alfred WARD	5 Thirlmere Street, Hartlepool
Edward WARD	
Jim WARD	55 Pilgrim Street, Hartlepool
Moss WARD	
Philip WARD	20 Water Street, Hartlepool
Thomas W. WARD	77 Studley Road, Hartlepool
William WARD	22 Clayton Street, Hartlepool
Willie WARD	
Stephen J. WARDMAN	249 York Road, Hartlepool
James WARMALD	34 Queens Street, Hartlepool
Thomas R. WARNES	6 Vane Street, Hartlepool
Walter WARNES	
David WARREN	
John J. WARREN	16 Ladysmith Street, Hartlepool
Arthur WARWICK	7 Essex Street, Hartlepool
James WATCHMAN	17 Christopher Street, Hartlepool
George W. WATERSWORTH	48 Blandford Street, Hartlepool
George WATKINS	57 Everard Street, Hartlepool
Richard H. WATKINS	8 Alice Street, Hartlepool
David WATSON	54 Alfred Street, Hartlepool
George A. WATSON	36 Dalton Street, Hartlepool
James F. WATSON	30 Alfred Street, Hartlepool
Reginald G. WATSON	30 Mulgrave Road, Hartlepool
Robert WATSON	21 Tower Street, Hartlepool
William P. WATSON	49 York Road, Hartlepool
Mattison WATT	15 Durham Street, Hartlepool
Robert WATT	4 Olive Street, Hartlepool
Thomas WATT	9 Henry Street, Hartlepool
James H. WATTEN	25 Topcliffe Street, Hartlepool
George H. WAUGH	13 Back Frederick Street, Hartlepool
William WEAR	37 Streatham Street, Hartlepool
W.H. WEATHERALL	12 Garibaldi Street, Hartlepool
Thomas WEATHERALL	10 Greenland Cottages, Hartlepool
John WEATHERALL	13 Union Street, Hartlepool
George W. WEATHERBURN	75 Milton Road, Hartlepool
John T. WEATHERHEAD	84 Northgate, Hartlepool
William H. WEATHERALL	

Albert WEATHERILL	20 Albion Street, Hartlepool
John T. WEATHERILL	29 Marmion Road, Hartlepool
Charles F. WEBBER	Sydenham Road, Hartlepool
G. WEBBER	
Thomas W. WEBSTER	
William B. WEBSTER	Brantford Cottages, West Hartlepool
Herbert WELDRAKE	15 Bowser Street, Hartlepool
J.H. WELFORD	27 Hampshire Street, Hartlepool
Albert G. WELLS	
Richard A. WELLS	314 Cornwall Street, Hartlepool
Robert WELLS	27 Durham Street, Hartlepool
William E.A. WELSH	17 Havelock Street, Hartlepool
Walter WEST	
Robert WESTHORP	11 Howard Street, Hartlepool
John WETHERALL	7 Sea View Terrace, Hartlepool
Frederick WETHERELL	
Thomas WETHERELL	
Benjamin WHEETMAN	31 Garibaldi Street, Hartlepool
Alfred A. WHITE	50 Stockton Road, Hartlepool
F.E. WHITE	
Frederick W. WHITE	
James C. WHITE	51 Brenda Street, Hartlepool
Robert H. WHITE	173 Burbank Street, Hartlepool
Reginald WHITEHEAD	41 Milton Road, Hartlepool
Vernon M WHITEHEAD	46 Alliance Street, Hartlepool
Thomas WHITEWAY	40 Kimerley Street, Hartlepool
John WHITFORD	45 Raby Road, Hartlepool
John WHITLOCK	4 Stephenson Street, Hartlepool
William WHITTAKER	64 Alice Street, Hartlepool
William W. WHITTON	4 Gordon Street, Hartlepool
Charles WIGHTMAN	120 Cornwall Street, Hartlepool
Robert WILEY	56 Cumberland Street, Hartlepool
William WILKIN	62 Milton Road, Hartlepool
Frederick WILKINSON	4 Burn Road, Hartlepool
H. WILKINSON	3 Burn Road, Hartlepool
James WILKINSON	
Smurthwaite WILKINSON	27 Tristram Avenue, Hartlepool
Thomas WILKINSON	57 Clarendon Road, Hartlepool
Harry C. WILLEY	139 Stockton Road, Hartlepool

Arthur E. WILLIAMS	9 Osborne Road, Hartlepool
John WILLIAMS	2 Dent Street, Hartlepool
Percy WILLIAMS	19 Wards Terrace, Hartlepool
Thomas R. WILLIAMS	13 Union Street, Hartlepool
William A. WILLIAMS	8 Pilot Street, Hartlepool
E. Ernest WILLIAMSON	34 Alderson Street, Hartlepool
Robert Edward WILLIAMSON	27 Dalton Street, Hartlepool
Tom WILLIAMSON	2 Houghton Street, Hartlepool
Walter WILLIAMSON	7 Memorial Homes, Hartlepool
Robert H. WILLIS	35 Wood Street, Hartlepool
Alexander WILLIS	5 Shiers Court, High Street, Hartlepool
John WILLOUGHBY	39 Lowthian Road, Hartlepool
Robert WILLSON	Haswell House, Foggy Furze, Hartlepool
George E. WILSON	78 Hermit Street, Hartlepool
Harold WILSON	3 South Road, Hartlepool
Isaac WILSON	
John WILSON	Cliff Terracece, Hartlepool
John R. WILSON	20 Queen Street, Hartlepool
Joseph WILSON	2 Wood Street, Hartlepool
Thomas WILSON	24 Jersey Street, Hartlepool
Thomas A.D. WILSON	1 Dent Street, Hartlepool
William A. WILSON	3 South Road, Hartlepool
Alfred WILYMAN	
Fredrick E. WINPENNY	64 Arncliffe Gardens, Hartlepool
John H. WINSHIP	
John W. WINSHIP	14 Elco Street, Hartlepool
William WINSPEAR	7 Vollum Buildings, Hartlepool
Basil WITHY	Brantford House, West Hartlepool
Richard A. WITTEN	
Fred WOMBWELL	25 George Street, Hartlepool
Charles W.D. WOOD	6 Pilgrim Street, Hartlepool
Frank WOOD	57 Lister Street, Hartlepool
Harold Duncan WOOD	Born in Hartlepool
James WOOD	16 Burbank Street, Hartlepool
J.T. WOOD	58 Montague Street, Hartlepool
Leon WOOD	38 Benson Street, Hartlepool
John W. WOODRUFF	40 Musgrave Street, Hartlepool
Wilfred WOODRUFF	11 Laurence Street, Hartlepool
Frederick G. WORMALD	70 Westmoreland Street, Hartlepool

James WORMALD	34 Queens Street, Hartlepool
John H N WORSTENHOLME	Old Farm Foggy Furze, Hartlepool
Albert WRIGHT	39 Winter Street, Hartlepool
Algernon WRIGHT	
Frank WRIGHT	12 Lancelot Street, Hartlepool
Frederick WRIGHT	4 Storeys Passage, Hartlepool
George E. WRIGHT	
Norman G. WRIGHT	127 Thornton Street, Hartlepool
Thomas R. WRIGHT	57 Stephen Street, Hartlepool
Bertie WYETH	29 Seamer Street, Hartlepool
Cyril R.M. YOUNG	
Ernest YOUNG	2 High Street, Hartlepool
Robert YOUNG	20 Casebourne Road, Hartlepool
Tom YOUNG	21 Alma Street, Hartlepool

There were so many names originally commemorated on the Hartlepool War Memorial, such was the sacrifice made by men from the district. Others who had a connection with the Hartlepools in one way or another have subsequently come to light. I hope that I haven't missed anyone, or spelt a name incorrectly. If I have, then I express my apologies, as it is due to a regrettable oversight on my part.

Redheugh Gardens War Memorial.

Hartlepool also has the Redheugh Gardens War Memorial which was unveiled by John Lambton, the 3rd Earl of Durham, on 17 December 1923, and commemorates the war dead of both World Wars, with the dedication carried out by the Rev. D. Patterson. It specifically mentions the names of the British soldiers from the towns of Scarborough, Whitby and Hartlepool, who were killed during the German bombardment of the town on 16 December 1914. A plaque, which included the names of a further 240 military personnel, both men and women, who had died whilst in the service of their country between 1919 and 1967, was attached to the memorial and unveiled in 2001.

Sources

Wikipedia

Commonwealth War Graves Commission (https://www.cwgc.org)

www.ancestry.co.uk

www.britishnewspaperarchive.co.uk

hmcoastguard.blogspot.co.uk

www.1914-1918.invisionzone.com

www.heughbattery.com

https://www.durhamatwar.org.uk

www.1914-1918.net

www.naval-history.net

www.merchant-navy.net

www.forceswarrecords.co.uk

Index

Aliens Registration Order, 36
Anderton, Mr, 26
Andree, SS, 58
Arethusa, HMS, 3
Arrowsmith, Capt James, 3

Battle of Heligoland Bight, 3
Battle of the Marne, 2
Bell, Coroner Mr J Hyslop, 26, 40, 47, 60, 64
Blake Street, 11
Blucher, SMS, 10, 22
Bradley, William, 49
Brook Street, 92

C9, HMS, 23
Carrigan, Annie, 47–8
Carrigan, Edward, 47
Char, HMS, 32–3
Christopher Street, 35
Cleveland Road, 37
Cliff Terrace, 12
Clio, HMS 88
Cornforth, John Robert, 28
Cressey, Albert Edward, 28
Cromwell Street, 44

Dene Street, 39, 43
Dixon, George Edward, 34
Doon, HMS, 16, 23
Durham Light Infantry, 51, 113
Durham, Lord, 12
Durham Royal Garrison Artillery, 22, 30, 41

Emden, SMS, 6–7

First Battle of Ypres, 2
Forward, HMS, 23
Fraser, John B. DCM, 103
Furness, Carl Einar, 5
Furness, Sir Stephen, 4–5

Grenadier, SS, 83
Gritten, Mr W.G. Howard, 4
Grosvenor Street, 48

Hartland, Guardsman John Edward, 8–9
Hartlepool Board of Guardians, 95
Hartlepool Engine Works, 126
Hartlepool General Hospital, 10
Hartlepool National Shell Factory, 99
Hartlepool War Memorial, 181
Hartlepool West View Cemetery, 14
Henry Smith School, 26
Heugh Battery, 23, 41
Horsley, Mr Vivian, 72–3
Hurworth, Bertrand James, 65
Hurworth, Frank Hannaford, 46

Jeffrey, Mr Thomas, 69–70
Jones, Theophilus, 12

Kings Own Yorkshire Light Infantry, 56

Mallins, Sgt F.W. MM, 66
Marmion, HMS, 87
Matterson, John Marshall, 46
Military Service Act, 62
Military Service Tribunal, 63

Moltke, SMS, 10
Mons-Condé Canal, 2

Newby, JP, Mr George, 94, 121–2
North Eastern Railway Company, 29, 42, 58, 114
North Gate Street, 60
Northern Cyclist Corps, 2–3
Northumberland, Duke of, 31

Parkinson, James Alfred, 45
Patrol, HMS, 17, 23
Picken, Mr Harry, 7–8
Pyott, 2nd Lt Ian Vernon, 80

Rae, Mr Hugh, 67–8
Randell, Frederick, 11
Richardson, John Robert, 6
Runciman, Sir Walter, 34

Scattergood, Samuel, 48
Seydlitz, SMS, 10
Shute, Ashley, 34
Silver War Badge, 91
St David, HMHS, 78
Stageman, Sgt Frederick James, 123
Storr, William John, 34

Stranton Cemetery, 13
Sucrerie Military Cemetery, 10

The Clan Matheson, 5
Thompson, L. Cpl T. MM, 72–3
Trafalgar Club, 115
Twizell, Ralph William, 45

Vanguard, HMS, 86–7
Volunteer Training Corps, 62, 67, 71
von Arnauld de la Perière, Kapitanleutnant, 84

War Service Badge, 63
Watson, Alderman T.W., 74, 79
West Hartlepool County Court, 97
West Hartlepool War Memorial, 130–1
White Swan, SS, 61
Winterbottom, Chief Constable Mr A., 104
Women's Army Auxiliary Corps, 114

York Road, 29
Yorkshire Regiment, 54, 101, 110

Zhemchug, 7

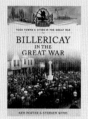
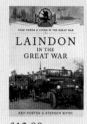

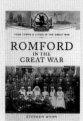
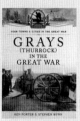
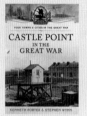
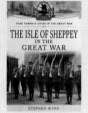
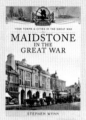

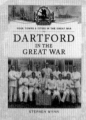

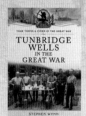

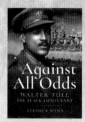